COUNTING DOWN

COUNTING DOWN

A Memoir of Foster Parenting and Beyond

Deborah Gold

Michael M.

OHIO UNIVERSITY PRESS • ATHENS, OHIO

Ohio University Press, Athens, Ohio 45701
ohioswallow.com

The essays listed below previously appeared in different form in the following publications:

"Cleaning Up for DSS" appeared as "Cleaning Up for D.S.S." in *Water~Stone Review*
"Cody" appeared as "Cody, Age 14 (or 15, if you ask him)" in *Gargoyle*
"DSS: Department of Social Services" appeared as "D.S.S.: Department of Social Services" in *Hotel Amerika*
"Counting Down: Reunification" appeared as "Counting Down" in *Press 53 Open Awards Anthology 2011* and, in abridged form, in *Fostering Families Today* magazine
"She Said Yes" appeared in *Floyd County Moonshine*
"Gel Pens" appeared in *J Journal*, literary journal of the John Jay College of Criminal Justice
"The Pickup Line" appeared in abridged form as "The Pick-Up Line" in *Fostering Families Today* magazine

All names and place names have been changed, along with many identifying details. This is my own recollection of events, which I've related to the best of my knowledge. I am grateful to all the family members and professionals who have supported these children and allowed them to become part of our lives.

Printed in the United States of America
Ohio University Press books are printed on acid-free paper ∞ ™

HARDCOVER ISBN: 978-0-8214-2296-0
PAPERBACK ISBN: 978-0-8214-2297-7
ELECTRONIC ISBN: 978-0-8214-4618-8

28 27 26 25 24 23 22 21 20 19 18 5 4 3 2 1

Library of Congress Control Number: 2017959985

And it seemed as though in a little while the solution would be found, and then a new and glorious life would begin; and it was clear to both of them that the end was still far off, and that what was to be most complicated and difficult for them was only just beginning.

—Anton Chekhov, *The Lady with the Pet Dog*

Contents

Mine & Yours

—Michael, age thirteen

In my life,
we had to hide the knife.
In your life,
you grew up right.
In my car,
we couldn't drive too far.
In your car,
you could probably go for a tour.
In my kitchen,
they talked of snitchin'.
In your kitchen,
all you could smell is chicken.
Near the trees
is where we grew the weed.
Near your trees,
you could hear the bees.
On my land,
there were lots of beer cans.
On your land
is a box of sand.

I

A FOSTER FAMILY'S INITIATION

Zero to One Hundred

AFTER A long and contentious spring semester, I was cleaning up the chaos of my university office. Our creaky old asbestos-ridden Language and Literature building was due to be renovated, and in the interim we were all getting moved across campus to a still older, creakier building pervaded by an untraceable smell of mold. Rumor had it that once renovations were complete, some newer, trendier departments might actually snap up our original building and trap us for good in that crummy location; the hallways were full of sniping and suspicion, which my staticky office radio couldn't block out. Tired of the grumbling, most of all my own, I just wanted to pack up my file cabinets—back then in 2002 most of us still had massive, dog-eared files and sheaves of Xeroxes and brittle newspaper clippings—and get things ready for the moving crew. At least we didn't have to do that part ourselves. Outside my windows, the pear trees were in blossom. I couldn't wait to get out into the mountain sunshine. I was ready to forget everything and launch into summer freedom.

Finishing up a publicity archive for our department's film series, I still had several newspaper issues to go through before I felt I could quit for the afternoon. All the local papers did was reprint verbatim the press releases we sent them, but I felt obliged to keep a record to show to potential donors or at least the department chair during my upcoming annual review. But as bored as I was restless, I stopped to read the lead article in the previous Sunday's *Sentinel*. As it was Foster Care Month and almost Mother's Day, the article profiled Laurie Marsh, a florist by day, who ran one of the county's longtime foster homes with her husband, an auto mechanic. Photographed holding her grandchild on her knee, she spoke of the dozens of children who had come through their home, staying anywhere from overnight to two years, and even returning as teen parents with their own infants; with Laurie's help they could learn to care for their babies before aging out of the system. Later I learned that Laurie framed a photograph of every foster kid who passed through their doors, eventually covering an entire living room wall. She spoke of offering a safe place to damaged children on the worst days of their lives. She didn't claim to save or fix or do anything more practical than offer a clean shirt, a dry diaper, or a hug, and she shrugged off the opportunity to condemn the parents whose actions had caused their children to be there.

At that time, fifteen years ago, I'd hazily imagined foster children as blank-eyed, abandoned waifs who were hopscotching between group and family homes while waiting for an adoption that might never come. Everything I knew I'd learned from TV, so it was no wonder I conjured up stereotypes: elfin boys hiding sullenly behind swept bangs, blonde girls with dirty cheeks clutching Band-Aided teddy bears, and of course the babies—the fabled stream of needy, crack-addicted babies so many of us yearn to have placed in our outstretched arms the moment the foster home license arrives in the mail. But where we lived, that's not what the need was.

I was surprised to read that many more children were removed because of neglect than because of abuse. But what did *neglect* even mean nowadays? I pictured a thin boy in an Oliver Twist tunic who was peeling lead paint off the walls and watching endless episodes of *Cops* on TV. That couldn't be right, I knew, but *abuse* sounded like the photographable, fixable stuff of TV movies, while *neglect* sounded more amorphous, lacking any concrete remedy.

I was intrigued by the article. Something clicked: maybe I could be a foster parent. I was all about fixing, as misguided as we've been told that is when it comes to spouses. As a university teacher, I fixed students' papers all day, didn't I? And found professionals to fix the students themselves when crises hit. I'd once saved a neighbor's horse from choking on a plastic bread bag by reaching down her throat, and I'd gotten certified in CPR every year since it was introduced, just in case I was ever the only one in a crisis who knew it. Fixing was not something I thought I could do better than others, but I was not afraid to try. I couldn't do much worse than your average Good Samaritan, could I? Especially when the odds already seemed stacked against success, whether that was reviving someone in cardiac arrest or, as a future foster parent, helping a girl avoid motherhood at fourteen.

How badly could I screw up something that had started out already broken? "You don't have to be perfect to be a perfect parent," the foster/adopt ad campaign says, although in the naive dramas of my imagination, I privately suspected I might be. Plus, like every foster parent I came to know, I viewed myself as being fairly organized and didn't mind tracking down information and calling strangers on the phone—basic advocacy skills—fueled by a useful middle-class presumption that the person on the other end of the phone ought to listen to me. And although I mostly ignored my carbon footprint, there was something ecologically pleasing about the notion of repairing something—someone—already here on Earth. Not that I had much choice about that, since I'd recently learned, in my late thirties, that I couldn't have children of my own. As I read that newspaper article, I decided I was ready to start foster parenting that day.

Right that day, without the first thought of licensing, training, fire inspections, or what my new second husband might think. The temporary nature of foster placements even sounded like a good thing—like some clear-cut work project with deadlines and spreadsheets, a sense of accomplishment and finality. Fixed, submitted, filed—then time for a vacation break or instantly produced screenplay before the next thing. *No prob, Bob,* in the words I'd later learn from a big-eyed backhoe on TV.

PUTTING OFF cleaning my office, I read the article from start to finish and was full of spring possibility and that end-of-semester rush of energy that made it feel like anything would be possible in the next twelve weeks—writing an entire novel, losing thirty-two pounds by running a marathon, and, most of all, enjoying the ecstasy of sleeping like a normal person instead of writing sure-to-be-ignored margin comments in tiny crabbed letters until 2 a.m.

At the end of the article was a phone number and the name of a social worker to call for information about becoming foster parents; dissemination of that information was the true purpose of this profile. So the next day, after my husband's equivocal *maybe,* I found myself sitting in my university office, dirty beige phone receiver in my clammy hand, heart pounding sickly—as it would so many times, for different reasons, in future calls to the Department of Social Services (DSS). I took a shaky breath and dialed, but the person I needed, like any good social worker, was out. (And I don't mean out getting her nails done, although somehow they all manage to have glossy, chipless manicures, but out in people's homes, interviewing kids at school, picking up a child for a visit or supervising one, appearing in court, or attending staff meetings. Frustrating, but what would it mean if social workers were always in their offices, waiting for a call?)

The next day and a hundred happy fantasies later, I reached Geraldine Taylor, the licensing and training coordinator. And all my excitement, my visions of cruising music festivals and craft shows with a backpacked toddler, came to an abrupt halt. All stopped by one question from Geraldine: "Can you tell me about your water source?"

CHUTES AND LADDERS

That was May 2002. Michael, the child around whom I would shape my entire future, did not yet exist. When eventually he was born, three weeks premature, the doctors watched and waited through the first hours of his life until the bubble—the hole in his lung—finally closed. At it happened, his first home lay just a few miles from our own, down the steep slope of a back road that I hadn't known existed. I would not see their trailer for several years, until it had been abandoned, condemned for meth contamination, and then mysteriously burned.

A year and a half into Michael's life, his chest rattled by asthma, we would meet him.

I'VE ALWAYS admired my husband, Will, for having kid charisma in spades, with the patience to spend summer mornings teaching his friends' kids to dig up plants or wade around our muddy pond and fish. Unlike me, he is a biological parent and a natural—my ambassador to the world of children. Still, I'd worked four years at a historic farm park and had spent a year as a live-in nanny, tightly bonded to a newborn, so I could stay in the Bay Area. *This can't be the only time you do this,* I remember instructing myself, amazed that even off duty and living two floors below, I'd waken at 3 a.m., seconds before the baby cried from the crib beside her parents' room. I'd hoped to mold her into an adventurer and so hauled her in the baby backpack up through the fragrant, urban hillside eucalyptus groves and pushed her stroller through the endless avenues, past the Asian fruit stores, and along the perpetually cold and foggy beach. I heard her first word, *leaf,* spent $25 for her to ride a pony around a ring, and watched her learn to toddle-run through the Jurassic carrot-top palms in the arboretum. Whatever my future held, I resolved I'd have this kind of experience again.

Years later, I had it to some degree when my stepson, Vince, would come to visit—although more often Will would drive a day and night to see him—but he and Will were so fiercely enfolded in their tent of time together that the best I could do was trail along on their outings and bite my tongue at their daily trips to Walmart to buy more worthless plastic, as even they called it. (To his lasting delight, Michael would inherit a whole closet full of those Lego pieces, Hot Wheels, netherworlds, and minigarages in the years to come.)

So a decade later and a continent away from my nanny days, with a home and barn filled with rescue pets, I was excited to move back to the human dimension—at least so long as no one brought us a teen as stubborn and secretive as I had been. (That karmic wheel spun around much later.) The thing I didn't realize then is that it's not just hardened teens or older children that people fear—by the time a baby is born, the damage can already have been done. For every baby who hears the poetry of Robert Frost or *Goodnight Moon* read to her *in utero,* dozens hear shrieked curses instead, dozens have synapses permanently frayed by alcohol. They don't just "move on." Whatever chain of misfortunes has landed them in foster care has already marked them and sent them careening down the very first game board chute, while everyone else their age is scrambling up the ladder.

BEFORE WILL and I could even start the training required for prospective foster parents, we ran into obstacles. First, the emotional kind—Will was basically on board, but obtaining the agreement of his then preteen son, who lived halfway across the country with his mother, was painful. Vince had sobbed over the phone, unable to bear the idea of another boy's getting so much time with his dad—time that Vince himself had missed. Impatient as I was to get a foster child in our home, I felt awful for provoking this.

But the physical obstacles were what made me gnaw my knuckles with frustration. We lived in the mountains, where pure springwater is bottled and sold region-wide, yet the environmental bureaucrats in the polluted, chlorinated state capital had deemed this very same mountain springwater unsafe for foster homes. Period. Our only alternative was to spend thousands drilling a well. So much for the supposed abuse, neglect, hunger, and epidemic meth and opioid use in infamous Appalachia. The problem was the premium mountain springwater. Miraculously, a state senator spent months pushing a bill through the legislature that relaxed the water restrictions, freeing us and scores of other families in the mountain counties to pursue foster care licensing.

I'm not one of those people who believe that everything happens for a reason, much as I wish I could. But if we'd been able to jump into fostering with no obstacles and delays, we'd likely have had a different child or two in our home already by the time Michael was removed, and then what would have become of him? Would my now beloved Michael have gone instead to one of our new friends? Would we ever even have met him? Sensed a cosmic missed connection? The whole thought of such a miserable parallel universe made me dizzy.

Will and I went through the standard foster parent training with an unusually small group—two single-mom best friends—led by the awesome social worker we now called Gerri, with her cynical optimism and equally awesome wardrobe of gypsy skirts. In addition to leading training for new and renewing foster parents, she was the one designated to assess and license homes, to find and make the best possible placement for a child coming into foster care, and to serve as foster families' liaison to the agency, offering ongoing support and addressing foster parents' questions or concerns. (A birth family involved with the agency was assigned a separate worker to serve as the family's advocate and guide.) With Gerri, we worked through six booklets; learned to inventory needs and strengths and to recast one as the other, like sides of an algebra equation; heard the words *love* and *logic* linked for the first time; went through background checks, for which we held our breath over Will's teen years and I thanked God for all I had gotten away with during my pre–midlife crisis in my twenties. Last stop was the sheriff's department, where we rolled our fingerprints over the new touch screen. Will's usual jokes went unreciprocated, while I studied the list of criminal charges posted on the wall, amazed at all the gradations.

As we finished the training, we grew ever more energized at the prospect of seeing the composite children in our workbooks, their strengths, needs, and behaviors neatly charted, come to life in three dimensions. We were ready, we thought, for bedwetting, fire starting, tears, crayoned walls, and tentative hugs. We were ready to dump massive quantities of abstract, unconditional love on a kid, despite having been warned that this was not the universal fix.

We were ready to respect the bioparents, as Gerri called them, as wounded grown children still dealing with their own unmet needs but always doing their best to cope. We were ready to accept that, no matter what, they were the parents "our" children would always love and need the most. Good students that we were, we believed such understanding could override our instincts.

AFTER CONQUERING the water situation, we did not expect trouble from the fire inspector. We'd thought we were ready for him as well—our ingenious, custom-built 1980s house had previously housed a family with disabled children and seemed perfectly safe; our smoke alarms worked only too well and could detect a bag of slightly singed popcorn before you'd even opened the microwave. We had our fire extinguishers, upstairs and down—okay, no problem to get bigger ones and fix them on mounting brackets. The door to the hot water heater had to be vented. The closet next to it had to be permanently emptied (and was every time we got a relicensing inspection). Thank goodness they did not measure the length of the dryer hose, which snakes its way through the basement before venting outdoors. But an upstairs bedroom window was a few inches short of standard width.

Who knew that becoming a foster parent would involve recutting a window so it would be wide enough for a fire ladder to fit through its frame? (Never mind the bigger question: Would that ladder truck, stationed in the center of town, actually get here in time?) In an endeavor driven by heart, soul, compassion, and angst, who would think so much comes down to measurements?

I understand, of course, why foster homes have to be physically safe in every aspect. And I understand why the inspections have to be picky. I understand why smoke detectors have to be placed seven feet high and not five, since smoke rises to the ceiling and then drops down. I just wish that the regulations went both ways, so that when foster children return to birth homes—where everyone smokes, does their own wiring, and produces heat by opening the oven doors, lighting unvented kerosene heaters, and stoking woodstoves illegally installed in trailers—those birth homes would have to have at least one working smoke detector with an unexpired nine-volt battery that hasn't been filched for use elsewhere. But there's no such requirement.

Eight hundred dollars and five months later, the fire marshal okayed our beautifully vented water heater door and a new window in a bedroom we hadn't even planned to use.

THAT WAS summer 2004, more than two years after I'd first read the newspaper story about Laurie Marsh and her husband. We were ready.

Ready to begin waiting.

All those websites and billboards about "waiting children"—with their dark-ringed eyes, dropped teddy bears, and reproving stares? Well, that waiting went both ways, we learned, especially as we were licensed by a county's social services agency. Thankfully, our local social workers were conscious of the need to make a good match, especially as we were just starting out, but we understood they couldn't predict when birth parents would mess up so badly that a judge would approve intervention. Even then, we knew from our licensing classes that social workers were required first to search for family members who could handle a kinship placement.

So we were waiting for a midnight phone call. Waiting for a placement. And waiting some more. Waiting until we'd forgotten we were waiting at all.

CHILDPROOF

I thought I had no illusions. I thought I might be the first person who'd bought into the official DSS line. After many years of pleasing teachers, I could parrot the workbooks right back: the actual goal of foster care is that children will go back home again. *Reunification.* A mouthful of a term I found oddly impersonal from the start. I learned that food cabinets could be filled and support services found to fit a family's needs; I believed that drug addictions and abusive relationships were problems weak parents sweated out, talked through, and moved on from. Not problems that some just got better at hiding. Ever the compliant student, I had the notion that foster kids were like library books taken briefly out of circulation, improved with new binding and taped-up pages, then returned to a rebuilt, sturdier shelf. At that point, I assumed, my real life would resume with its movie dates, trail rides, and the spontaneous girlfriend weekends I'd read about in *Oprah*.

I didn't want to adopt. I'd said that up front once we started the licensing process—a conviction that would change the instant a real child was in our home. Until that point, I saw foster kids as theoretical beings in transit—souls in purgatory—whose wait might be made more pleasant by a stopover in our home. But what would make the next decade so wrenching—seeing children going back to seemingly unchanged situations, again, again, again—was largely absent from my early fantasies.

For Will the thorny issue about foster parenting was rules: he's a true product of the sixties, who endears himself as a teacher by never doing anything the way he's supposed to. He was not about to change that approach for this foster parenting venture driven by state regulations, court orders, and restrictions, which include not being allowed to introduce foster children *as* foster children ("our friend who's staying with us right now" was the trainer's suggestion). I knew that Will would be fantastic with actual kids, but his resentful reluctance to accede to requirements like getting twelve hours of training per year even while we were waiting to get our first placement, or taking the deadbolt off the front door as the fire marshal required, was already causing tension between us. Entirely predictable tension, but I constantly feared he might back out of the whole endeavor.

MIDWAY THROUGH that winter of 2005, we finally got a call from Gerri, the social worker who'd licensed us. She knew I'd be terrified to start with an older child, no matter how she'd tried to dispel my wrong belief that the youngest children were blank slates psychologically. Today I understand that even a fetus can experience stress, connecting shouting voices with surging cortisol, even if Mom is not punched in the stomach or pushed down stairs. Before these babies are even born, their reflexes are set.

But, okay, it was our first time out, and there was a sixteen-month-old, Michael, who had two older siblings—all were with a relative for the moment, but when she went back to work in a few weeks, Michael would come to us, Gerri said. No county foster home was available that could take all three children, plus Michael had to-be-expected developmental delays and might benefit from individual attention. (It was almost funny that I'd expected those delays to be emotional: *He needs to learn to bond, to love, to trust.* Instead I was shocked at the prosaic nature of his preschool services worker's goals for him: "We want him to learn how to hold a spoon. To drink from a cup.")

WERE WE ready for this?

Between grading midterms, Will got caught up on his HBO and snow shoveling, while I calculated how to rework my teaching schedule, plugged up the electrical outlets, and figured out the puzzles of child locks and stair gates—all good preparation for working the mystery latches and Möbius straps of a car seat. Two days later, though, Gerri called back and said stop, don't buy anything yet—at the first hearing, the judge sent the kids back.

That was the first big "huh?" of our lives as foster parents. One day parents are unfit and the next day they aren't? A different judge can turn things around just like that?

Judges seemed to be the wild card in every birth and foster family's outcome. And this was months before another foster mother told me about an infant who had recently left her care: the three-month-old had arrived with twenty-eight broken bones and a terror of bathwater; the detectives were still trying to pin this abuse on the birth father when a judge sent the baby back to the grandmother's home, next door to the father's place, on one hour's notice.

ONE HUNDRED

I didn't expect to hear anything more about Michael or his family—I assumed we'd just go back on the roster of families open for a placement. Then the night before the end of our spring university semester, a new, young social worker called. "Mom isn't doing what she's supposed to" was the worker's only tight-lipped remark. Something had happened; I never found out what. (It's the first thing everyone wants to know, however obliquely they ask . . . and you can't tell anyone anyway. Later, the question changes to "So, is *she* doing better now?" *She* always means "Mom," while people rarely ask about the dad. Like our opinions would make any difference. Like we could be the judge.)

Michael, now a full-fledged toddler, would be brought to our house from day care the next day, while his brother and sister would be taken on to be placed with two other families. Zero to one hundred: nine months in one night. My head was reeling. We went directly to Walmart and got diapers, two baby bottles, a sippy cup (a term I couldn't believe I'd hear so many adults say with a straight face), and a crib, which Will spent most of that night piecing together. He would wait at home to greet Michael while I was teaching my last class.

I got through that class in a fog, pinching my forearms with excitement. *Would I think back on this, like a movie character, as a true before-and-after moment? One of the few in life you could distinctly recognize? This was the day my life would change—maybe.* I thought this in actual words, yet words were all they seemed to be.

The next day DSS called after the family's social worker had raced from court to pick up the siblings from school and day care before Mom could zoom up and confront her. But Michael was coming with just the clothes on his back, as is commonly the case. I might want to head back to Walmart, I was warned, and pick up a couple of outfits for him to start with. In training we'd learned we could spend $160 every six months on clothes and shoes for a foster child. Walmart wasn't required, but shopping there and at consignment stores was the only way to make that budget work, no matter how you felt about the store's sweatshop supply chain.

I zombie-walked into Walmart for the second time in twenty-four hours, hardly able to grasp that Will was having our life-changing experience, while I was out buying a Cookie-Monster-plays-soccer outfit in stretchy gray and pajamas adorned with a red-haired Rugrat in a pith helmet. This was the dawning of yet another realization—that you have to pay a lot more for toddler clothes that don't advertise something. And even the expensive clothes—Old Navy or OshKosh—either have a brand logo front and center or they're advertising fake brands of surfboards or safari lodges. If you want an outfit with a plain picture of your basic steamroller—one that doesn't have eyes and a name and well-known catchphrase—you pay a premium.

It was evening by that point. Will called to say that Michael had arrived, eaten a cut-up hot dog and some scrambled egg, and was settling with a bottle while they waited for me. I knew Michael would have had a bewildering day, and that he'd have to go to sleep soon so he'd be ready to go to his required educational day care in the morning. Yet I walked through Walmart stunned, unable to focus. I hadn't even realized toddlers' clothes were sized by years, months, and the letter *T*. Or that diapers were sized by weight—a weight I couldn't begin to estimate. I felt like an imposter in the children's department, and I sensed the eyes of other new parents on me as I scrutinized clothing tags and held combo outfits up to gauge the fit for a child I hadn't ever seen. Would they peg me as a kidnapper? Or what if his mom was actually there and saw me? All the experienced foster parents had horror stories of running into angry birth parents, invariably at Walmart.

I got home at 7 p.m., turned the doorknob, and eased over the threshold, hoping to get close enough to see Michael before he saw me. I found him and Will in our bedroom, where Will was lying on our bed, flying Michael over him in the classic airplane maneuver. A half-full milk bottle stood on the nightstand. Will set the boy on his chest so that Michael was on hands and knees. I didn't want to startle Michael because I knew he'd be wary. So I said hello, and we were silent for minutes, as he turned his blond head slowly to the left and stared at me.

Who does he think I am? I wondered. *And what is he seeing? Shouldn't I be feeling something?* But ballooning stillness itself became a feeling, and my lungs filled with an immensely tranquil emptiness I've never found in meditation. It was the space love would rush into as soon as I let go and let the next breath in.

BY THE second morning I wanted to adopt. Could we? Was it even remotely possible? But of course we were *foster* parents—that's what we'd signed up for. His mom was complying with the plan Social Services had drawn up, and Dad was temporarily "out of the picture," in the shorthand expression that everyone I met seemed to like to use.

At first we had no idea how long Michael would stay with us, and little understanding of the stages of the court process. Terms like *adjudication* and *stipulation* were as alien to us as they probably were to the "bios"; I know of one determined foster mom who attended every hearing and always tried to find a way to slip the judge photos of the kids who were thriving in her care, hoping the judge would grasp the stakes. Other foster parents I met felt it was their duty to be present and, for the sake of the kids in their care, attended and squelched whatever discomfort they felt. Coward that I was—and completely shaken the first time I encountered Michael's mom in an agency hallway—the notion of attending court (which is apparently more commonplace now, a decade later, as is education about the process) seemed incredibly confrontational to me. Foster parents were rarely, if ever, invited to testify, and we were pledged to support the agency's decisions about the case anyway. Simply sitting in court, I felt, would have seemed to spell out the us-versus-them divide that we tried so hard to erase from our hearts and minds. Worst of all, to me, it seemed invasive of the bioparents' privacy. Curious as I was, I didn't think any bioparents would see us as their allies. If I showed up at court, I didn't think they would ever forgive me.

For Michael and his siblings, sometimes I heard when court dates were coming up, while other times they were mentioned after the fact, in passing—a reminder of our irrelevance, was how I took this. Like everything the children's first social worker, Kayla, said, I constantly found myself wanting to say, "Please, wait, slow down, explain." I didn't know if I was snooping or stupid or if it seemed like I was overstepping and second-guessing her plan. But pushy was not how I wanted to seem with a social worker, and I knew it would not get results. In hindsight, I think this worker was almost as new as I was in my very different role; still, I was relieved when another Child Protective Services director took over the office after Michael's case closed. It was too late for all my questions, but from that point on, it seemed to me that transparency increased for the foster parents.

All I really cared about was knowing our sentence—how soon we'd have to give up our toddler. When I first heard that Michael would be with us for three months, I was baffled—what kind of change could happen in that time? The parents had split before the children were removed, his mom had a new boyfriend who planned to come to several visits, and Dad would soon end up in jail for unrelated reasons. I didn't want to get into the family's business, but weren't we supposed to be some kind of partners in this? Was some kind of change not the point? Three months—twelve weeks—barely a season—seemed like nothing. I was confused, and if I didn't know why we had Michael in the first place, how could I know what progress they were seeking? Or was it none of my business?

("You didn't know why they were removed?" an agency staff member asks me now, aghast. "The children's social worker never told you?" My usual assertiveness had failed me, I'm chagrined to say, the second I thought I might displease an authority or seem a pest. And back then I'd had no comparable experience to go by.)

Later, we would hear the estimate of a three-month time frame miraculously grow to six, due to some time-consuming practical issues. Anything that meant Michael would be with us longer was manna to me. But his mother had rights, and her social worker was determined that Mom would have a successful reunification with her children, no matter what obstacles might arise. Or, as a more diplomatic staff member eventually told us, "Mom's done everything we've asked her, and she deserves the right to fail. Or to succeed on her own terms, even if it's not the future you'd most like to see." If I'd read that in a training manual, I know I would have agreed wholeheartedly.

FROM OUR first moments face to face with Michael, we had every bit of the staggering love-and-wonder rush that I imagine every new parent experiences, and more. We always knew there was an expiration date ahead—the snapshots of memory weren't going to be wistful nostalgia to laugh over with a teen. More like a Snapchat photo, for once that child was gone, those memories would surely vaporize: the sweet, clean, pointed face; the little sailor suit I crammed him into for a Walmart portrait; a love of chicken nuggets so great that he brought his stuffed toy rooster into the kitchen and begged me to cook it; the laughter at a bubble in the stream; his mania for cars, motors, and real, dangerous tools (this was a kid not fooled by their colorful plastic facsimiles); the "God bless" litanies I helped him recite with names of people I didn't know; the untraceable, lingering smell of his room and hair. Every gain was a loss as well, in the moment it occurred.

SWEET HOME

During one of the hearings leading up to the reunification, the lawyer representing Luke, the children's dad (who was in jail), told the judge that the children's still-married mother should not be allowed to take them to live with another man—and the judge agreed. It was his lawyer's idea, not Dad's, as it turned out: he despised Benny, the new boyfriend, but Luke hated DSS more and wanted the kids taken out of foster care and returned to one parent, that is, to their mom.

At first this ruling had meant an unexpected gift of time—instead of having the children returned to her after just three months, Jessica first would have to get a home of her own, apart from her boyfriend. This meant a long process of qualifying for a federally subsidized housing voucher, then finding one of the scarce rentals that would accept the government payments, then furnishing it using Goodwill coupons and somebody's borrowed pickup truck, and so on. Even with the constant hurried help of her social worker, it would take months. It was a huge reprieve for Will and me. Not only would we have more days with Michael and further opportunity for him to grow and learn but, less charitably—as many foster parents know—such a delay also would mean time for the birth parent to screw up—or more time for old screwups to come to light.

JESSICA WAS always sweet and complimentary to me when she carried Michael down the stairs and buckled him into my car after the weekly supervised visits at DSS. His siblings would be rocketing around, and Jessica would talk to them sternly, calling the kids ma'am and sir as the social worker looked on approvingly. Jessica's hair was often a completely different color from visit to visit, but she always looked like she'd made an effort to think about how she'd be seen, as I did myself.

I glimpsed small lapses, though, once the family progressed to unsupervised visits. To me, this new stage of the case plan was awkward and unwelcome, as no social workers were even in the vicinity; the agency was short-staffed that summer and I was asked to meet Jessica and Benny alone for the weekly rendezvous to drop off and pick up Michael and his siblings for full Saturday visits. Suddenly Jessica was wearing tiny halters or tube tops instead of Coke-branded sweatshirts, with her hair pulled up in a streaky knot instead of clean and brushed. She and Benny would drive off with the children to a vaguely located lake—and come back with balled-up wet clothes turned inside out, half belonging to kids unknown and half of Michael's missing. Brother Ryan would be talking in fragmented riddles and sister Isabelle would be in a speechless huff. The swimming diapers Michael had been wearing that morning would be gone, of course, and so would all the extras; when Jessica returned him to us, he'd be shirtless and in a wet swimsuit. By the time we'd get back to our home, the padding of his car seat would be soaked in urine.

I PICKED up all three kids from these daylong unsupervised visits, because Isabelle's foster mom ran her florist business out of her house and was minding a baby, while Ryan's had four or five other kids to juggle. But much more unnerving than the extra driving and messy car was being all alone to hear Benny's recountings of jet-skiing and of how toddler Michael had gone underwater, but—no problem—Benny had scooped him out of the water and held him aloft overhead in triumph, like a football at the goal line. No mention of life jackets for any of the kids; clearly no use of sunscreen, even though I'd put it in the diaper bag and tried to coat Michael with it before leaving. Ryan, always, would come back exhausted, with a shirtless red blaze that often covered his torso.

Jessica and Benny must have thought my mania about sun exposure was a middle-class phobia and a predictable failure to realize that sunburns, spankings, and all-day soda were just part of growing up. Of toughening up. I said something about the jet skis and seeming lack of life jackets to the kids' by-then third social worker, who was just out of college and substituting in to cover staff vacation time. Basically I got the message that this was Mom's time, not mine, and it was up to Jessica to determine what was safe. But thanks for "transporting" them.

WHEN I was consumed with the imperfect details, the big picture was elusive, but even at the time I realized there was no greater blessing for us than the motion made by Luke's lawyer and the judge's requiring Jessica to secure housing separate from Benny's. The extra months we gained with Michael as a result were an irreplaceable gift, giving our hearts more time to knit, allowing Michael more time to live free of cigarette smoke and learn to take asthma meds through a tube, and permitting us to go to the beach with Michael and his sister. Ryan too was able to go on the first vacation of his life with his foster family, traveling to the World of Coca-Cola and Stone Mountain, Georgia; the colored lasers that illuminated the cliff carvings at night impressed him more than anything he'd yet seen.

Then, in late summer, we heard that Jessica indeed had found a trailer that qualified for a rent subsidy. Like Benny's place, it was also in the next county—not only remote but out of the jurisdiction of our DSS, which gave Jessica and the kids a clean slate and, if a crisis should come, different foster homes. And as slow to react as we thought our DSS was, this neighboring one was rumored to be slower. But at least our own DSS would have to monitor Jessica's family for what we hoped and believed would be six months after reunification—in fact, it turned out to be two months, barely—before their case was closed.

Early on, Jessica had wrinkled her nose and mentioned that the rental was in a pretty crummy small trailer court, but that was it. (*Well, at least there'll be people around*, I remember thinking.) Yet once the kids started going for weekend visits, the penultimate step of the whole reunification process, we heard nothing, oddly, about the new trailer. Jessica and Benny now brought the children all the way back to us, which cost them significant gas money but was no doubt worth it to keep us out of their lives and their business. The kids said little—even the older two, who could speak. What these visits were like was perplexing to piece together, and surely they'd been told not to say anything for fear of never getting their family back—but I remember sitting with their paternal grandmother, Irene, and looking at the patterned walls of her trailer, while she tried to find out what they'd eaten that day, and if they'd had lunch, because she said they'd never had lunch in the past. (Yes, we learned, they'd had box macaroni and lettuce, which I hated myself for thinking sounded suspiciously balanced to impress DSS.) I was also trying to decipher what Ryan, who always spoke cryptically, even when he wasn't covering for adults, meant by "the new Hardee's, you know, the *new* one," in an unnameable county or town.

Ryan's more experienced foster mom, Mona, was equally disgusted at the vagueness and confusion of the whole transition, even though she had pressed for a plan for Ryan to leave as her twin nieces had just moved in to stay while both of their parents were deployed overseas. Since he had started spending weekends with Benny, Ryan had come back to her house saying things like "I don't eat with brown people," and he was refusing to sit at the dinner table with Mona's nieces. So Mona was well ready for him to be gone, but not like this.

As for Michael, he would walk around the day care on Monday mornings, saying, "Belt, belt, spank, spank," while the director and I looked at each other with big eyes and pressed lips.

Somehow, we learned that the kids had been in the new trailer once and found a nail to hang a backpack on but that it had no furniture. ("Sweet Home in a Trailer," the boys always loved to screech—the *8 Mile* version of the classic—oblivious to Eminem's bitterness.) I think perhaps the new trailer became their storage space, because I remember some commotion when the year's lease was up, their vehicle was down, and the landlord wanted their stuff the hell out of it.

We never understood how this arrangement could go undetected—and by *we*, I mean the children's Grandma Irene, Ryan's foster mom, and me. Clearly the kids were spending all their visiting time at Benny's place, cruising around bareheaded on dirt bikes and four-wheelers with Benny's grandson. Yes, I shuddered to think that Jessica's boyfriend had *grandchildren* who were older than Michael. This was pre-reunification, so surely all we had to do was to somehow get DSS to see this, to *realize* that the judge's order was being violated and that Jessica and the kids were not staying in that new place at all! Mom was still married, albeit to an inmate, yet she wanted the kids to spend their nights with a man they vividly remembered watching fight with their dad? Just a quick, pointed disclosure and DSS would realize that the whole housing situation was a scam, and then surely the reunification would dissolve and we'd have the children and be home free! They could even send Isabelle to our home, I thought, beneficent in abstraction.

The one big *but*? Somehow, this exposure of the children's new living arrangements had to happen without appearing to come from us, because once the kids were back with their mom for good, she could cut all of us, even Grandma Irene, off completely. So how to move forward?

Isabelle's foster mom had her business to run and a baby to consume her time; brisk and efficient, after caring for many dozen foster kids, she had seen it all and had a caring but more logical perspective than the rest of us did. Nothing that a judge or social worker did surprised her, and the process was just the process, in her view. So Ryan's foster mom, Mona, would be the one to speak up, we decided. She was the one with nothing to lose, as she was in a hurry for Ryan to leave in the first place so she could settle her nieces, so she started to wonder aloud to the social worker if the kids actually were getting fed during these weekend days, because Ryan came back so hungry. Shouldn't DSS be monitoring those weekend visits? Dropping in unannounced?

Mona raised enough doubt that the agency promised someone would drop in on the family—and, in fact, the head of our Child Protective Services unit at the time lived closer, so she would do it, rather than Kayla, the young social worker who had first worked so hard to get the children into custody and now seemed so determined to push them back out again.

And so the supervisor did stop by, on a Sunday morning, we were informed. And all was fine. Food in the cabinets. "No concerns." Full speed ahead.

"Benny's place is much more appropriate for kids," Kayla quickly told me later that week while not meeting my eye. I was stunned; Mona and Grandma Irene were stunned. So Kayla had known—and her supervisor had known—that the family was at Benny's place? Yet, in their view, apparently, Jessica had met the letter of the law—and maybe they just gambled that the law wouldn't look. After all, I guessed, if Mom and the kids could live where she didn't have to work to support herself, and could slide off their caseload and budget . . . "More appropriate than a trailer park—and, honestly," Kayla shrugged, "Mom's going to need the help."

Also irrelevant was that neither Jessica nor Benny could drive legally, although they always had a vehicle. "We don't get into law enforcement issues," Kayla said.

(The only one who did care about licenses, it turned out, was the secretary of the new day care to which Jessica was slated to send Michael.

She later confronted Jessica once or twice about dropping him off but having no driver's license. And so the developmentally delayed Michael stopped going there and just stayed home or with Benny's grown daughter instead.)

Unreal. Everyone knew—they'd just agreed to leave us out of the loop. And now, even worse, Jessica and Benny, who hated scrutiny more than anything, would know why DSS had come that weekend to check. Someone had put them up to it. Jessica, Benny, and the family social worker were all on one side, and we—Irene, Mona, and I—were on the other. Leaving the kids in the middle, obediently keeping the secret.

DO A quick search of internet comments about social worker interventions, and suddenly every commenter, left wing to right, is a Tea Party libertarian, so certain everything social workers do is government interference and overreach—"Getting in our business" is the all-purpose description. Whether it's free-range kids, homesteading megafamilies living in tents, poverty rates of investigated families—the latest media outrage seems to bring liberals and libertarians together in judgment of social work. But at the time, when we were facing Michael's imminent return to a new home with a sudden near stepdad, I wanted to demand: *Where does all this "interference" happen? Because it sure isn't here.* Everything our social workers did, they ascribed to state codes and mandates that protect the primacy of parents' rights, so was it really just our little agency that seemed so conscientiously cautious? So careful in their prescribed responses? So full of belief in the parental potential of people most of the rest of us would have written off? At the time I didn't know what to believe or whom. I simply knew that my own beliefs, complaints, and hopes were entirely beside the point.

MY FEARS took deeper root when the children began to leave us—first brother Ryan, five, and sister Isabelle, almost seven, went back together to Jessica; then, two weeks later, at just over two years of age, Michael left foster care with us and joined his siblings and mother in her boyfriend's remote, phoneless trailer, more than seventy minutes from our home. How could this be called reunification, I bitterly asked Mona, when the children were moving—I certainly couldn't say *returning*—to a family configuration that had never existed, to a home in a county where they had never officially lived, to a home that was not leased in their mother's name, and to a situation in which a judge had ordered the children should not live? At the same time, to fulfill the court's decree the family was renting a crummier and more expensive town trailer in which they had never spent a night, paid for by government housing funds; the unused trailer was the essence of government waste, which perfectly suited the landlord.

I STILL don't understand how this situation could have happened, but neither that supervisor nor the social worker stayed at the agency much longer. Yet, if we'd made any kind of a protest, well . . . we'd signed the foster parent agreement that we would actively support the agency's reunification goals and never interfere.

"You're not going to stop this," the social worker told the director of our day care who had called to report Michael's "belt, belt" warnings after the weekend visits. They would all go to live with the boyfriend with the ice-blue eyes and endless suitcases of Busch beer in the trunk of his car. "Nothing's going to stop this."

And nothing did.

NIGHT OR DAY

Our experience as foster parents was unusual. Unusually unusual, given how different each child and family's experience can be. Michael had indeed stayed with us six months before being returned to this new incarnation of his family (Dad newly out of jail and Mom living in the next county with a much older boyfriend—hardly an uncommon relationship dynamic, I was to discover). Amazingly, we were able to remain involved after reunification, thanks to Michael's paternal grandmother and his still-young mother, Jessica. At first I was filled with cold doubt and despair when Jessica hesitated to let me plan a visit during Michael's first weeks back home; I didn't know whether to blame the social worker, who might well have advised a break from us to let Michael settle, or Jessica's boyfriend, who seemed eager to fence his new family off from any more prying eyes or interference, or my own voracious need to cling to Michael and nail down some assurance of a future with him. Most likely, it was a combination of the three that initially scared Jessica away. But after a couple of false starts, she stayed true to her word: Michael had lost enough people already, she'd often said, and didn't have to lose Will and me. Jessica had lost plenty of special people herself, she would tell me, from her only protective and nurturing relative to the afterschool support team that had cheered her through middle school to the teachers who'd wept when she was pulled out of ninth grade to tend her siblings at home. Even the destruction of her first hard-earned car, which had been borrowed without her permission and wrecked, sounded like the soul-killing loss of one more treasured relationship. So whatever resistance, natural jealousy, or awkwardness Jessica might have faced in allowing Will and me to maintain our bond with Michael as he grew, she would not let her youngest child lose the love and support of which she had been robbed repeatedly herself. I longed to believe this, but I knew there were conditions—and that Benny held sway over all decisions.

For Michael and his siblings, home life was often chaotic, traumatic, dangerous, exciting, and unpredictable—sometimes visibly so and always weighted with secrets and adult pressures. Before, during, and after foster care, older sister Isabelle clung to the role of little mother to Michael, while Ryan and Michael often believed themselves responsible for the well-being of Jessica and Benny.

Despite how friendly and bluntly honest he could be, I was terrified of Benny, whose background check had not raised concerns at DSS: his record showed prison time and lost driver's licenses—but no substantiated child abuse. The same boyfriend taught the boys one of their favorite sayings—"It's not a threat, it's a promise"—and never went anywhere without a knife pouch on his belt. To this day, the teenage Michael hates walking in the dark, even if he is holding my hand, because he remembers running for his life from Benny's shouted threats through the night, pulling his mom along as she stumbled. Benny's white-blue eyes shock even now when called up on a computer image search; in a nonstop stream of talk, he'd enumerate for any stranger the elements of his swirling inner turmoil, an uproar that Michael came to believe only he could quell. And when Michael was a teen and at last in our custody, he would ask if our family could get into the witness protection program, although we were never part of any case against Benny.

Also unsettling was that Jessica was almost young enough to have been my daughter, while Benny and I were of the same generation, albeit worlds apart culturally and economically. And I eventually heard that before their removal, Michael's siblings had seen Benny and their father fighting and supposedly trying to stab each other in a parking lot; for years the boys revisited this story, insisting it was "over a dog." They later admitted seeing Benny choke their mother as well, but they knew to keep that a secret from us. From fear of Benny, but even more, I guessed, of betraying the family and losing the mother they had only recently regained. The idea that such violence might cause her to leave Benny and take the children with her was not the simple option it might appear, no matter how much help she was offered; the kids seemed to know that keeping their mom was a package deal, bound to the very force that might destroy her.

These children breathed fear on a daily basis—fear mingled with the ever-present cigarette smoke so its scent was no longer detectable, just part of the air. Unsurprisingly, that was how Benny said he had spent his childhood as well, trying to protect himself and his mother from alcohol-fueled violence, and never knowing safety or freedom until he'd grown big enough to fight back. That such cycles repeat is news to no one; the question of how to stop them in the next generation is what confounds parents of all kinds.

Back before reunification, I thought I understood why Michael needed to return to his mother and siblings—so long as Jessica fit my version of single-mom nobility. So long, I guess, as her choices of how and where to live and with whom were not hers to make. But, of course, those choices were all part of the basic American freedom package of having her life and kids back. And I shared the social worker's muttered doubt that still-fragile Jessica could handle and financially support three spirited kids on her own.

IN THE PICTURE

At DSS you learn that every birth parent is called "Mom," or, more rarely, "Dad," as in "Mom was appropriate" or "Dad's in jail" or "We've given Mom a month to get it together." Maybe it's shorthand that saves the trouble of remembering names; or maybe all clients have somehow blended into one dysfunctional parent. It's this way as well, we learned, in school, mental health, and juvenile court counselors' offices, where the kids always have first names, often infamous ones, and the parents don't; where Mom and Dad get pronounced with practiced neutrality. "But Mom's got to do her part," social workers will warn, or, more charitably, "We can give Mom some vouchers." Meaning she can get a couch she has no means of transporting to her home, and all the used blue jeans she can stuff into a grocery sack at the church-run thrift store. Given a month, wouldn't that help anyone get it together?

INTO THE WOODS

The Path of Needles, The Path of Pins . . . this was the choice offered Red Riding Hood by the wolf in an early version of her story. Both were bad options for navigating the deep, dark woods on the way to the Grandmother's house, where the wolf would famously wait, ready to spring his trap. *Needles? Pins?* I've seen explanations that range from sexual metaphors to evocation of a dressmaking apprenticeship—no one seems to know the original source; to me, these routes described the always painful, always hazardous paths I trod toward and around Michael's family, with forks that offered only bad choices. I knew, too, that a stumble over the thinnest root can send you back to the starting place. You can never put your foot down securely, never even know if you are moving forward—or toward what.

There was no right way to walk this walk, so I picked my way through the dark wood from day to day, straining to spot breadcrumb clues, always fearing I'd never find my way back into Michael's life again.

PATH OF NEEDLES

I had never fully believed we'd get to visit after Michael went back to his mother, especially after Jessica pulled the plug on the very first visit we'd planned. She had asked the confused DSS director to call at the last minute to inform me the visit was off—a call that had sent me cascading into grief and the certainty that the family would deliberately disappear into the cliffs and chasms of the next county. Then, a month after his return, Jessica offered to let Michael come visit us the weekend after Thanksgiving. Everything went perfectly until I took Michael back that Sunday evening: we met halfway in a Wendy's parking lot, and as I handed Michael to his mother and Benny, Michael cried my name and he reached out to come back to me instead of going to Jessica. I saw Benny's eyes flare—as the all but official stepdad, he clearly gave the orders now, and he pulled Michael sharply away. Michael reached for me again, wailing. I couldn't reach back: I had to pin my arms to my sides and keep the dumb plastic grin glued to my mouth, the ultimate betrayal. I drove back home in despair, sure this was the end.

But thanks to their grandmother Irene, who continued to keep the children every other weekend as she had before and during foster care, I was able to spend many Sunday afternoons hugging and playing cars with two-year-old Michael. It was incredible good luck: simply getting to see him this way gave me the patience to hang on when I started to panic. I even got to experience an approximation of Christmas that first winter when Irene invited me to spend the Saturday afternoon before the holiday with all three kids at her home, sharing lunch and watching them go through the Christmas motions. Michael sat on my lap, playing with the antenna on his new remote control truck as Ryan and Isabelle leapt from couch to coffee table in new onesie leopard pajamas, tearing open presents and Precious Moments bibles, while I-Carly and Sam bickered from the TV.

After Christmas, I got my nerve up and asked Jessica to let Michael visit again for several days of our university break and for weekends now and then, to which she agreed as if nothing had happened. But I always feared this arrangement might suddenly end, simply because Benny had decided that Michael and I were too close. At the end of each visit, I begged Will to make the drive with me and be the one to pass Michael back, just in case.

SHORTLY AFTER New Year's I found out the family's case had been closed. DSS had released them, and months earlier than I'd expected. Full stop. So I was shocked, a few weeks into January, when Irene called and asked me to stop by her work. Breathless, she told me that the boys' sister had raised alarms at her new school and that the guidance counselor had summoned their county's DSS in response to her disclosure.

Isabelle? I was staggered. The first-grader who had cried and pined and begged through half a year of foster care to go back with her mother? I knew she hated Benny, who had usurped her beloved father's place. But how terrible must things be if Isabelle was the one causing an alarm?

She had seen Mom's new boyfriend smoking from a pipe, like her dad used to, the girl had said. "A pipe" could have meant marijuana; it could have meant crack or meth. Regardless, she must have hoped that telling the counselor would bring the ceiling crashing in. Maybe Isabelle pictured her mom, brothers, and estranged dad coming back together for a happily-ever-after ending.

"She doesn't like my rules," Jessica explained, "all because I wouldn't let her eat potato chips for breakfast that day. Was I wrong not to let her?"

Was this what I'd been praying for? Didn't something have to happen now? My lungs inflated with an impure mix of hope and dread.

But then—nothing.

Michael did not magically reappear in our crib, and Jessica and Benny's TracFone was perennially out of minutes. All we heard was that Benny had been required to show up at the courthouse for a drug test. And that he'd been furious. And that then, when one of the new county's social workers had come out to Benny's trailer, Isabelle had run up into the woods and hidden until the worker had heard Jessica's story and left again. There was a missing piece somewhere: Why didn't the social worker go talk to Isabelle at school? Ask the child why she was afraid? With my usual trust in authority, I assumed something was going on behind the scenes with the new DSS, something we couldn't see or know.

For two or three weeks, apparently, Isabelle was not allowed to eat with her brothers, and she had to sit apart at the Little Tikes table. With the whole family in the car, Benny drove her down the road in the dark and threatened to keep driving her right back to the foster home where she'd had to eat all her food and go off to her room if she wanted to cry. Then, abruptly, still attributing what Isabelle had said to revenge for being denied potato chips, Jessica and Benny sent Isabelle to live with Irene, where she remained, going back only for visits. And given the strange lifelong tension between Benny and Isabelle, Jessica must have sensed her daughter would be much safer growing up there.

Once Isabelle was gone, I held my breath, elated for her liberation despite the loss of her dream. Plus, she had been especially close to her father's mother, so it seemed like a natural fit that could provide the family comfort she seemed to have been craving. "I think the kids are all coming out of there," said a friend's cousin who knew the family through a different service agency. Maybe it would all be over, just like that! Maybe my months of fearful longing since Michael had moved home and out of DSS custody had all been a necessary nightmare. Maybe we'd paid our dues karmically, and Michael—maybe even his brother—would be back with us for good!

It was February, and my hopes soared that things might go wrong enough that Michael would be removed and sent back to us. That was when I first started proposing all manner of bargains to God—a compulsion that would continue for years—for I was painfully aware it would take a catastrophe for Social Services to intervene to that degree. Whatever the possible disaster, I prayed ceaselessly that the children would escape unscathed physically and not die in the process. While that might sound like any parent's daily irrational fear, the only irrational part was the conviction that my own constant panic kept him safe, in some strange, cosmic balance. If I relaxed my vigilance for a second or let myself get lost in an enjoyable moment, I felt the worst might befall Michael and his family. I kept thinking of the high-rise apartment block in an old Monty Python sketch, which collapses to rubble the minute its tenants forget to believe in it. But it was no joke to me. I was relieved eventually to learn there was an actual name for this—"vicarious trauma," which caregivers, along with counselors, are prone to suffer.

AS MUCH as everyone had wanted Jessica to be the very model of the bootstrap Single Mom, keep her fast-food job, and strike out on her own with all three kids and their electronic welfare (EBT) card, clearly that was not ever going to be: sending Isabelle to live with her Grandma Irene was for the best. Jessica believed I was the only person who considered her a good parent, and not a bad one, for doing it, and I did. I still do. And yet I had secretly, selfishly hoped that having three kids to juggle would make everything break down more quickly and visibly. And I worried: What if having only two kids made life manageable or made the chaos more concealable, at least?

Isabelle's departure made clear to both boys what happened when someone failed the basic loyalty test. Ryan, especially, never forgot this and made keeping family secrets his specialty. And like his elders, he often spoke of facts, arrangements, and events in a rushed, jumbled, confounding, broken way that, purposely or not, further obscured any truth and avoided confrontation while leaving the listener unsure of what he'd said and afraid or embarrassed to press for specifics. It was the perfect cloaking device.

DAY AND NIGHT

My acquaintance's prophecy to the contrary, the boys did not "come out of there" as their sister did, but on and off, as Benny and Jessica gradually allowed Michael to visit with Will and me, we became more friendly and operated with the illusion of trust. We let that polite illusion settle over everything, but it seemed then as delicate as one of those foil emergency blankets that reflects body heat but seems likely to blow away or be crumpled up and thrown away in an instant. Even so, absolutely nothing required that Jessica allow Michael to see us, and at almost any point for the next decade she had the full right to cut our ties completely and at any moment.

No matter how illusory that veneer of trust was, I sincerely believed that anything I might do to help any close or extended family member, child or adult, find medical care or community opportunities or simply to get from one place to another would strengthen the whole in some small way and bond us through experience and goodwill.

Beyond that, I tried to use my letter-writing skills to help Benny resolve any number of bureaucratic issues. My reliable phone and computer gave me the ability and persistence to track down answers, while my convenient credit card too often made utility cutoffs and medical bills magically disappear. Will hired Jessica's brother, father, and Benny to re-roof our garage; we shared Thanksgiving and Scout potlucks, where conservative Christian parents overlooked the long hair and alcohol-infused slurring, accepted Benny's offers to assemble the pinewood derby track for the boys' annual wooden car competition, and said nothing when he cussed out the judge for the regional race.

But Benny seemed never more purposeful than when it would fall to him to take Michael or Ryan up into the hills on his four-wheeler and comfort them about the most recent failings of their birth father, Luke—everything from a missed visit to another prison sentence. Benny was there for them, he wanted them to know: for good and bad, this understanding sank in. Certainly at times the boys loved Benny and felt sorry for him when he suffered days-long spells of silent sadness. The boys would creep around the house, watching videos or playing Guitar Hero on mute, or they messed around outside in the woods with scavenged car parts for hours, as Benny lay in the corner of a darkened room, haunted by old losses, a sheet draped over the window to mute the light. Often at these times, Jessica would call to ask if I wanted to come get the boys for a few days, knowing I'd jump at the chance. "Can't Mom come with us, too?" the boys would often beg me, fearing they'd return to find her dead, not knowing I'd asked her myself, out of their hearing. Occasionally, she would allow me to drop her off somewhere, but usually she'd say that Benny was harmless at that point and that she was afraid to leave him alone in a depressed condition. Relieved as the boys seemed once they'd climbed into my car, I was sure they felt guilty to leave her behind.

Seeing Benny laid low, it was hard to picture his frightening rages, much less the usual brassy cheer and party spirit he brought to everything when he felt okay. In good times, Benny loved to work and seemed to feel most himself when working, whether work was crawling across a roof in blistering July heat, replacing spark plugs for a neighbor, or rolling paint down a wall in invisibly blended strokes. Work was his salvation, but there was never enough of it to last long.

As time went on, though, I noticed that Jessica began to arrange never to be alone with Benny, whether that was by babysitting cousins' kids, offering a couch to semihomeless friends, or even allowing Michael to stay behind to soothe Benny through an extra-bad morning and saddle himself with the impossible burden of curing an adult's grief.

Jessica watched the moon phases, as I began to, half-believing the full moon predicted the times of greatest danger. I worried Benny might die at his low times, but that they all might die at the peak ones. I tried hard never to be out of phone range. I didn't travel out of state or overnight without them. And I knowingly missed the last years of my only grandmother's life because she lived across the ocean. No one asked me to do this. I just knew I couldn't leave them.

FOR ONCE in my life, I wanted people to tell me my dread was baseless—that I was being paranoid and overreacting. I never doubted that Benny loved Jessica and her kids, yet no one who knew Michael's family, from within or without, thought my fear for their lives an exaggeration, least of all the children. ("We're a *re-active* agency," different social workers would tell me apologetically the few times I directly dared to seek them out. "We can't react to something that hasn't happened yet.") For a decade my heart twisted coldly in my chest every time I read or heard about a father, stepfather, or boyfriend who had killed an entire family. Sometimes these killings came out of fury, revenge, or impending loss. Even more alarming was when the killer reportedly had decided that life was too painful to live, so he would spare his loved ones in advance. And who could predict the amplifying effects of alcohol and drugs on moods that could shift from day to night within an hour?

Plus it wasn't just *self*-medication: Jessica's desperate fix when marijuana failed to soothe Benny's fury or despair was to stuff as many Valium as she could find down his throat and hope he'd sleep his way out of it. It's not even that he was averse to seeking help or spilling a blue streak of terrifying emotions and histories to any professional who would listen; it wasn't that there were no basic resources for the uninsured and desperate. The help was there, at least to the frustration-filled degree it may be for those who lack means and reliable transportation and are tired of being told what to do, but to me Benny seemed just too ill for the system—too damaged by life and chemistry; too numbed by mood stabilizers; too pulled by his morning beer and all day vodka-spiked Sprite; too yoked by the addictions from which he claimed he'd saved girlfriends; and too purely dangerous for any woman or child to live with.

Except that they did. So why would no one, least of all DSS—or Mom herself—put a stop to it? When, Will and I implored each other, would Jessica ever really leave him? I ranted for years to anyone foolish or caring enough to ask how Michael was doing or, with a worried glance, how "Mom" was doing. And Grandma—biodad Luke's mom, Irene—and I would rage together to each other, demanding answers of the air.

To her great credit, Jessica often would call me when Benny was near his worst—although I realized I would never see his actual worst, and hers, which might have gotten the kids removed. Jessica knew I'd drive over to get them at any hour, whether they were a county away and it was snowing, or (later) back in this county, which meant winding across eleven miles of gravel above the river's edge. "Please, phone me anytime," I begged her.

"Hopefully, she'll keep calling you" was all our social worker Gerri would say—*could* say. Until the kids were in imminent, concrete danger, awaiting a midnight rescue by police whom the kids couldn't call with a crushed or drowned cell phone, by police whom Jessica, the boys, and her parents had been taught from birth never, ever to call. That was the moment when Social Services could legally step in.

NEED TO KNOW

Eight months later the state was doing a random check on the disposition of the county's cases and picked Jessica's family file, apparently by chance. A representative from the state was coming to the area, and each of us had to show up and speak with him—separately, like criminals, I thought, to see if our stories matched. We were getting to visit with Michael every couple of weeks then, so I had already started treading lightly, feeling for tremors, ever alert for a misstep. What if I said something negative that the representative would then question Jessica about? She would see I'd known more than she'd realized and that she was right not to trust me. (The one card I held—both major asset and liability—was Jessica's mistaken belief that I could bring in the authorities.)

The representative was young and looked like any gigantic college boy suddenly boxed into a borrowed suit. The state's questions were designed to elicit nothing but predetermined short answers—no open-ended questions, none of the "tell me about *x*" openings that workers from Child Protective Services used to coax information from kids.

I do wonder what he would have done if I'd asked about where the family had been allowed to live and described how they'd gone against the judge's order. But alienating Jessica would mean losing access to Michael—and she was definitely slated to be interviewed after I was. More important, I could not afford to alienate DSS now, in case Michael and his siblings did come back into the system. Our section of DSS had as its new director a former social worker, someone I deeply trusted. So I was careful as I sat in that dark little office going through unexpected questions. For some reason I was seated beside the representative instead of across from him; the arrangement meant no subtext could possibly show through my expression. He leaned up against a desk and wrote brief answers on a clipboard; as he read the list of questions, his main focus was on what we'd been told about the reasons for Michael's coming into foster care. Surprised, I explained that we had not been told much of anything, aside from the frustrated remark by the social worker that "Mom's not doing what she's supposed to"—an explanation that could have described virtually any case in the system.

I'd always had the impression that "need to know" was the social workers' standard for sharing anything—coupled with the understanding that we might expect most of the behavior we saw from children in foster care but never comprehend the reasons for it. Jessica had frequently complained to me that they had never told her why they were taking the kids and that she'd been "clean" at the point they did; I believed her and could not understand the reason either.

Yet I also could not understand why DSS had not taken the kids far sooner, especially after they heard about the dog urine smell and chest rattle that Michael brought to day care when he attended, and the stories that his sister Isabelle began to whisper. Back during that first summer when we fostered Michael, Isabelle had directed me along a series of steep and rutted back roads to take her to see their old trailer, neither of us knowing it had been condemned and burned; Jessica often mentioned bitterly that Michael's father had carried him as an infant into another trailer across the county that had caught fire and exploded a mere two hours later. So why hadn't the kids been removed much sooner? Whatever the story, those two blackened, toxic trailers seemed like reason enough.

"Had the workers mentioned domestic violence?" the representative kept asking, and I was mystified. Well, no, but Michael's parents were no longer together, and it had sounded like things were still in a honeymoon phase with Benny. Maybe this was just a generic question asked of everyone—or could it be the real purpose of a state survey? It was clear to me that Michael had been exposed to fighting: he could not bear even slightly raised voices at the dinner table the couple of times Will and I stupidly had argued in front of him. Michael had put his hands on his ears and bellowed. So I knew that fighting or domestic violence had to be part of the problem, but, given all the chatter about the chronic problems of our region—dropout rates, child hunger, child neglect, meth labs, oxycodone, lack of transportation, lack of housing, lack of jobs, lack of healthcare, lack of fathers, and overall generational poverty—I'd figured that adult domestic violence was just one more standard ingredient in a poisonous brew that was causing foster care case numbers to rise. ("There's no meth case I've seen that has *not* involved domestic violence," a detective told our training group a couple of years later.)

Maybe the representative asked other families about the whole meth situation, which was exploding in the county's consciousness at that point, front and center. Or maybe, like the benefits of our spring water, it somehow had not yet registered on the consciousness of the capital.

Locally, sheriff's deputies were going around to all the civic groups and presenting slide shows of crime scenes and pictures of the kitchen sinks where dirty baby bottles were jumbled together with old matchboxes, turpentine cans, and other meth-manufacturing crap. I must have seen that slide show at least three times, wondering at the flip-book-style progression of a dozen real faces before, during, and after meth, going from firefighters' carnival beauty queen to skin-draped skull. Trainers told us repeatedly that during meth busts of trailers, kids were sprayed with fire hoses to decontaminate them—as if being carried from their homes by strangers in the dark was not horror enough—before being taken to the hospital for late-night evaluation. Their hair strands were plucked to test for meth exposure, and they moved on to emergency placements wearing hospital bracelets and oversized new tracksuits. All their clothes and toys were supposed to be confiscated, further amplifying their loss, but kids' consignment stores were booming at the time, and who was really watching to see if adults came sneaking back?

RACCOON RIDGE

Through the long, snowy spring after Michael had left his new day care following the dispute over who could drive him, Jessica allowed me to keep him from early morning until evening every Wednesday—the day I had set aside for grading, which I then crammed into the overnight hours or any others I could, just to have those eleven hours to pour into Michael.

That summer, he came for more weekends and another beach vacation week, but for much of it I was consumed with jealousy as Jessica worked sporadically at a fast-food job and sent him over to Destinee, one of Benny's grown daughters who lived a few miles away with her son and husband, Denver. Long-limbed and pretty, with Snow White's heart-shaped face and raven hair, she wore thick eyeliner and mascara that gave her eyes a harsh cast; in conversation she moved up close and entertained whoever was present with rowdy charisma and a frequent smoker's laugh. For no visible cost, she kept Michael and Ryan every day with her own son and some neighboring kids who seemed to wander in. She fed them hot dogs on forks, obsessively cleaned their ears with bobby pins, and toilet trained Michael (after all my tedious race car potty sticker charts and praise) by having him spend the day naked and going like a dog outside. This method worked great, his mom and others agreed—it was how everyone potty-trained in summer, diapers cost too damn much. And now, in Jessica and Benny's car, he wore big kids' underwear beneath gigantic T-shirts.

Destinee's home on Raccoon Ridge sat atop a series of sharp switchbacks flanked by dizzying drop-offs that seemed as effective as a medieval moat for keeping strangers away. A three-sided deck was built onto the house, and although it was then early in the super-electronics age, their living/dining room had the largest-screen TV I've still ever seen—no doubt salvaged from one of Denver's commercial jobs—with gigantic soap opera faces talking desperately, their stereo-amplified dialogue dogging every real-life conversation.

Relentlessly competitive, Destinee was either Jessica's best friend or treacherous enemy, depending on the week. From what I gathered, she hadn't actually lived with Benny during her childhood, but her uncanny knack for reading people's vulnerabilities, drawing them in and getting them to meet her needs, and lying convincingly about the plain truth even when the stakes were nonexistent—all this seemed to signal that wherever she'd grown up, it had been in round-the-clock survival mode, having to struggle for every scrap. Such survival tactics are hard enough to accept compassionately in a child; when they've hardened into adult behavior, they are near-impossible to respond to with anything but outrage. With Destinee you never knew if she knew she was purposely pushing your buttons or if it had long become second nature—but she was so good at it that I'd always blame myself and bite back a reaction. In her party-girl rasp, Destinee would talk about Michael possessively—"you just love hot dogs the way I fix 'em, don't you, honey?"—then laugh about how he'd suddenly disappeared and was found outside, pooping in the yard. She was planning to fix him a Thomas the Tank Engine birthday cake because he adored trains—how could I fault her for that? How could she have known I wanted to buy him the perfect Thomas sheet cake, tracks and all, from the grocery store bakery? I just wanted to either cry or scream.

Why, if Michael wasn't staying home with his mom—why, if he was spending the days at Destinee's—could he not just come to me? Clutching the steering wheel around the bends, I drove up Raccoon Ridge twice to pick him up and felt my stomach curl with resentment. I tried to drop hints to Jessica, because I knew that if I asked outright to keep him on these summer days, she would refuse in some utterly confusing way to avoid the discomfort of having to say no directly. I would appreciate Michael, teach him, love him (*spoil him,* I could guarantee Benny would say—and I knew they said that among themselves all the time, meaning the normal, unextravagant things I did for Michael, such as taking him to a swimming pool or library magic show). I'd happily drive him back and forth twice a day, whatever. Ryan too, gladly. But Jessica's job seemed to vaporize, and then she and the kids were hanging out all day and evening with Destinee while Benny and Denver were out working. I took what time I could get, drawing comfort from Michael's carrying around in his pocket a tiny plastic farm wife figurine that he thought was modeled on me—he called it "my Debbie," and he also had one he called "Will" that perched, cowless, on a milking stool. But Michael's face still looked narrow and pinched, like that of an aging elf, as it had since he'd first gone back home. Now only when he was asleep did I see his nose, his cheeks, his lips regain their soft, round shape. How long before he would forget about me?

IT WAS hard to get a read on Destinee, for she always seemed always to be "on" and poised for action. I wondered how she'd come to live in this state, when Benny was from elsewhere, but I knew that asking would be rude if not disastrous. She was an indoor chain smoker; crewcut her son's and Ryan's hair for summer, as most local families did; and thought nothing of "popping" children on the wrist or behind if they "needed it." Her voice was always a little too loud, as if she had grown used to speaking over blasting metal music or TV, and her thickly lined eyes were always brimming with energy. And consciously or otherwise, she could pack more subtext and landmines into a sentence than any playwright I'd ever read.

The second time I picked Michael and Ryan up on Raccoon's Ridge, Destinee cornered me—although it was not in a corner but in the middle of her living room. I felt cornered anyway.

"So Ryan says you're a Jewish." No noun.

True to Destinee's instincts, this was something I had tried to keep unstated. I didn't need anything to differentiate me even further—it was quite enough to be the strait-laced foster parent among the family's four-wheeling Don't-Tread-on-Me crowd.

I steeled my smile for some hostile comment or, worse, some request for financial advice. She stood two inches from me, her large blue eyes paling. I could tell from her tone that she was not going to issue the usual invitation to come to church—and even though Destinee wore a cross, I'd never heard any mention of their actually going to one of the fundamentalist churches around them.

Yet this turned out to be the most human interchange we'd ever have. "I loved *The Passion of the Christ,*" Destinee told me. Mel Gibson's movie, with its infamously sadistic gore, had just come out on video, and she and all the kids had watched it three times on the enormous living room screen. "I've been looking for someone to ask—what was that language they were speaking? When Ryan told me what you were, I thought you would know."

So of all the terrible accusations that she might have made about Jews, especially after seeing that movie, hers was just a simple, burning fan question about Aramaic. And somehow I knew the answer. I learned then that she had been raised Catholic, which both surprised and reassured me a little, though I'm not sure of what. I'd definitely gotten off easy.

"You and Will should come to our four-wheeler parties," Destinee told me another time, in front of Benny and a garage full of his friends who were assembling for Michael a ride-in plastic car I'd bought him. I was hoping they'd help *him* do it, as I was unable to, but these grown men were having too much fun solving the tricolor plastic puzzle themselves. "We go for, like, three days," Destinee continued. "Y'all should come." I cringed, hoping no specific dates would follow. Whatever went on in those parties, I didn't want to be trapped in complicity.

Four-wheelers were the enemy, in my predictable view, bringing a daily roulette of death, paralysis, or brain damage for these kids. I was hugely relieved every time they had to pawn one of the ATVs. Although Benny often promised to take us on one of the unreliable four-wheelers when it was running, Destinee and Denver's alcohol-driven four-wheeler weekend was the last place Benny and Jessica would want Will and me. I didn't know if Destinee meant this invitation sincerely—it was the greatest thing she had to offer—or whether it was just to laugh at us or rile Jessica. Destinee's first impulse was always triangulation, I would soon learn—so automatic and perfectly executed that I couldn't even tell if she knew she was doing it. Another hardwon survival skill, no doubt, but hard to appreciate when I was the one in the middle of it. Still, I was always mystified that they didn't all always act like we were extensions of the DSS machinery. (Jessica claimed to like the social workers—and well she might, for all the practical help and encouragement they had given her.) Was it because they knew I had everything to lose or because they actually saw the sincere ally I often tried to be? Was I just overthinking everything, as usual? As for Destinee in particular, did the invitation come from her disruptive reflexes or did she simply see everyone as potential party material?

THROUGH THE few years I witnessed, Destinee sowed chaos and was fueled by it, provoking feuds and betrayals, building brief alliances, and even likely saving Jessica's life by a well-timed call to the police, which went unappreciated, to say the least.

In truth, she was severely ill and addicted. The kids believed she had made her own young son smoke and then cough for the doctor so she could get codeine; and when a padlock was picked and half of Ryan's huge bottle of tonsillectomy pain medication disappeared, the suspicion immediately fell on Destinee and her friends. Jessica would have to make a police report to replace it, I told her; seething as she was, she chose to gamble that Ryan wouldn't really need it all—and he didn't. My urging Jessica to report it, I see now, was typically naive—in Jessica's world, suffering from the actions of others was always preferable to snitching. And although at that point they were not speaking, Destinee's life had fallen apart and she was living on Jessica and Benny's couch and eating their food—because she had nowhere else to go. Having "nowhere else to go" was a reason I came to realize trumped everything, on both sides of the family, no matter the difficult situations it led to. Was there a line between being Christian and enabling? Between protecting family members and being consumed by them? Who was I to say? Was it actually my family?

STEPPING STONES

Before he'd been home a year, we began getting Michael every other weekend. I was thrilled, and I lived by counting down to those days. Friday evenings I was filled with the joy of reunion and the need to make every little meal and activity perfect; I would lie down and sleep curled to him, just to absorb every possible moment through my skin. Sunday mornings my heart would fill with dread and I would be counting down hours in the other direction instead. Will and I took both boys back to Benny's place on Sunday afternoons—Ryan had come to us from his grandmother's—and Ryan would often have tantrums in our Subaru, kicking the seat and hammering the ceiling. Why didn't I think that our destination might be the cause? Instead, I thought his incoherent tantrums were directed at us or stemmed from his inability to spend more than ten minutes in a car. Ryan didn't really seem to notice us otherwise, so I was surprised when Jessica sent Ryan to us by himself for a weekend to distract him from a week of extreme distress after his father was in a serious accident. I was amazed but glad that Jessica thought we could be some comfort or provide some distraction.

I was always sweating over what would be too much to ask for and what would scare Michael's family off. But Jessica said yes to almost everything I asked to do with Michael or Ryan. Once their school year started, I did anything I could think of to be with them, driving more than an hour each way to take Ryan home from an after-school Cub Scout meeting, both so he could have that all-American normalizing experience and so I could push Michael on the playground swings. That winter and spring I babysat them weekly at a horrible pizza joint (burned crust, dry pizza topping)—flipping the jukebox cards and giving up quarters to blast Lynyrd Skynyrd and Hank Williams Jr., pulling the boys down off the wooden booth dividers, chasing them, policing their squabbles, and finding new ways to waste time in a boring place when I didn't want that time to end—all while Benny went to a required treatment group in the town hall basement. He couldn't be seen illegally driving himself to the meeting, so he and Jessica would switch places in a shopping center parking lot.

I didn't care if I was enabling, helping, whatever—I just hoarded the minutes and hours with Michael, wherever and whenever. As for my three classes, my sixty students—the upside was that I no longer obsessed so much about grading and teaching. Or at least I piled another, much heavier, obsession on top of my anxiety about work. I barely slept, except in two-hour spurts, and my goal was to plow through the grading of stacks of student stories. I was just doing what I could—at home, at school—to make it through to the next moment of relief when I'd see Michael's face break into a smile—"It's my Debba!" Wherever and whenever. Whatever it took, it was worth it.

PICNIC

For several years I supported Jessica in all the practical ways I could, including helping her attend community college and a workforce readiness program. Yes, I wanted more chances to see Michael and Ryan, but part of me also genuinely wanted to see justice done: Surely it was not too late for Jessica to get back some of the life she'd been robbed of as a teen? Against her wishes, she often told me, her parents had forced her to quit the school she loved in ninth grade so she could take care of her younger siblings. And these were not homesteading, haymaking farm days—this was the early 1990s, and her parents wanted their eldest girl at home so they could go out and party.

I continued to run into Jessica's former teachers who, after seeing us together, would pull me aside and say, "Oh, I worried so about her every time she came to school" and "I was so sorry when she quit." I would want to reward their sympathy with a glimpse of a happy ending and an *Educating Rita* optimism about the power of education, but if I mentioned she was in a community college class, their eyes would narrow nonetheless and they'd say, referring to Michael and Ryan, "I'm so glad those boys have you." Unlike me, then, perhaps these grade-school teachers saw the big picture, sensing without knowing what lay ahead: that despite passing a semester, Jessica would not be able to go back to classes after receiving financial aid and disappearing mid-semester, once for serious health reasons but once coerced, in my opinion.

I never did know what to say when people I looked up to, like those retired teachers, would say they were glad the boys had Will and me or something similar. Usually, I'd unravel their comfort and set them straight, saying I was deeply grateful to Jessica for keeping the boys in my life but that I had no power to keep them safe. An abrupt way to repay a kind sentiment, but why should anyone rest easy if I didn't? I am superstitious as well, so I often felt that a kind comment was a bad omen I had to undercut—don't let down your guard, I wanted to say. My foster parent friends would have said, "Pray for us"—words I often wanted to say but, as a Jewish atheist, didn't have the nerve to speak. "If you see something, say something" was more the gist of it—please go ahead and make the call about whatever it might be. (A Big Brother–type volunteer told me, almost offhand, ten months after he'd gone to pick up Michael at home for the first and only time, that he'd been shocked to find Michael's mom unable even to get up to see them off—if only he'd told his mentoring supervisor right away, they'd have had to report it, and perhaps Michael's whole house of cards might have folded. He could have avoided so much. Instead, the well-meaning mentor's solution had been to have me bring Michael directly from school to meet him.)

I was so sure the last days were coming—it was just a matter of when and where the boys would be when the perfect storm of triggers hit, setting off Benny's personal apocalypse. I didn't mean to be rude or just shrug off any stranger's kindness, but the more comfortable and complacent anyone felt about the boys' fate, I believed, the more surely disaster was bound to come.

BUT IN the meantime all Jessica had had to say was that she wanted to go back to school and I snapped to it, concocting a plan that exhausts me to even think about now. For half of a fall semester and all of the following summer one, I drove from my county to the next, picked up Jessica, brought her back to the community college, turned around and got Michael from his third new preschool and took him to work with me, taught my class, went and got Jessica, and took them back again to pick up Ryan from afterschool care and then home again. In the summer semester, I wasn't working and it was all much simpler—just long days spent with Jessica and the boys that were as gratifying to me as the experience seemed to be for her.

For Jessica, even attending the community college as a regular part-time student with a basic course plan was a triumph. It was even more of a boost when she realized that she was one of the few students consistently doing the work outside of class in a room full of dour recent high school graduates. The teachers liked her for this, she said, and respected her for being a mom. It was probably the first time in her life she had felt like a role model. I wanted her to bask in it, and I was thrilled when she would talk about the book they were analyzing or phone me simply to ask about a verb form. The mini-essays she wrote and printed out on a rickety dot matrix printer were all connected to her life and opinions—another thing she rarely had been invited to express, other than personal gripes about people.

The biggest triumph of all came a few weeks into her second, restarted semester after difficult surgery had made it impossible to complete the first. This was in the summer, when she was made class note taker for her math course, an honor that also paid $10 a day. But it seemed that even small victories flew from her grasp, like the enchanted golden Snitch of Harry Potter's Quidditch that was driven to escape: only a few weeks into this new position, she realized that the whiteboard markers in the poorly ventilated amphitheater were triggering the migraines that so crippled her that she left class in tears daily.

For me, the lowest point also came during that summer session. I'd had an idyllic, if consuming, schedule, when I'd drive Monday through Thursday to pick up Jessica for class in the morning, and we'd bring the boys along. I reveled in the triumph of getting them away from the TV and into safety for even a few brief hours. We'd drop Jessica off, then spend the time hitting balls on crumbling tennis courts with giant rackets—Ryan's favorite activity—or we'd attend the library story hour or play miniature golf or hang out at the county rec center—all the fun, really normal, low-key summer things I wanted them to get to do. I loved the time with them, loved the morning breezes and the sunshine reflecting off the deep green, towering trees.

The night before, I'd spend an hour making beautiful lunches for us, with little tubs of mandarin oranges and quesadillas for Michael; sandwiches with pickles and hot peppers for Ryan, who craved eye-tearing heat and sensation; sensible, adult whole wheat sandwiches for Jessica and me; and uncrushable, portion-controlled pods of Pringles. I'd pack it all into an insulated backpack, chilled with ice packs and sweating frozen juice boxes wrapped up in grocery bags to keep them from waterlogging everything. Once Jessica finished her two classes, we'd have lunch at the new, raw wood picnic tables the community college had just put up behind the main building on the austere campus.

The picnic area looked out onto forested slopes and over a dark blue reservoir, the peaceful view softened by the summer haze. The boys would eat briefly, then run around after each other in the short grass, shrieking at bees and climbing onto the tabletops and benches to jump back off them again. I cringed at the marks their shoes left on the unfinished wood—I imagined the picnic tables were a construction class project that had yet to be stained and sealed. There behind the building we couldn't see people coming and going from their cars in the parking lot—really couldn't see anybody. As busy as I would have thought a community college might be in summer, most of that activity must have happened in the evenings, because it seemed quite empty and serene.

No matter where we'd been before arriving on campus, or how many times I'd prompted the boys to use the restroom before we got there, Ryan would always have to go into the college building to use the men's room. Michael was still young enough that I could whisk him in and out of the ladies' room, which was near the back entrance, and we rarely encountered anyone in there. But Ryan was old enough to use the men's and absolutely refused to do otherwise; I suspected he just liked going into the novel, air-conditioned building and all the way down the long, cool central hallway. As much as I wanted to stay out of the building, I itched to at least accompany him inside and stand outside the restroom door, to make sure no stranger danger could reach him, but Jessica would say, "Oh, no, he's fine."

Other than taking something off a bulletin board or trying to put pennies into a vending machine, there was little trouble he could have gotten into, and quite possibly, he didn't cause any. Nonetheless, I would cringe and hold my breath, literally clamping my teeth on my tongue, when Ryan would once again clank through the smoked glass doorway and go down the hall and out of sight. Sometimes I couldn't restrain myself and would anxiously ask Jessica if she wanted to go in after him; I knew she was annoyed by the nervously corrective tone that so often colored my voice, but if he had been gone a little while, sometimes she would.

Why I was the one suffering nerves, I don't know—as was so often true, I should have taken the advice I'd heard many times on videos from the Love and Logic Institute, which DSS used in training both foster and birth families, when they say to parents, "Now, who has the units of concern?" What they mean is that parents should not carry the worry for kids' actions when the kids should shoulder that worry. But in this case, at Ryan's age, it was not the kid's so much as the mother's burden to carry. So I would lie awake at night, mourning the hours of lost sleep because I knew I'd have to be up at six in order to get Jessica to her nine o'clock class, and last in my rosary chain of worries would be the one about Ryan going into the community college building to use the bathroom. So much for the Serenity Prayer—by this point, I'd completely lost any wisdom to know the difference.

All was good between Jessica and me so long as I offered no advice, which would be the case with any mother-friend, really. So Ryan's men's room trips were definitely not my burden to carry, yet I felt absolutely mortified one day, a few weeks into the summer session, when Jessica met us at our usual wooden table where I was unpacking our picnic and snatching after the blowing paper towel napkins.

Jessica was white faced and narrow eyed. "My kids can't be in there anymore," she said. "I can't bring them here at all. They can't be anywhere on the grounds." We had been told to leave.

She was furious and confused; I felt like I'd been slapped. And I was baffled. What in the world could either of the kids have done that was so bad? Wasn't this a *community* college? A no-frills one, to be sure, but wasn't it *for* parents trying to better their lives, among others? Wasn't Jessica practically a poster child for her generation's struggles and here fighting to walk a good path? "I knew Ryan shouldn't have gone in the building," I blurted, even as I tried to muffle my words.

But really, whatever had happened, it was one of those rare times, I realize, when both Jessica and I were angry, and we were actually both angry at, and hurt by, the same thing. By that point, she was probably used to authorities issuing orders without explanation, but all these years later, I still wonder about the reason.

Then, at night, I fumed for all of them. How many more worlds would Jessica be told her family didn't belong in?

INDEPENDENCE DAY

Why did I continue to help? I didn't have to do those things for and with Jessica to keep seeing Michael—that was always entirely clear to me. All

I really had to do was not betray Jessica and Benny to any authorities—a much more difficult challenge. I didn't have to help get the power restored or take Jessica on special outings with us. All that was my choosing. If I couldn't have my first prize of Michael free and clear, then, like Benny, I wanted us to be a family. And I wanted Jessica to break free of everything that had held her back—to be free to have some fulfillment in life. Everyone else in the family was busily wishing she would break free of Benny, but I accepted that this was a lost cause—she'd seemed tantalizingly close to doing that at times, but I just wanted her to have the chance to live more fully. To read, to have real work, to be.

Helping or "helping"? Now, I might see my efforts of those years as enabling, patronizing, naive—but at least it was in the direction of health and for the purpose of good. Yes, my own unproductive hours on the university tenure clock and unwritten pages went whizzing by, and if I'd invested even half the hours I spent on Jessica, much less the boys, on our marriage instead, who knows how much healthier and better a wife I would be. Nonetheless, I hoped that Jessica would acquire some momentum and agency, recover some long-stolen sense of what still could be. I didn't think her life would change or that she would ever break into some Martina McBride chart buster and walk away from Benny, but Jessica surely deserved the simple experience of being in a place where adults read, write, and calculate—where she could be the adult mom in a small comp class of eighteen-year-olds who wants to be there and makes it worth the teacher's time, as virtually all her instructors had told her she could be. Every week she would write her one-page compositions and have me check the spelling before typing them on her antiquated desktop computer—the most memorable for me was an argument paper against a proposed state lottery, based on her experience as a new mother whose husband would insist they end their pressure-washing workweek by driving to the state line and spending all their diaper and rent money on the lottery tickets he was convinced were one number from making them rich. Her husband was not bad at math, he'd told her, and he'd figured the odds.

JESSICA'S PARENTS, who often leaned on her for help, were the least supportive of all when it came to any post-GED education: I doubted this when she told me, until the day her father looked up from working on a car in the driveway and told her she was "gettin' above your raising"—a phrase I'd only ever heard used as a joke. I didn't think real people still said it. He said he couldn't understand the words she used anymore. When she was in grade school, the teachers were still trying to make kids lose their Appalachian accents, and she'd had speech therapy galore. That seemed to have made no difference, luckily, but now six weeks of community college had her speaking to her family like a Hogwarts professor? I didn't think so.

Jessica had a genuine hunger to learn and, like everyone, needed to be listened to by someone who cared about her opinions—yet the peremptory wishes of men quickly overrode her instincts. She would devour any book: her class reading of *Into the Wild*, an account of the fatal adventure of a young survivalist in Alaska; the boys' hardcover library copies of Harry Potters, which she would finish in a night; the Lee Smith novels I passed along; *Fried Green Tomatoes, The Color Purple*, and *The Glass Castle*; and the cover-stripped romance novels she found in the dump's Swap Shop shed. She often spoke of loving to read and told the boys how important it was, even though Ryan could go for weeks without a signature on his school reading log.

More puzzling was that when Michael was in primary school years later, long after Jessica's community college dream had folded, she began doing his homework for him. He did have a lot of it, and he struggled with handwriting, so initially Jessica would take his dictation, writing down words or math numbers in big, looping, girl-cute printing, then have him trace over it in faltering pencil. This in itself was not always a bad thing, but she soon was literally doing the homework for him, not even with him, even when he wanted to do it on his own, he'd tell me; often the work he turned in contained mistakes he would not have made himself. He didn't want to hurt his mother's feelings, Michael said. The homework pages became almost a weird game of keep-away, with me trying to have him do it in my car or with me rather than taking it home. "Please tell Michael he *has* to do it himself," I would beg his new and astonished teacher, whispering so Michael wouldn't hear me and repeat it.

To this day, I am guilty of helping him with homework too much myself, always with the intention of keeping him on track once the afternoon spells of attention deficit and hyperactivity kick in full force; I prod him to do a better job, write in complete sentences, restate questions, show his work, find the evidence, and I simply try to get him to think. Or, as many parents of children with these problems may recognize, to keep him from spending all his energy on studying for the test he already took or writing a paragraph that addresses something entirely different from the narrowly prescribed topic—I was well aware that he would burn the house down before he'd redo it. So I don't have much standing to admonish anyone for helping with homework, although I also know Michael would not do it if I didn't at least try to corral him and keep him on track.

As frustrated as I was, and as hard as it became to get Michael to do the barrage of elementary homework, or even to hold a pencil instead of snapping it, I felt sure, I told the teacher, that his mom was just entirely bored and sad that she had never gotten to finish high school herself. I was sure, I said, that she found these small daily challenges as satisfying as others might find guessing *Wheel of Fortune* phrases or doing crossword puzzles. Jessica might have been pulled from high school by her parents and from community college by her boyfriend's jealousy—but she could still do these simple assignments while feeling like a good parent who was helping her child get to a better life than she'd had. Even when Benny's teenage son lived with them, she took copious notes from his math book on his behalf—notes that she longed to explain to him and that I doubt he even looked at. For once, I thought, I could understand exactly what she felt.

"I expect you to go to college," she'd say to Ryan and Michael, and simply saying it means something, even without a clear path to reach it, and even if the person saying it puts up one obstacle after the next. Needles and pins.

AS MUCH as I wanted to do some tangible good, my reasons for helping the family in practical ways were selfish. In addition to my being able to keep Michael on alternate weekends, I was elated that I could spend time with him and his brother while their mother was in classes, or we were all driving back and forth; soon Jessica incorporated me in the boys' many medical appointments, which gradually became entirely my responsibility. I bought her a cell phone and calling plan in the hope the boys would call to escape Benny's rages—and so I'd always have a way to call and make arrangements to see Michael; this also meant replacing a series of phones the enraged Benny broke to cut them off from me or other help, events that Jessica explained away as "accidentally dropping the phone in the toilet" or in a glass of water—an excuse designed to forestall questions.

At least I never bought the endless cigarettes, but every year I wondered if the kids' Christmas money did. It was always clear to Michael that the first and last of all money always went to cigarettes. Indeed, the price of cigarettes seems to be a constant unit of measurement in foster parents' complaints—and even from the children's grandmother, who is a heavy smoker herself but said she never bought cigarettes until the week's food was in the house. For foster parents, every basic item or experience the birth parents fail to provide is always expressed in terms of something the children could have had: for the price of a pack of Camels, that child could have had at least thrift store sneakers, gone to a school dance, had spare underwear to keep for accidents at school. It was the measure I heard most often—and used myself.

JESSICA AND I kept up a friendly and warily trusting relationship for several years, though, by talking about books and the pride we shared in her children. The first time she sent the boys to stay for an extended time with Will and me was just before Halloween, two years after they'd gone home and halfway through her first community college semester, before and after the surgery that went wrong. The feverish infection and complications that followed seemed likely because she was on Medicaid at that time and the surgery was the last low-reimbursement one the surgeon performed before heading to a Caribbean cruise. Initially, the boys were to stay with us for just two weeks, but this stretched through Christmas Eve, and then again after. I was glad that Jessica was getting some rest and help for her pain before her Medicaid coverage ran out, and I was thrilled to have the boys with us for that much time, even though it meant driving them from one county to the next for elementary and preschool each weekday. Gas and road hours seemed like no price at all to pay, and it was a relief to get to pick matching clothes and smell hair that was clean and smoke-free. The hours on the road meant all the more opportunity to play hand-me-down purple cassette tapes of nursery rhymes and folk songs, pumping in those essential memories and rhythms, vocabulary, and classic images they needed a chance to absorb. First nursery rhymes, then Bible stories, then mythology, information I always thought needed to simply lie dormant in a child's consciousness. Aren't they are the building blocks of—something, surely?

After her ordeal I tried to help Jessica get better health care, with worrying results: when I accompanied her to a follow-up appointment with the surgeon and, at her request, tried gently to assert the concerns of family and friends about her rocky recovery, the surgeon told her never to bring another person into her appointment again; a replacement doctor I helped her find turned out to be even worse. Then her time on Medicaid ran out, leaving her without a doctor or any of the follow-up medications she was going to need and always suffered without. I found Jessica an overloaded but free health clinic that would go the many extra miles needed for its patients—so long as they managed to get there and keep appointments.

ORIENTEERING

The Path of Needles, the Path of Pins.

"Y'all are family," Benny would say when it suited him, and, even though I was slightly younger than he was, he introduced me once as "the mother of all of us."

Mother of us all, with the bottomless checkbook; but Mother of Dragons is what I needed to be.

The Path of Beercans, the Path of Weed.

I know there are stories they still haven't told me.

The Path of Pit Bulls, the Path of Switches.

Path of Shotgun Shells, Path of Blades.

For a week at the worst point, sheriff's deputies patrolled our road overnight and ran their engines at the end of our driveway.

The Path of Big Gulps, the Path of Pills.

The Path of Cigarette Butts, picked up and resmoked down to the filter.

The Path of Dollar-Brand Trash Bags, burst and leaking in the rain.

Map of Trauma.

The Map of Secrets.

THE PATH of Lice. Just to put it all in concrete, miserable perspective. Head lice are on the path that almost every kindergarten family walks. By first grade, at least. Everyone shared these, but the boys came to us to treat them, to wash all their clothes and graying towels with the hottest water and chemicals, to buy can after can of useless furniture and linen spray. Shuddering at the thought, I combed and combed their hair, searching for nits, until my eyes teared and burned beneath the yellow bathroom light. I've finally forgotten the scorching smell of

RID shampoo, but for years, whenever I got tired, or was lying on the verge of exhausted sleep, behind my eyes I would see the bugs moving along the hair parts, see those tiny gray hyphens wiggling their routes through pale scalp, and I'd know that they weren't gone, we didn't get them all, they were coming back from somewhere, and we would have to start over.

"Come on, please check my head," Michael would beg me for years to come, at the slightest itch of anxiety.

The only good thing: the lice kept crawling up Michael's long, thin hair, so finally we were able to get it cut. For three years he'd had to grow it to fit the cute image of a baby biker or junior outlaw for Benny, with constant pressure on Michael to say that was his wish. His long hair infuriated his father's family, which only intensified the unspoken battle. I had to smash down my opinions, but I couldn't understand why, long or short, his beautiful hair had to be unshaped and raggedly uneven. But saying the first word about it would have conjured up a massive wave of critical subtext that could have shut everything down. "At least it makes him *look* neglected," I said to his aggrieved grandmother Irene more than once, "so maybe someone will stop and pay attention." "It's just not the style anymore," she'd always answer. "The least they could do is trim his bangs so he could see."

I'd grown up through the 1970s, so to me, long hair was not so bad, though I recoiled from the idea of his being Benny's mini-me. "But he has such a pretty face," my mother would say, convinced the girlish angel-look made him more of a target than he was anyway. Plus, "looking like a girl" definitely mattered to Michael, causing him endless pain and fury, equaled only by his dread of causing Benny a single hurt feeling.

I hid behind the advice of teachers, who spoke carefully but unmistakably about hair length and the spread of lice. Michael and a girl in his class kept infesting each other, putting their heads together while working on the kindergarten learning center projects, the teacher said—that was how it always happened in their classes.

"It's what the teacher said," I told Jessica the third time around. "And the school nurse. That they'll keep passing it back and forth." The girl came to school with her hair in French braids, pulled back, or under a bandana.

And what Michael's angry tears at being mistaken daily for a pretty girl couldn't do, at least the lice did. His mother conceded that Michael could decide for himself about his hair, although he knew what she wanted. He was scared. He wavered. I know it's now not acceptable to say what a boy should look like. But he got his hair cut, and afterward he looked like a boy. The lice never came back. To both of us, I think, it was an immense relief.

THE ROAD

My car was the constant—with or without children, Jessica and I seemed always to be in it. She had no license or car of her own for reasons both practical and dubious. She did drive at the times it suited her or when she could get access to a vehicle. (Benny had no license either, but he seemed more fearless and often found some roundabout way to get the uninsured cars registered, although one of Michael's most persistent memories is seeing Benny unscrewing a license plate from a neighbor's car and being told to go back inside.) And every time I see another economy car spray-painted flat black, as theirs was following one of Benny's close calls with the highway patrol, I wonder why the occupants don't realize it makes them a more obvious target. However, the overall lack of legal transportation seemed to be one way Benny kept a tight rein on Jessica and corralled her movements. Having lost multiple licenses, Benny really ran the bigger risk, but to me his gallantry in running that risk was one more control trap. Yes, when Jessica wanted something and had a car available, she did drive, although she seemed to prefer that I didn't know it. In general, though, the notion that she could drive off on her own and be down the road and free, out from under Benny's thumb, was little more than a fantasy.

But I don't think Benny minded her going off with me. At least it didn't arouse his usual suspicions of cheating—although he certainly didn't share her excitement about school and her newly forming identity. Jessica loved being the good student, the one who talked in class, who was chapters ahead in the reading. It's not that Benny was against education itself (the very thing he should have feared, had Jessica taken it much further), but the immediate possibility of Jessica's meeting other men at the community college set him on edge, she told me. God forbid she might ask some random guy to light her cigarette, back in those days when you could smoke freely in entranceways and parking lots. Of all the forces working against her, from within and without, I'd bet that Benny's possessiveness was the biggest factor in what ultimately doomed her efforts to take classes.

As we drove, Jessica shared grueling stories from her childhood; it's a wonder she survived it and, understandably, generously, wanted better for her kids. It was from her I first understood that the notion of moving on from the past is just one more comfortable myth.

There's moving, yes. Moving in spirals, sometimes in and sometimes out. And then there's moving on, the comforting, hear-no-evil myth.

"The past is never dead. It's not even past." Like any good twentieth-century English major, I'd learned that from Faulkner. But for the next ten years—and easily foreseeable for the next twenty—I was about to learn it the hard way.

I NEVER found the right balance of helping versus enabling. To put it mildly. And was a balance even possible? For someone as guilt ridden, class conscious, and habitually apologetic as I was? Someone who went overboard with everything, from grading feedback to birthday presents to counting calories as a once-anorexic teen? Most of all, how was keeping a balance possible when all I wanted was for the boys to have every chance in life? Or at least every chance to survive childhood?

Still, I tried to show the boys we could all be one family, because even with the lies, secrets, and constant subtext, that was the only way to persist. And I meant it. It wasn't just that Jessica would let me take the boys off for a few days or a vacation week—no, Jessica included me in all kinds of things she didn't have to—not only the medical appointments but also scout potlucks, teacher conferences, and the near-sacred ritual of the first-grade Mother's Day school tea. This was remarkable, given that my public presence was a constant reminder that I had been their foster mother and that her children had been "in care," as the social workers always called it.

Jessica, the boys, and I—and sometimes Isabelle or Benny's visiting teen son, Edwin—traveled together, to Atlanta, the circus, amusement parks, and to any historic place or fair where guides would be in costume, speak in fake half-British accents, forge knife blades or dip candles, blow glass, weave mats, or eat giant turkey drumsticks. It wasn't like Jessica had had a childhood herself, or had anyone else to talk books with. We went on the Cub Scout family camping trips together; she came with me to see musicals and attend music festivals with the boys, and, usually alone, to hear authors speak. I was not the least surprised when the author, Dorothy Allison (*Bastard Out of Carolina*), came up and hugged her after a reading, picking her out of a long line of starry-eyed young college women—and told Jessica she looked like Dorothy's aunts and cousins. To me their kinship through terrible times was visible.

It's true, as they always tell us in foster training workshops, that simply driving in the car makes teens open up about their secrets, and this was true for Jessica as well, in her late twenties. As the miles rolled by, I absorbed so many of her unbelievably painful stories and fleeting instants of nostalgia that I felt I had witnessed them, and my mind's eye is still full of faces, places, and losses that came long before our acquaintance. I could see the skeleton of her grandpa's old cabin, the wormy chestnut siding stripped away for cash; sense her anguish over the poisoned Jack Russell terrier; feel the locked knees from standing Wednesday evenings in church; and taste the sugared cherry slices her diabetic cousin stashed away. Our partnership was genuine on my part, and I still hope it was genuine on hers, even when she had something to hide or a secret to keep, which, I realize now, was always.

ALL GOOD GIFTS

With the gift of a rocket ship for Michael's sixth birthday, the ever-so-slightly upward trajectory began its slow downward arc to a crash landing. At least, that's what I think. Maybe no upward ever existed, but it was how I saw things.

I can pinpoint the day Jessica began to hide things from me again—or, rather, to hide them more noticeably. She had always hoarded secrets and used them as a confidential, shared currency. With me, with the boys, with her whole ever-shifting network of allies and enemies. "Don't tell X, but"—preceded many of them, often with my name or Irene's in place of *X*. Even more than cigarettes, weren't secrets the last comfort Jessica could own, keep, and dispense? In times of no money, you could always dole out secrets, like a stash of Hershey's kisses. They were her *Precious,* it often seemed, and she could not begin to keep all the lies and secrets straight, instead resorting to confusion and loss of phone signal, if pressed.

Secrets were the treasured gift she had to bestow upon the special, and sometimes cursed, recipient. I have no doubt that "Don't tell Deborah" was a phrase the children heard as often as the reflexive "I love you" phone sign-off; even as the facts concealed in the secrets weighed upon the boys, they were thrilled with the recognition of their greater loyalty. As their family life fell further and further apart, the shared secrets proved that, even in tatters, even without a roof to call home, at least something remained for them to be loyal to.

HOW DID I know so instinctively that Jessica was hiding secrets—that is, more secrets—again? For one thing, as I stood in her latest tiny, dark living room that Sunday, I knew it from the dread in my gut—that single, nonexistent animal organ we are told to trust above all else. I could feel the truth in the cold-sweat prickle along my arms and between my shoulder blades. I knew it in the way that a family dog senses sorrow or tumors. Second, and most unmistakably, Jessica had long since spelled it out for me: she had always proudly told me that when Luke, the children's dad, would accuse her of being on drugs—same as *he* always was—she'd tell him, "If I was, then Deborah would be the last person I'd want to be around. And I'm with her all the time." So when suddenly she wasn't, I felt my stomach sink. And I knew this meant some kind of ending.

The first sign had come the day we had a birthday party at our house for Michael. All of Jessica's family lived in our county, so she'd let me host this year's party. In addition to the usual family, I'd invited a few actual kid-friends and parents. This was something I'd badly wanted to do, so I could make it nice and store bought, with matching theme plates and napkins. Not a Martha Stewart deal by any means—but just something like the parties other children had. The kids would all wear shirts and wouldn't race four-wheelers and bikes down the driveway as guests were coming in, and we'd have Domino's pizza and a SpongeBob piñata for them to descend upon. I hoped for RSVPs and for family feuds to stay temporarily buried. All one more stab at normality, even if cigarette smoke clouded the outdoor spaces and some adults brought single 7-Up bottles laced with liquor. I was even more excited than Michael was. We'd had a big birthday party for him when he turned two, back before he left foster care—that one, foreseeably, had overwhelmed him, but now he'd experienced other parties, and I thought he was ready.

Despite the bad blood between Jessica's family and the boys' father, Luke, even he came, dropped off by a muscled, sun-weathered man who Jessica previously said had threatened and abused her. As much as I knew what Luke's presence would mean to Michael and his grandmother, I'd almost hoped Luke wouldn't show, for I feared Luke would first have words, and then get into a fight, with Benny, and that would be the end of Michael's having any friends visit. Days later I found a sickeningly hooked switchblade that had dropped between the sofa cushions; I saved it for a while in an overhead cabinet, as I might anyone's lost property, but it began to feel radioactive to me or, like Tolkien's Ring, summoning someone to its thrall, so one night I buried it in the kitchen garbage, superstitiously preempting the taking of a life someday. I couldn't remember Luke's having sat on the couch, but I knew beyond a doubt that this weapon had belonged to him.

There wasn't a fight that day, to my huge relief, although the force field became palpable when Jessica strangely spent a long time sitting on the grass, close-talking with Luke, who was still technically her husband, despite her much broadcast hatred of him and Benny's pretense of not watching them from the porch above while he was talking to Jessica's dad through a haze of Lucky Strike smoke. I had a hunch about what this could mean, for making a little extra meth to sell was Luke's only plausible way of making a living. As he and Jessica sat on my lawn with their knees almost touching, their heads bent so close (*how* could *they,* I thought, *right here*?), the unwelcome idea seemed as visible as skywriting. How stupid could I be?

LUKE'S ACTUAL birthday gift to Michael locked down my naive realization. Luke gave him a gigantic fantasy rocket ship model that must have had a zillion tiny pieces, most no bigger than Monopoly houses. It was the kind of toy sold on the Kmart remainder aisle because it was too complex for real kids to use it—its thousands of pieces seemed fated to clog an army of vacuum cleaners. Nonetheless, it was more of an actual, storebought gift than Luke had given either boy in years—a new gift, that is, that was not a knife, sword, or exotic bladed weapon and was not bought or traded from a flea market dealer to pay off some dubious debt. Invariably such secondhand gifts were both achingly desirable and completely frustrating—the broken electric guitar that seemed like it could be fixed with just the right part, or the frozen-up X-Box still in its original packaging. These gifts always ignited such hope and tinkering, requiring special follow-up trips to find odd-sized new batteries or new strings, yet these gifts never failed to crush. Whatever their dad's good intentions and longing to impress, Michael would end up in tears, saying, "My daddy always gives me broken things," never recognizing that it was the same for his brother. For his part, Ryan would just keep tinkering with that latest obscure object of desire, convinced he was on the verge of mechanical success, with bragging rights to the amazing dirt bike or video game console just one tweak or discontinued part away; he'd take it apart to fix it until he could no longer tell whether he'd broken it himself or it had come that way. It wasn't that Luke didn't care—on the contrary, he wanted to impress them—and with the current state of his life, they were the best gifts he had to give. Still, Luke was there for the excitement generated by those gifts, which he had usually broadcast ahead, and I was there for the inevitable crash of disappointment and fury.

At any rate, this gigantic rocket ship model was new, and Michael was bowled over by the size alone. The package, shrouded in Kmart sacks (the same thing an aunt had earlier apologized for as "redneck wrapping paper"), had stolen the show with its grand hidden promise, and Michael had plowed dazedly through the opening of other gifts just to get to it. And then—oh, well. Cool. That was it. For a five-year-old whom our neighbors called "all boy," Michael was strangely unimpressed by dinosaurs, *Star Wars,* and rocket ships. The picture on the gigantic box made me feel obsessive and crazy—the rocket's wide cylinder housed a full-fledged space station with tiny astronauts doing jobs inside it. The toy looked like something no regular person could put together, much less a child. And how would he even play with it, if it was assembled?

AT THE DSS-supervised visits, back when Michael and Ryan were small kids, the social workers discouraged gifts from birth parents. Regardless, the kids were thrilled with the SpyKids trinkets, comics, and other plastic-packed gimmes of the week that their mom brought from the kids' meal stash after her fast-food shift was over—a job that DSS made her work to pay child support to the agency and therefore forced—or allowed—her to keep much longer than Benny otherwise might have let her. Even today, as a young teen, Michael still brags to friends about all the free kids' meal loot he got.

Once the kids had come home and for years into the future, her gifts to the boys—other than a memorable wooden train set, dream catcher, bikes or MP3 players from the local Angel Tree, or an expensive weapon of some form that Benny had bought—were usually something that she could purchase with an EBT card—bags of Sourpatch Kids or, for Ryan, smoked sausage or hot sauce sets—a reflection, I guessed, of Benny's relentless control. For most of their years together, the EBT card in her name was the closest Jessica could get to having her own money.

And when Benny did have a real gift for the boys—a guitar or DVD player—he thought it was funny to first give Michael a box with rocks in it or actual charcoal briquettes, as if seeing the child's face fall into tears and then beam again minutes later when the real present appeared somehow made the gift all that much more benevolent. Plus, it made for a good story, in his view. It was some family tradition of Benny's, I supposed, and once, delighted, he and Jessica even told me ahead of time about their elaborate plan to trick Michael this way. I had cringed inside, imagining the pain it would bring, and yet, like so much I disagreed with in that decade, I felt I had no alternative but to nod and smile. I'd heard enough from Luke's mother about the retribution even the mildest confrontation or implied criticism would bring.

Jessica's parents, MeMa and Poppa, would usually bring the boys big bags of assorted Dollar Store toys—bubble guns, camo doodads, and magnet fishing sets in neon plastic. They had no visible income themselves yet never came empty-handed to a birthday celebration. Poppa, who, like Michael, could practically manufacture anything from water, air, and bent nails, would also make them slingshots (which the boys naturally aimed at each other as much as at crows or chipmunks) and later carved wooden eagles, Indian heads, and trout that we prized as much as the boys did.

What I—Will and I, but really I—gave was of course always too much yet all carefully chosen over months to perfectly meet Michael's current obsessions, from trains to cars to electricity to the Simpsons. I was careful to give his gifts to him well before the parties, though; since he kept almost all our gifts to play with at our house during his visits and sojourns, no one in the family had to know or think I was trying to outdo them. Yes, they were already convinced I spoiled him (although they never said that of Ryan, on whom we spent equally), so why make it any worse or make it seem like a heavy-handed competition? Even when the boys were living at home, somehow we were blessed to have both boys spend a number of birthday nights and mornings with us. We all have our own traditions, and mine from my childhood was leaving wrapped birthday presents on Michael's bed for him to find when he woke up—even now, he reminds me to do that.

Luke's mother always planned painstakingly for the children's birthday and Christmas gifts, usually buying them on layaway from her full-time but ridiculously small paycheck. For weeks she'd crave the first glimpse of "the smiles on their faces" and would insist the boys not save her gifts for weekends with her but immediately take them back to their family home, trusting that their mom would make sure they were properly taken care of. Without fail, these much-appreciated, high-stakes gifts would be left out in the rain or pine forest for days or, even worse, left at someone's house, or the boys would lose the one-of-a-kind charger or remote control. No doubt their grandmother resented Jessica's failure to keep an eye on these things, but even under the best circumstances Jessica had the opposite view—and one I knew I should adopt—when it came to the boys' responsibility for their belongings. Even the amazing trio of kid-sized, drivable mega-battery-powered cars for which Grandma Irene saved and scraped to delight the children when they were reunited with Jessica never functioned correctly after the first time they needed a full charge. Benny's terrifying assortment of four-wheelers made many more circuits of the yard than these expensive cars ever did.

But the kids weren't their own worst enemies when it came to their birthday and Christmas gifts, and at this sixth birthday party Irene had made it her mission to police the birthday present opening to prevent the swarm of excited cousins from removing all the toys from their near-childproof boxes, after several toys had been destroyed mere moments into an earlier party. Naturally, every cousin always wanted to help Michael, Ryan, or Isabelle open their gifts; usually Jessica would help instead and ensure the birthday child made eye contact with the givers and said thank you. But as soon as she looked away, the cousins piled on like zombies rushing a carcass, surrounding and prying the newest shiny, remote-controlled gift from its molded plastic sarcophagus and antitheft wires, then rushing it out to the porch or yard, where the demo-only battery died within minutes and someone would find the whole thing in pieces weeks later.

PATH OF PINS

Michael spent that birthday party night with us, but when I took him home on Sunday, his mom was putting together the gigantic rocket ship, which was balanced on bar stools in the living room. Normally she would have scoffed at anything Michael's dad had given him, but this time she'd put together an amazing number of the tiny pieces. I took a closer look at the diagram on the box—it showed not just the outside but also the inside of the rocket ship, which looked like a gigantic ant farm or miniature colony where sea monkey aliens could take command. I stood there and tried politely to visit, as Jessica kept fitting pieces together and never really turning to look at me.

Was she mad at me? I wondered. I used to obsess about things like that. Had I unknowingly done something wrong? Crossed the class lines I tried so hard to pretend did not exist? Usually, my radar let me know when I had breached a taboo, but I knew that if I even posed the question gently, she'd deny it. Jessica never dealt with unpleasantness head-on anyway but through harsh complaints to others or fast, scrambled statements. So being up front and direct never worked. But all those crazy, tiny pieces, and that puzzle of compartments and passages, I thought, and the way she won't even look at me—what kind of compulsion could drive this?

That was the moment I thought I knew.

A mental snapshot of that three-foot rocket ship, headed sideways, still haunts me. Because I'd heard a narcotics detective say that they never made a bust without finding dark rooms full of disassembled lamps and radios, that meth or other amphetamines drove users to take things apart. This rocket was being put together, not taken apart, but I got the same feeling of compulsion. I'm always the last person to figure things out, but on that day, seeing Michael's mom simply putting his birthday present together felt like nothing but bad news.

Usually I think that such distinct moments, the sharp before and after shots, are for fiction—those distilled moments of clarity after which, as my beloved old teacher said, nothing will ever be the same again. I thought those moments were as much of a fiction as a coherent cause-and-effect plot line, but in my time with Michael, so many of those photo moments stood out—my phone call about Benny's driving and drinking; the good-bye glimpse of Michael through the truck window; the instant he told the DSS worker he was afraid Benny would kill his mom with a knife—and this one.

Only a meth-fueled person could do this. I heard these words in my head spelling out what I feared; I froze the mask of my face and forced my voice up the scale. I could almost feel the earth shift.

I WANTED to believe I'd imagined it. I was paranoid. Too sensitive. Or that even without words, I'd let my judgment show. But then my fears were confirmed when a few days later, Jessica decided that she didn't need for me to pick her up and take her to the community college anymore. No worries, she and Benny said—they had it all figured out. I would have my mornings and evenings back, and God knows I needed them. Benny would take Jessica to school, he said, when he came into town to go to work. They didn't owe me any explanation, but I badly wanted to believe this.

So Benny had to know what I thought I knew, and he was as calm and polished as I'd ever seen him, smoothly rearranging our lives with a big-toothed smile. It was always bad news when he did most of the talking. I felt a circle closing, and I was on the outside of it.

UNITS OF CONCERN

There was no reason that this new plan of having Benny drive Jessica to and from the community college when he commuted to his job should not have worked—and worked far better than our long-standing convoluted arrangement, especially now that Michael was in all-day kindergarten and afterschool. But I did not for a second believe that it would. I also told myself that no matter my own past investment of hours and miles in Jessica's new education, it was not my business, but I was vexed that Benny didn't care like I did. Possibly the opposite. Somehow it felt like Jessica was the powerless child in the middle and he and I were the parents, arguing over what was best for her. Except that nothing was overt, she could have spoken up for herself, and I should have asked myself that same old Love and Logic question: whose were the units of concern here? And why did she suddenly seem so uncomfortable around me?

I don't know how long that new commuting arrangement lasted, but I kept up a polite pretense and didn't ask Jessica my usual school-related questions. I was dying to know what was really going on but didn't want to force her to lie to me. Feeling guilty, I was nonetheless glad to be free: first, all the back-and-forth driving was simply impossible for me to keep up; and second, my feelings about the community college had soured after the children had been banned—during the final weeks of that summer semester, I'd dropped Jessica off quickly and zipped back down the drive, lest their lone security guard think he needed to warn us off. Honestly, I had found it was glorious to have my freedom back now—the freedom to focus on my actual job, that is, with so many new hours in the week. Plus, to my great relief, I still got to keep Michael on the weekends.

Several months later, though, when Ryan and Michael's offhand comments had made it clear she was no longer a student, Jessica asked me to stop by the community college and pick up a piece of paperwork—some transcript or form she needed to show somewhere else for some purpose—only to find the college office would not release it to me or anyone until Jessica came in and responded to their demand, unknown to me, that she repay the grants for unattended and failed courses. Two administrators, one of whom I already knew as a kindly, thoughtful, supportive person, emerged from their cubicles, their faces pinched and angry. "Why didn't Jessica come get this herself? Why are you here getting it for her?"

I was amazed they even knew who she was. I felt myself blush. Little did I realize that the community college itself suffered because the federal government held it accountable for those grants. Flustered and embarrassed, I tried to explain how life worked against Jessica, how her boyfriend controlled and scared her, how—but they had seen this a million times. They knew how things worked, and, worse, they thought I did too—first they thought I was in on a scam, then that she had duped me.

I was stunned that they didn't see Jessica as an individual with a hard row to hoe, someone doing the best she could. Where was their sympathy for the surgery complications that had forced her to quit midway into her breakthrough first semester? Disappointed she had quit a second time, I blamed it on Benny for insisting he'd drive her this time around and then, quite openly, paying off a major fine as soon as her grant stipend came in. As much as I'd doubted his commitment back when he dismissed me as driver, I'd known it was time to relinquish my role as self-appointed chauffeur and smoother of the path.

I'd never messed with Jessica's dream, though. She wanted to become a traveling art teacher for preschools—a position I wasn't even sure existed. She had tried this as a volunteer in her workforce readiness program with satisfying success, and I felt sure she would have been excellent at it, given any chance. Every time she mentioned it to an actual teacher or social worker, though, they would tell me under their breath, "You know she can't do that." "Can't" because of the past Social Services involvement was what they meant—the result being that she could never be approved for teaching or any other job that meant working with kids. So much for the myth of rebuilding your life.

They acted like they expected me to break this news to Jessica. I knew how distant a dream it was, though—far enough for her dream to change entirely, or for other doors to open, along the way. Simply having a dream, having a concrete goal—surely, for Jessica, that in itself was a best-case scenario. Why be crushed at the outset, when *any* time spent along the path to that goal was healthy for everyone? For once I curbed my impulse to correct the facts of another's situation.

LOOKING BACK I can see that I should have given up . . . yet it was during those drives to and from the community college that Jessica had seemed the most confident and alive. Of all that she'd been robbed of in her youth, education was the one area that could be reclaimed. It was also the one area, besides our hopes for the children, where we could speak the same language. Where our roles were balanced—she wasn't the helpless victim, and I wasn't the eternal helper. So later on, after she'd moved back to our county and expressed interest in trying again, I slunk into the community college's registration office and paid cash for two courses in a last bid for her success, only to have her drop one on the second day and tell me they'd send a refund in the mail, that they had my address. The other course had a weekly lab attached and did not last long either. Okay, Jessica had attempted and quit three times now with my support—I guess I was getting the message. Maybe it had all been *my* dream for her, but I'm pretty sure it was hers as well. I still wonder what would have happened had she been able to go through the whole program at her own pace, unimpeded, even if that had taken five or six years.

"FINE"

Through all of this, my mind was never at rest. Therapists talk about children's becoming hypervigilant in dangerous and unpredictable situations like Ryan and Michael's, yet I felt myself becoming too finely attuned as well. In the silence of my own home, day and night, I'd hear my cellphone ringing faintly when it wasn't, like tinnitus but from the outside, and I'd find myself taking the temperature of the universe, feeling doom settle like mist. I couldn't relax and watch TV unless the boys were here and sleeping, couldn't let my stomach unclench unless I knew they'd be returning to our home after school.

The more I heard about family murder-suicides on the news, even states away, the more likely it seemed it would happen here, at their home. I drove myself crazy, daily calculating intangible odds.

The knife always on Benny's belt was no different from the kind worn daily by working men, hunters, and farmers everywhere, yet it was also a constant reminder not to cross him, and he surely knew that. At one point, I heard that Benny held it to Jessica's throat for hours, but because the children were already with me when it happened, DSS once again gave her credit for having sent them to a safe place rather than counting this as a reason the children should stay away. (And she herself never would use the word *safe* in the context of the boys returning home—everything was always just breezily *fine*, as if nothing had ever happened that necessitated their running out of the house to a waiting car at midnight, while someone out on the road could hear yelling in the house. She would not even make the tacit admission that everything was fine *now*.)

"Everything's fine" became one of the expressions I hated most, with its Orwellian erasure of danger and drama and its summons to send Michael and Ryan back home that afternoon. I even thought Jessica would deliberately call me in Benny's presence so I could hear by her bright tone deflecting my queries of "Are you sure?" that she couldn't speak freely. Even when I was driving them a long way back and forth to school, I never wanted them to leave our house. I wanted to get them any time for any reason. When they were with us, I could breathe.

For years, I felt I never fully slept, except when the boys were under our roof, because I was always waiting—for a tearful call to come get them or something worse. I lived in a permanent state of stress in their absence, yet this was nothing compared with the stress they lived with and stuffed down daily. When we finally, unbelievably, got even temporary custody, I felt myself exhale all the way down to the bottom of my lungs for the first time in over a decade. From the start I had feared the weapons both child and adult family members took for granted, from slingshots to BBs to knives and switchblades to rifles—and I suspected more that I didn't see. I knew such weapons—other than switchblades—were second nature in the rural families around us, but when it came to the boys' extended family, the constant presence of weapons just compounded my worry. This went on for years, starting two weeks after the children first returned home, when Ryan told his grandmother Irene that "Benny shot the dog." At six, Ryan's statements were often confusing, and only became more painfully convoluted in response to questions, so his grandmother and I strained to figure out what else those words could mean. At a party I vented to a kind and patient stranger whose professional life made me think he'd understand; he in turn passed my fears on to Michael's former early childhood intervention worker. She invited me to come by on the pretext of having me return a book I thought she had given to Michael. *So how do you think everything's going for the family?* she asked. Knowing it would set off a chain reaction of disclosures, I forfeited the chance to blurt my panic over a likely dead dog and instead sat silent on her office couch, feeling like a bad student, my conscience twisting before this young woman who had helped so much and who had seemed to communicate, through her veneer of professional neutrality, that she wished DSS had not reunified Michael's family so quickly.

I kept my guilty silence, though, certain that Jessica was alert to the first glimmer of a hint that I would turn them in. Plus, when Irene had met me at Hardee's for coffee and comfort the Sunday morning of Michael's reunification, she told me that Jessica had made a general statement about me: "I don't know if I can trust her." (Jessica was a champion at sending the message that would be passed on—her method of indirect, and often conveniently jumbled, communication was like one giant game of telephone.) But for once, reticence had served me well: a few days later Irene called to tell me she had seen the still-living dog—thank God, thank God—when she had gone to pick the children up that Friday. So I'd failed my own morality test but passed the family's: if the cops or DSS had swarmed the family to investigate the supposedly dead dog and existence of a gun, who'd sent them would have been obvious and would have meant the absolute end of my relationship with Michael—a calculation I would have to make countless times during the next decade. "Please don't count on me to say something—you need to just keep watching them," I'd beg our social workers when Michael's family later moved back to our county. "If they were really in danger," the director would counter, "we know you'd share it." An infuriating Möbius strip from which I saw no escape.

But the first time I went to pick up Michael from their new home in Benny's trailer, my heart dropped: wedged between Benny's recliner and the wall was what looked to me like some kind of handgun—real or fake, I was too ignorant to know. I tried to look like I was looking away. Outside, the chained dog—a liver-spotted pit bull that Michael still mourns—lunged for attention, a ridged, fresh, hairless, never-explained scar on her head. I tried to pet the dog, as if nothing was there, knowing I couldn't ask, even by way of a nervous joke. But Jessica saw me register the scar, just as surely as she'd seen me register the gun, and so she mentioned it, too casually, a week later. The "pellet gun" or the "airsoft pistol" or whatever phrase she slipped in had to do with the dog's being in heat and Benny's having to scare other dogs off. *Sure,* I'd muttered to myself later in the car, *firing off warning shots sounds like a lot more fun and cheaper than spaying.* Just like dumping gasoline and burning the trash sounded like a lot more fun and much cheaper than spending thirty minutes and two dollars' worth of gas on going to the dump—at least the kids sure thought so.

Again, I was grateful I had not asked about the dog. How ridiculous I would have appeared, to not know the difference between a pellet gun and a—whatever. How into their business. How gun-shy, literally; how hyperreactive and wimpy. At least they didn't think in terms of red and blue, liberal and conservative, Democrat and Republican; no, if anything, it was rebel versus the meek. Rebel—as in, let your outlaw Confederate flag fly, whether it was duct-taped across windows to block out prying eyes or hanging from an actual flagpole cemented into the ground. Offense was intended, but why didn't they care that, at least here in these mountains, the relatively rare flag is a beacon to cops? There might as well be a giant arrow flashing "weed grown here" or "expired license plates." The word "Confederate" was never used, however: racists though they unashamedly were, the flag's true point for them was *rebel.* As in *not like you and wouldn't want to be.* Live free or die.

How unsurprising, Benny and Jessica would have snickered, that someone too weak to believe in belts and spanking—me—would fail to recognize a fake firearm. Or was it fake? As I lay awake, midnight after midnight, my fears would balloon as if I had a high fever. Could the kids pick up that weapon and kill each other on a dare, or would it just pop like a clown's gun in the circus? My eyes flew to that spot between the chair and wall each time I entered their home. But it was all a red flag clearly proclaiming, *Don't ask, don't tell* about this and endless other suspicions—about violence or the scales on the coffee table but also about the countless things that might start a fire, prevent escape, or cause asphyxiation: kerosene heaters in doorways, plastic-sheeted windows that didn't open at the best of times. And whether that pistol was real or fake, I felt certain there was a real, unlocked, and loaded revolver hidden somewhere. (Only yesterday, years after the fact, did I hear Michael suddenly say, in the context of never knowing what Benny would do next, that he never knew when he'd get out the gun and threaten to shoot their mother. *What gun?* I wanted to grab him and say. *What gun where?* But that reaction is still the fastest way to stop Michael from talking.) I never did understand how that dog got the scar on her head.

But everything was *fine.*

As usual.

SOON ENOUGH, the boys got BB guns for Christmas and birthdays, along with day-old grocery store birthday cakes. Not that BB guns were unusual in a mountain town or would have been anything but the norm anywhere in America a generation earlier. It's just that neither boy would have thought twice about putting someone's eye out—and the lost eye would have been just one more story, one more jealous lashing out, one more inevitable misfortune. The counselors at the boys' Cub Scout camp taught BB and rifle shooting with an almost nauseating nostalgic reverence for safety and tradition, with goggles, crewcuts, and all—but back at home the boys were on their own with a whole raft of weapons, to say nothing of such tools as hatchets, box cutters, sledgehammers, and machetes. And, of course, the three-foot sword—one of the flea market gifts that Ryan's dad had given him. Freed of Scout safety strictures, the boys thought nothing of throwing rocks at each other, so how much more provocation, boredom, or dare would it take to shoot? Or swing a blade? The boys were chronically, giddily impulsive, bubbling over with jealousy, and quick to take offense. "Do that one more time—see what happens," they'd challenge each other, then and now, and although I'd never heard Benny say those words, I heard their voices channeling his.

Although much of the boys' Christmas usually arrived in green lawn and leaf bags from the Salvation Army Angel Tree, somehow the cash was always miraculously there to get them not only pocket knives and airsoft rifles but also used crossbows, viciously serrated switchblades with rebel flag or wolf handles, and, before long, hunting rifles for the occasional backdoor shots at deer, the good old rite of passage that would conveniently put one more illegal weapon in Benny's hands when he was consumed by rage and alcohol.

If one boy didn't kill the other with it first.

IT DIDN'T take a liberal to be outraged: How did a felon have no shortage of firearms at hand? And how did they remain unnoticed and unconfiscated when the police searched the house for pot, tipped off by a bitter ex-friend? These firearms were hunting rifles for the kids or other unspecified guns that their mom would reassure me her "Daddy came and took away" when Benny was getting to the edge. She never did tell me he had returned the guns, though—if they ever really left in the first place.

I KNOW I sound like your classic left-wing, knee-jerk, party-line antigun crusader. But there's more to it than that. I'd been held up at an old movie theater job with a gun we all thought might have been a toy, until the next day when we found the holes and bullets in the outside wall; I'd stood next to the robber outside the counter, trying to look like I wasn't memorizing his face or watching his scarred hands shake. The boys never tired of this story and asked for it over and over, willfully ignoring my righteous point that real guns and toy guns can be hard to distinguish. Before the holdup, I'd once unwrapped a mystery object in a white T-shirt that I found on top of the theater's concession counter. It turned out to be the handgun the projectionist had just bought. It seemed alive, like an oily gray organ excised from the body. I was angry at the projectionist for springing this on me, like some weird gift, but he was trembling with excitement. He lived out in a tiny rural town in New Hampshire—why in the world did he need it? But later I lived for three years with an avid hunter and member of the National Rifle Association—the boyfriend who'd first broken my heart back in high school—and I didn't bat an eye at the rifles, magazines, skinned squirrels in plastic wrap in the freezer, deer carcass hanging like a death-to-America effigy from a tree, the deer sawed up into pieces over days on sawhorses on the porch. I loved him and loved our every difference, and I knew that guns and hunting, when they didn't bring him utter frustration out in the woods, were the only thing that brought him peace.

So it wasn't the guns or the rifles, in principle. And I knew that where I lived now, "gun owner" was practically synonymous with home owner. Totally mainstream. There were lots of guns, but very few PEEL MY COLD, DEAD FINGERS OFF THEM bumper stickers and belt buckles. Gun ownership was assumed of everyone who did not teach at the university. (The gun population, I recently learned, is twice the actual population of this superficially peaceful county.) But I also assumed that at least the gun owners who were parents wouldn't keep their loaded weapons in children's easy reach.

Several years later, the landlord supposedly stole the rifles from the boys' padlocked house, in payment for overdue rent, shortly before their eviction. Even if they had been the kind of people to call police, which they were not, they simply could not report the theft of guns from the home of a felon. While the boys seemed to shrug it off, I was thrilled to hear the rifles were gone.

A PROMISE

For all the fear and tedium, for all the meals they missed when adults were sleeping or when staying out of the house and collecting cans and scrap metal in the woods was a good idea, the very things I wish the boys would forget about their past are the very things they most miss: riding four-wheelers and the superhero miraculous saves by Benny when they tipped; the all-nighters watching *Saw,* Freddy Krueger, Jason, and worse, and of being the only one awake when those monsters then scratched at the windows; the stoned laughter at Cheech and Chong, the only minorities Benny would tolerate; the fuel-propelled trash bonfires and weirdly melting plastic; their Confederate flag symbols, which seemed like an invasive species introduced in Appalachia; year-round drunken fireworks; and "Deep Purple" played over and over on stringless *Guitar Hero* guitars.

Yet underlying all these hilarious and sacred recollections was Michael's indelible memory of the roared promise: "I'll bury your mother, dead or alive. I'll put you all under the ground." These were words I couldn't unhear; my vision of a wooden door covering a pit of bodies by the driveway was one I couldn't unsee. Luke's mother had repeated Benny's threat to me thirdhand, months after the fact, at her birthday dinner. We sat in my favorite seafood restaurant, forever ruined now, as the cold sweet tea expanded the rock-heavy hush puppies in my stomach, and Irene told me how the kids had all run down the road into the night as Benny roared these words after them, and how their mother had stumbled into a hole and called the kids to wait, stop, come back and help her, then telling them to run again to safety.

The oldest, Isabelle, had been staying with them that week, and although the kids had been sworn to utmost secrecy about this whole night and Benny's not-a-threat-but-a-promise, Isabelle had told her grandmother, who, a month or more too late, had now told me. I felt like the grandmother, my greatest and only ally, was always handing me these horrible hot potatoes—terrible news about which I could do nothing but let it burn into me. The kids would clam up and never corroborate it to any authority, and there always seemed to be a reason DSS could not get involved—elapsed time was the biggest, along with the supposed lack of an imminent threat—and yet, if I called at this point, weeks or months later, and tried to insist they do something, some brand-new social worker was likely to stop by and talk to Jessica or summon her and Benny in and give them a warning. Not even half-measures, as the *Breaking Bad* henchman would later famously say, but just enough to let Jessica and Benny know that indeed they couldn't trust me, that I would sell them out at the first opportunity, just as they'd always suspected. (Someone can always make an anonymous report, a social worker told me, "and legally, we can't tell them who made it, but, you know, from the details, they can pretty much figure out who it is.") And that would be the absolute end of my seeing Michael. Or Ryan. Period. Weigh all that against the hours and weekends of joy and relief I increasingly had with Michael and whatever little practical good I could do for any of them.

It took almost a year for the words of this incident to come from Michael himself. I'd so hoped it hadn't really happened or that Isabelle had blown it up dramatically. But Michael told exactly the same story, with the same terrible words—*I'll put you all under the ground*—even worse for the flatness with which he uttered them at eight years old. We were a hundred miles away, at a four-day Cub Scout camp, when he told me about it as we packed up because of a tornado warning. We were alone in the log lean-to, and the sky was full of licorice-dark thunderheads. Michael was sure he'd go to hell and that Benny would be the one to make good on his promise and send him there. Nothing I said could console or reassure him, and, as he told it, I could see them running down the road, with Jessica stumbling and panicked, pulling her children back down into the dark with her.

Once we were home, all I could think to do was to somehow get Michael to confide in the kind pastor who was helping the small group of Cub Scouts get their religion pin. I'm not sure how much Michael told him, but I could hear the pastor tell him about having to blockade himself in closets as a child when he could hear his own parents fighting. Whatever passed between them, Michael at least seemed relieved of his conviction that he'd go to hell whenever a raging Benny ultimately caught up with him.

REWIRING

The summer before Michael started second grade, Benny's son, Edwin, now an older teen who had always lived hundreds of miles away, moved in with them, touching off many additional crises. I'd felt deeply sympathetic anger on his behalf when he'd visited one summer: I learned he'd been allowed little time with his father through much of his youth and that back home he was basically raising two younger half-siblings. And finally, the night before he was to go on vacation with us, his custodial grandparents forced him to return home instead. Yes, I wrote letters to help him get enrolled in our local high school, picked him up when he broke a bone there, let him use my computer to Facebook friends back home, and took him to get summer tutoring. But I never forgave his teaching the boys' cousin to hollow out an apple and use it to smoke pot or for inviting another former foster teen and the teen's mother to walk away from a birthday party at our house and smoke a joint with him.

Perhaps there had been hope that Edwin's presence would unify and complete the family and make Benny whole again. Or that Edwin would be a helpful distraction, at the least, filling the air with busy teen noise. Or serve as another, larger human shield against violence or despair. I don't know, and I am probably just projecting my own thoughts.

At any rate, Edwin's arrival was generating excitement—how many kids get a cool, tan, good-looking, instant big brother?—and the boys' beds had been switched around in some way. The top bed of the bunks we'd given them quickly became Edwin's storage space / closet, and he seemed to sleep in the bottom bunk, leaving the boys to sleep on the couch or recliner—another matter the boys kept hazy, but it was clearly a game of musical chairs with far fewer beds than people. Polite, smiling, and easy for me to talk to, Edwin nonetheless did not turn out to be the hoped-for ally to Jessica. No doubt that was too much to expect from an unrelated teen dealing with his own trauma. Edwin's arrival offered novel distraction, but even I felt uneasily let down when I'd see him glassy eyed and slouching against the porch rails, hiding nothing.

During the crises when Jessica would send Michael and Ryan to us, Edwin never joined them, to my guilty relief; he was in no danger, according to Jessica, who implied he was a lot safer than she was—whatever the truth, he never left the house when I arrived at night, and I was more than relieved not to have to take him.

But Edwin was so damaged himself, and had lost so much, that I couldn't help but feel for him. I tried taking him, along with Ryan, to swim and have reading tutoring with one of my university students through his second summer, and he even made it through most of *The Lightning Thief.* But that weekly dose of wholesomeness in months filled with the temptations of boredom of course could not make a dent. He badly damaged his ankle in gym class, and that seemed like the beginning of the end: the weeks of crutches made all the frustration and unfairness visible. When eventually Jessica's family was evicted and it looked as if they'd all go to the homeless shelter, someone drove up the hundreds of miles and retrieved Edwin permanently. He'd arrived as a young teen, relieved of raising his younger siblings, but left with no childhood remaining.

As that November eviction date approached, Jessica began to assert her belief that if adults went to the homeless shelter with kids, they'd be fast-tracked for housing and put up in a motel, as some friends of hers once had been. She knew I would grab the opportunity for Michael and Ryan to come stay with us, though, while she and Benny stayed in the shelter, and that I would think it barbarically selfish to put the boys through that disruption and despair. This belief in shelter-funded motel rooms for families was a wishful myth, I thought, or at least not worth the gamble, but it was close to a right in Jessica's view.

I dreaded the idea that the children would spend any time in a shelter, and being crammed indefinitely into a crummy single motel room with all their possessions—the best-case scenario—sounded awful as well. At the very least, they'd have to change schools and live out of a suitcase. But of course it was not my call.

Irene worried with me, but my husband shrugged it off. They'd never go to a shelter—Jessica could go with the flow, he argued, but Benny was too much of a Don't-Tread-on-Me rebel to conform to the rules: job counseling, schedules, and a nightly breathalyzer test to gain admission.

Instead, Benny quickly found them a place blessedly near us, on land where he'd lived several years before. The new home needed major renovation, which sounded to me kind of odd for a manufactured trailer. If they renovated, they would not have to pay rent for six months, and I bitterly marveled at how they always seemed to land on their feet—when I wished fervently that things would just fall apart, once and for all, so the boys could be free. But love and loyalty aside, so long as work for Benny was sporadic, they needed the food stamps and tax credits yoked to the boys' ostensible presence to survive.

Then it clicked: this new place looked suspiciously like a meth-busted trailer, which, instead of being condemned, as the county fire marshal claimed meth labs always were, had simply been stripped of its paneling and meager insulation. At some point much of the wiring had been scavenged or stolen. As scary as the idea of his amateur rewiring was, even scarier was Benny's installation of a giant woodstove that looked great but violated every mobile home code. But even if someone were to blow the whistle on this toxic firetrap, I knew that the county had no housing code whatsoever and that, even if asked, county building inspectors could not even go look at a place where the electricity had not been disconnected for a year.

At least the renovation work would be difficult to do with kids underfoot every day, to say nothing of camping out in the dark, with only candles and a VCR powered by a neighbor's extension cord. So to my great relief, Jessica did send the boys to stay with us for what turned out to be four months, which included a record winter month of ice and blizzard. It was Michael's third-grade year and Ryan's seventh. I prayed for delays of any kind.

HOLY NIGHT

Christmas was always the most volatile time of year, with all its treacherous expectations and empty time. Between the new BB guns, airsoft rifles, and actual .22s and all the newest contributions to the kids' medieval metal armory, it seemed anything could happen. So long as they received a new Christmas weapon of some kind, the boys plowed through and then shrugged off the inevitable pile of stuffed animals, video game cartridges, movie compilation DVDs, and the annual Elves' Workshop bikes that replaced the snow-rusted ones of the year before. There were also grocery bags full of useless filler gifts from a dubious new church and charity—Shepherd's Way—that would make families sit through hours of glib preaching and staticky musical crooning by a Ken doll lookalike and his Duggar-haired daughters, then coerce moms into signing the kids up for well-meaning sponsors in distant states, who would send the kids "in Appalachia" Bibles and the church money—but everything was crummy surplus, consisting mostly of imitation Beanie Babies, expired Avon products, moth-ridden sacks of flour, and brand-new but untradable store-donated clothes or shoes in random sizes.

Jessica often let the boys stay with us until Christmas Eve and would agree to let us take them again Christmas night to visit my extended family a state away for a week: for this I am infinitely grateful. Imagining Christmas afternoon and then night at their house with new weapons, disappointment, mountain-high emotions, and cases of Busch Lite made it the most terrifying holiday. There's an urban legend that the Superbowl is the most domestically violent day of the year, but I would bet the rates for Christmas are higher, especially for Christmas night. I was never so relieved to get the boys out and away.

WORSE

Content in our new routines of Christmas, snow days, and school, I didn't realize things could turn for the worse until I learned that Jessica and Benny considered this new trailer to be only a temporary home. Two days after a New Year's trip south for an old friend's funeral, Benny and Jessica came to our house to talk with Will and me upstairs in the TV room, where they'd never been. Benny did all the talking, as Jessica sidestepped confrontation, and, I must admit, I generally did as well. Sounding unusually rehearsed, Benny said it was "time to go home." He needed to help his widowed aunts do repairs and a cousin was going to set him up with steady work, so they were going to move hundreds of miles south. As a family. At some unspecified point in the future. We shouldn't worry—we could come get Michael for big chunks of the summers, and we could deliver Ryan to Luke.

Worry? That the boys would be doomed to drop out seemed all but certain to Will and me, and, even before that, they would grow into shirtless teen drinkers and fighters, then into sunburned, melanoma-ridden addicts—if they even lived that long. This might be catastrophic thinking, but recognizing that made me no less certain of the outcome. And seven weeks of summer back in the mountains with us couldn't fix them. If summer visits even ended up happening.

Life went cold for me.

THE WHEEL

It never stopped turning. Never slowed down.

Halfway through the decade between our foster care and custody, the boys' mother and Luke, the husband she had finally divorced, had been arrested in our pickup truck. Will often lent it out to friends to haul mulch or rototillers; days earlier Jessica had borrowed it for an afternoon's moving back to the outskirts of our town, to a house near her parents, and, we'd thought, away from Benny and an increasingly volatile web of relationships in that county. I held my breath, daring to hope she'd actually strike out alone. Then the police caught Luke and Jessica with a meth lab in a backpack, whatever that meant, entrapped by a man we'd all heard trying to flirt with Jessica the week before. To say that the boundaries of all these relationships—with boyfriend, boys' father, friends—were fluid is to suggest that there was an actual belief in boundaries to start with. Luke ended up going to jail and then prison for this arrest, but Jessica was released after a week, uncharged; following a basic inspection of the rental house, DSS okayed the children to move from our house, where they'd been already at the time of the arrest, into her newly rented house, where Benny, whose threats she'd supposedly been escaping, had already anchored himself.

Two years later, after the eviction and move to that fixer-upper trailer near us, even after the renovations were completed, Jessica allowed Michael to stay with us during the week so I could keep taking him to his same excellent school; one crisis after another led to his spending many weekends in our home as well. Ryan would often stay with us for weeks at a time, but he basically lived with his mother and Benny, buffering adult fights and attending the district middle school. Then his beloved, newly divorced uncle, who used to hunt, fish, and own a business, truck, and boat, took over the boys' room/storeroom with his pregnant girlfriend and, one night after a party a few miles away, died of a drug overdose. It was the beginning of yet another ending.

THROUGH THOSE years I found the title of a Grace Paley story collection stuck in my head: *Enormous Changes at the Last Minute.* I couldn't even remember what the title story was about, but I found myself repeating those words to myself like a calming mantra each time the ground shifted.

But that was just me. To the boys and their sister, always alert to the slightest tremor, seismic change must have been their normal.

A SEASON after Jessica's brother died, she and Benny secretly went south to avoid pending court dates for seemingly mundane traffic offenses, making good on the plan to move away they'd told us about a year or so earlier—an apparent brick wall of certainty that had put Michael and me in a state of sheer misery until the plan somehow faded. (Sensibly but infuriatingly, Will refused ever to worry about things until they happened.) This time, though, they really did leave. At Jessica's request we kept both boys to "finish out the school year," but it was coldly clear to me that they'd both have to move hundreds of miles away to live with their mother and Benny after that. I was counting down to separation all over again but with even more sickness and anguish this time. Desperately, I tried to figure out how to get an academic job there, a whole day's journey away, or to do some distance teaching online, even with my severe technological ineptitude, and commute hundreds of miles every two weeks to meet a class and return. I ignored the likelihood that my popping up in Jessica and Benny's new life might be entirely unwelcome. My plan was completely insane, I knew, but our incredibly kind department chair okayed it, if the need ultimately should arise. In addition, I was also facing hospitalization for major surgery for a suspicious ovarian cyst, and whatever further horror that might bring.

Yet even if Jessica conceded that the boys would be better off with us, I was sure Benny would insist on moving them, with that steely control he masked as pride and caring. I believed Michael and Ryan made him look good and feel needed—he genuinely loved the boys, and they often loved and admired him back, yet too often when they spent days around him, they were poisoned and deadened with fear.

Once the school year was over, first Michael, then Ryan went to join their mother and Benny. Luckily, Michael spent most of his nights at the home of Benny's aunts while he, Jessica, and Benny spent the days renovating yet another gutted trailer in an even more treacherous trailer park. Their lot was flanked by yet another trailer they would watch burn down and from which they would scavenge toys, tools, and the left-behind fireman's hatchet that Ryan treasures to this day. Their summer stay at the home of Benny's aunts helped me believe there'd be at least a veneer of sobriety and safety, but later I heard that they'd spent a week lakeside camping with all the passed-out drunkies, as Michael called them, and I saw the phone photos of him—still a weak swimmer—flipping into a lake from the roof of a boat at dusk.

Ryan spent much of that summer with us, sweating out the decision to stay or go—a decision he believed was his to make, and which everyone from family members to camp counselors to doctors weighed in against. Behind the scenes, I asked everyone I could think of to talk to him. Knowing how conflicted he was, Will and I strove to appear neutral and to simply listen. Finally, he mustered the resolve to say he wanted to stay on with us, in his home community—resolve that shattered the instant he heard his mother weeping over the phone. After all his agonized wavering, Ryan's mind was set and I helped him box up every memento, magazine cutting collage (his summertime hobby), and piece of clothing. I wrestled with whether to buy his back-to-school clothing and shoes, as I had done almost every year I'd known him, but finally determined that if he was going, it was his mom and Benny's place to do that for him. Sure that they either wouldn't or couldn't, though, his Grandma Irene insisted on buying clothes for him from her bare-bones budget before he went, leaving me both guilty and irrationally angry. We'd had a middle school graduation party for Ryan in June, but as much as he hinted he also wanted a going-away party, it felt to the rest of us like nothing to celebrate.

To my profound relief, Jessica let me pick up Michael in August, when we drove the still reluctant but resigned Ryan down to start high school there. I promised Ryan the unused phone and minutes I'd bought for Michael to use to call us, and I begged Ryan to hide the phone and keep it charged for his safety; yet when I asked Michael to go find it for him, he barely remembered what it was, only that it was either lost or broken.

Ecstatic as I was to have Michael safely with us, none of us could stop worrying about his brother. Ryan called three times mid-crisis on a borrowed phone, giving no details but anxious to be brought back north to us, yet each time we got Jessica's father mobilized to go to the rescue, pressing gas cards or cash on him, along with hopes that his old pickup truck would survive the rush trip, Ryan would call back that night or the next day to say all was okay, that he and his mom didn't have to leave. I would hear the flatness of his voice and try not to ask too many questions, knowing that others were listening.

Bleakly sober, Ryan came back with Jessica after his fourth call, a week before Halloween. Whatever dreams he might have spun of rescuing his mother were dashed when she returned south alone just six weeks later, dismaying the whole family. Ryan had already made another move to live with cousins who stretched every dime they had to keep him; he then came back to live with us ten months later, just as his sophomore year of high school was to begin. After all Michael and Ryan had been through, their family and we agreed they needed to finish growing up together.

It seemed miraculous that both boys had returned to us—and returned at all—from their perilous southern exile, although it was with lasting ill effects that included nightmares, a need to see who was inside certain types of vehicles, eavesdropping on conversations, and freezing every time a car drove up our remote dirt road or the phone rang.

ENOUGH

So what does it take to get children removed from their home? We'd learned the textbook answers back in our first training class, but the real-life answer seemed to lie at an ever-receding horizon. Gathering monthly with other foster parents to share our stresses and stories, I heard it all from them and they from me: Why does only the photographable bruise or hostage situation constitute danger and not the slow burn of fear, boredom, smoke, and adults sleeping it all off, to the twenty-four-hour drone of pirated cable TV? Or when medication prescribed for kids gets hijacked for adult use, or a sex offender is openly allowed to move into a child's home? When a parent is evasive about plans to send their newly returned kids to unknown relatives outside the country? And then, just when you have documented proof that danger is imminent, you're told that action can be taken only after a catastrophic event? From where I stand, it seems the horizon always shifts.

FOR MORE than a decade the Social Services staff was hearteningly supportive of the network of relationships we've kept up, reminding us of studies crediting the success of severely at-risk children to their having even one caring adult who believed in them. "*If* they survive," I'm sure I answered with a wince, for the irony persisted that because the boys either were already at our home or were sent to us when dangerous situations arose, social workers didn't have the circumstances they needed to get involved. Yet the boys were never sent before they became stunned with fear; ever vigilant for bad news, they sensed just when to listen in on a phone call.

Many times over the years I've agonized about disclosing all the little and big secrets I've been handed, despite my wish not to know about things I couldn't change—and most of the time, I learned about these matters too long after the fact to be any use. The social workers are always clear about how high the bar is and how little is actually actionable if not caught at exactly the moment it is happening: any report I might make, I always knew, would lead to questions but no change and would likely cut us off from the boys for good. I'd already seen how little would change, even when I took the risk. Shortly before two-year-old Michael was to be returned to his mother, for instance, I told the social worker that Benny had driven Michael's siblings down the highway with liquor on his breath—and even though DSS knew he also had no license, they did nothing but chastise him, which made him furious at me at the fragile time when Michael was leaving us.

Even when police found twelve pot plants growing outside their home—his flowers, Benny had told the not-stupid kids, though he routinely smoked pot in front of them—nothing happened that was visible to me or Luke's mother. The police obtained a search warrant, and saw that kids lived there, but kept everything superquiet, without so much as an anonymous report in the newspaper's crime log. And years later, after he and Jessica had gone south, Benny left a death threat against her—"Jessica's coming home, in a pinewood box"—recorded on our home answering machine. Yet when I played it for DSS, begging them to intervene while the boys were still safely in our state, with us, the social workers apologetically reminded me that they couldn't act on something that hadn't happened yet.

The catch-22's seemed never to end, although the social workers still tried to help with good insights and suggestions. I'd like to say that that horrible, unerasable, unforgettable message, which I felt compelled to capture and replay, was Benny's biggest gift to us—but even so, nothing could be done when Jessica made the inevitable "it's all fine, he just ran out of his meds, but he's got more now" call. But even though DSS couldn't step in and forbid us to take the boys out of state to Benny and Jessica for a planned school break visit, our social worker Gerri said, "I'd tell her *you* just aren't going to take the boys down there because of the threat." Gerri advised me: "Tell her she can come get them herself." Fine, but if she did, would the boys ever come back? Yet when I did try out those lines, with well-rehearsed but bullshit confidence, amazingly, Jessica acquiesced.

But for Michael and Ryan, enough finally happened. For all the years DSS had praised our situation as a successful case of the kind of co-parenting that so many foster and birth families resisted, eventually even the most optimistic social workers could see the scaffold collapsing beneath us. Later that same year, after we'd refused to make the visit, Jessica returned north for the third time, voicing her determination to start over in a place of safety. It seemed like a turning point, and when we picked her up from a distant bus station, the boys melted with relief and excitement. She stayed with her family, bringing the boys over there to visit and promising them that she'd soon get an apartment where they could come for whole weekends. Reflexively, I fretted through all the potential problems with that scenario, but I took care not to let my nerves dampen the boys' spirits. All that mattered to them was that she was back where they could see and hug her, alive, alone, and free from danger.

And then, within a month or two, came rumors that Benny had reappeared in our town. Perhaps at Jessica's parents' house, where the boys went to visit their mom—and maybe Ryan had seen him there—or not. The familiar veil of secrets descended. Maybe Benny had simply come to bring Jessica the belongings she couldn't haul on a bus, or maybe, again, to persuade her to move back away with him. Our lives became more frightening and frustrating than ever. In turn, the boys became more anxious and vigilant than ever, as did Irene, Isabelle, and I. As usual, Will alone held things steady, waiting to see what would happen. The boys fought over which one would have the big dog sleep on his bed—they were beside themselves with anxiety, afraid to lose their mother again, but just as afraid she'd take them with her. Even this far along, she had every right to come to our home and take them away anywhere she chose, on a second's notice. And the boys believed that she'd still do whatever Benny told her. They watched me lock every door each night, torn up with fear, uncertainty, and the fresh secrets they weren't supposed to tell us. At last, Social Services called us all in, and the situation began to shift, first to conditions of safety and security and then, over several months, to both of the boys' parents agreeing to let us take custody and set the circumstances for visits, with the understanding of continued relationships.

THROUGHOUT THOSE years and to this day, it's been other foster and adoptive parents on whom we most depend for support and sanity. Diverse as our local support group is, I believe we're all the only people who truly understand what the others go through. That too is a miracle, for how many places in our culturally segregated society would you still find such a range of people coming together—Baptist homeschoolers, gay parents, biology professors and university housekeeping crew, Hispanic, Appalachian, insurance agents, window and bathtub replacement specialists, fans of *Fox News* and *Focus on the Family*, MSNBC addicts, IT specialists, classroom assistants, gun owners, and home health aides, all sharing the same frustrations, values, and sorrows—and sometimes sets of siblings.

And while we all have "a heart for the children," as the most sincere say, like many of the others who started out as liberals I've unwillingly come to a jaded view of food stamps, tax deductions, HUD housing vouchers, and all the other supports I saw and heard about being bought, traded, and otherwise used to gain things like alcohol, cigarettes, drugs, and cash, and only sometimes for the benefit of the children for whom they were intended. (Our local grocery store even has a poster in the front window cautioning that the sale and transfer of EBT benefits is a crime that can carry a jail sentence.) I'm ashamed to think this way, in my greatly privileged position. The only thing that makes me feel slightly less ashamed of having become so cynical is that it's children's kinship placements and working relatives—the "good" ones, as they call each other—who are the most furious of all about the abuse of benefits and donations. And these are the people who either choose not to take that help, can't get foster board payments from the state, or don't qualify, often marginally, precisely because they work. They are the ones who would actually use the food stamps or kids' Medicaid as intended. No matter the government's short-term savings, what kind of sense does that make?

FLASH

We all had our suspicions and disappointments. Ryan had the expensive and required high school calculator we'd bought him stolen out of his mother's parents' home; elsewhere, an aunt warned me to take Christmas toys out of the package before giving them to her nephews, knowing how easily they could be resold.

One December Jessica proudly read to me an advance letter from the school about the tubs of wrapped gifts it discreetly gave out every year. The letter said the gifts would include disposable flash cameras that were to be used to take pictures of the happy kids opening their gifts on Christmas morning. The school *required* that the cameras be returned, and the family would get one set of the developed pictures. It was the strangest mixed message. In my old life I would have been disgusted, regarding it as condescension for the purpose of letting the sponsors feel good about their charity and the requisite smiles on children's faces. But by the time I saw that letter, I knew exactly what it was—an uncomfortable sugar-coated way of requiring proof that the wrapped gifts stayed wrapped and were given to the actual children, and a gamble that, after letting a child tear open a package, even the most desperate addicts would not be so heartless as to trade it for the drugs they needed themselves.

I believe Michael's family actually took a few photos and most likely lost the camera—at any rate, I'm sure the kids got their gifts, but I imagine the cardboard-encased camera washed up in the same purgatory where all the unreturned permission slips, unsigned reading logs, and pointless pencils went. Now the school asks parents receiving Christmas help to commit to helping with the school's annual rummage sale, but I've never heard about cameras being sent out again. It's not just school social workers who leave nothing to trust: a local women's service league, using referrals from guidance counselors, chooses a hundred county kids and teens to meet Santa and then go shopping for winter clothes and boots. The last step for the volunteers is to cut off all the price tags and turn them in with the receipts so no one can make returns after the items go home with the kids. Everyone wants to help the *kids*.

I know how bad this sounds—I'm a Bad Democrat, to echo Roxane (*Bad Feminist*) Gay—especially since I come from a rabidly pro–New Deal, War on Poverty, British Labour, Clinton's-too-conservative, southern, liberal Jewish family. To say nothing of coming from the monolithically enlightened bastion of a university humanities department.

As for drug-testing food stamp recipients, which *Salon* and Bill Maher cite as one more right-wing conspiracy to thwart and humiliate the poor, I've heard this same group of foster parents and many others applauding and amen-ing this idea, even the most libertarian and Christian among them. I know it's wrong if it denies even one child one meal, but I understand some of their frustration. They don't want to deny food to kids, of course, but they believe that the kids often don't get it anyway. At least here, where the minority population is minuscule, the racist subtext attached to many discussions about this or any other welfare issue on national TV seems largely absent; in our small circle, at least, the desire to see urine samples exchanged for food stamps is apparently connected to specific experiences and people—often their neighbors and relatives.

My own prejudices and stereotypes definitely play a role, as do my picturesque default images of what Appalachia should be—but while the welfare system does have some multigenerational families as clients, many more recipients find themselves in trouble in this region because they moved from elsewhere, without a traditional extended support system.

Of course, it's not poverty or even homelessness that gets children into the child welfare system. Although I wanted to be the good MSNBC liberal, I nevertheless shared the irritation when one of our support group kinship caregivers talked of running into her stepsister in a grocery store as she trailed after a friend who had given her a ride; the stepsister was carrying a handbasket while the friend had a buggy full of food, which the caregiver felt sure her nieces' food stamps were going to buy. I'd felt guilty enough when Jessica would ask me to stop to get cigarettes and then use the welfare card to buy me and the kids sodas at the convenience store as thanks for giving her a ride somewhere—a small, face-saving gesture that I tried to accept with grace. Another foster parent told of their child lying to a doctor about having worms so that a surely frantic afflicted parent could get the antidote prescribed through the child's Medicaid. While there might have been legal and more time-consuming ways to get treatment, the panic behind getting a secondhand prescription to kill parasites was one I could relate to. I could get self-righteous about a kid smoking to get a parent prescription cough medicine, but I couldn't feel any sense of outrage about wanting worms out of your system. The lice on the outside had been bad enough. And I still feel badly for Jessica, who was on Medicaid herself just long enough to get the surgery she needed, but not long enough to get more than one round of the expensive lifelong medication the surgery necessitated before her eligibility ran out.

While we've all routinely heard foster parents accused of being "in it for the money"—a cliche that always draws a laugh from any group of foster parents—the payments intended to help feed and clothe the children never begin to match what foster parents actually spend to meet the children's needs, much less to provide the "more" we all long to give them; except for those first six months with Michael and some of the respite care we've done, we have not received board reimbursements. At least we can afford it, unlike the countless relatives who provide court-sanctioned kinship care and, at least in the past, often got no help at all from the state. The boys lost eligibility for free school lunches once they returned to live with us outside of foster care, but even with our getting custody, both boys have been able to keep Medicaid, which has been an enormous blessing, miraculously covering the many appointments, procedures, therapies, and medications that kids born prematurely who've grown up in severe stress so often need. I knew Medicaid would cover braces only if they were judged to be "non-cosmetic" and if I was again willing to drive two hundred miles monthly, which I did for two years with a former foster teen, so we decided to just pay out of pocket for orthodontics locally instead. While a huge and necessary expense, it has had the unexpected benefit of further normalizing Michael with the kids at his school—with the dental practice's movies on the ceiling and laptop X-boxes, and exchanging serious-faced fist bumps with kids he knows in the waiting room, he's suddenly out of the world of the clinic dentist and into the world the middle-class kids have always lived in. I think that one of the proudest moments of his middle school years came two weeks after his braces first went on, when another seventh-grader casually asked if he had a spare rubber band.

CODY

Despite our overwhelming but unofficial commitment to Michael and his family over the years, we continued to call ourselves foster parents and worked to remain licensed. But looking back, I always felt guilty that we were not of enough use to the agency, other than doing respite care for other foster families or children in residential care. So why did we stay licensed, with all the renewal requirements, inspections, and twenty training hours required every two years?

Primarily because it seemed for a decade that Michael and Ryan could always abruptly return to foster care. So I needed to be sure they always would be able to stay with us legally. They visited and stayed overnight often, of course, but I was afraid to give away the space I felt I had to save for Michael, and later for his brother—not just in my heart but physically, in the two officially allotted, fire marshal–approved rooms of our house.

Halfway through our decade with Michael's extended family, however, when Michael was about seven, we also served as short-term foster parents for a voluntary placement of Cody, a teen with invisible disabilities. We got along with his stressed but good-humored working mother, Risa, who needed temporary care for him that she could count on. Cody's older, adult brother, Logan, came and went, dropping in at his mother's home now and then for pizza, video games, horror movies, or a break from the several girlfriends and relatives he stayed with, but Risa knew better than to leave them alone together while she went out of town to care for a relative.

Michael and Ryan were unfazed—they were used to people of all ages coming in and out of their lives, and Cody lived so immersed in his own world of the moment that he paid the boys—and me—only surface attention. It was Will he liked and would seek to engage, as all kids magically did, and Will got a kick out of Cody's love of tinkering and enthusiasm for chopping wood or helping Will haul dirt and fertilizer around our garden.

We remained a close support for Cody and his mom for the three years that she let us—until she became involved with a man who stole his medications, followed my car, wouldn't let Cody talk to his mom alone, and cut them off from everyone else. Weirdest of all for us, he eventually moved them into the same remote, hazardous house from which Michael's family had been evicted, and Risa lost her longtime job for lack of transportation.

Although a teacher tried frequently to get DSS back on the case, this had only temporary effect, even when Cody went to school bruised and with a black eye, saying he had been thrown out of his mother's home on Valentine's Day night. (As crazily as he always exaggerated, his knowing it was Valentine's Day, when he couldn't even tell you his own birthday, confirmed for me the accuracy of his report more vividly than the bruises.) I missed seeing Cody as often once his mom's new boyfriend came in and took over—I'd felt close to this wild teenager, even though the feeling wasn't mutual, and I'd marveled at his standard hyperbole ("Come on, Deb, speed up—the limit's 120 on this road") through hundreds of hours taking him to a summer landscaping job, to Special Olympics swim team workouts, to church food box pickups, and monthly to the Medicaid orthodontist a hundred miles away, or making him peanut butter and mallow whip sandwiches and finding him old stereo parts to dissect while his mother was at work. He'd somehow revived his mother's previous boyfriend with his own version of CPR when he was only nine or ten; when the man died a few years later, Cody never stopped being terrified of the closet in which he'd found him unconscious.

Predictably, neither Cody nor his mom ever forgave me for the trouble provoked when I told his school nurse that he'd told me he planned to take a big rope he had stored away and hang himself from a specific tree behind his old trailer park. Did I truly believe he would? No, but is that really supposed to make a difference when someone tells you a soup-to-nuts suicide plan? And did I believe Cody's threat to the counselor that he would kill me for telling her this? Not really—for, like everything else that passed through his mind, I knew he'd forget the threat and move on to talk of sneakers, cars, and milkshakes when it was time to drive the two hours to the orthodontist. Unfortunately, that was for his final visit, because he was still refusing to brush his teeth and the braces that should have changed his life and bite instead were going to rot his teeth, so they had to be removed.

Cody was a unique but completely troubled, illiterate, and often out-of-control teen, and it broke my heart that he eluded all the community resources that could have allowed his future to be other than the totally foreseeable one it has turned out to be. I hate to think what will happen—what has already happened—to the two children he fathered while still a teen.

SURROUNDED

Here's the other Lynyrd Skynyrd song all the kids bellow: not just *Sweet Home Alabama*—beloved by Michael and Ryan even before the Eminem version—but *That Smell.* They cackle. *Oo-oo, that smell. Can't you smell that smell? The smell of it surrounds you.* Oh-so-knowing laughter from seventh-graders about the waft of weed, when in fact "that smell," to me, to some other foster parents, to child welfare investigators I've met, is something else entirely—the smell of neglect in winter. I've heard people say that the smell of kerosene is the smell of poverty, but the smell I mean is something else altogether: a heavy, choking mix of, yes, unvented kerosene but also indoor dog crap, cigarette smoke, dog pee on furniture, and bacon grease, all rising up and ballooning against plastic-sheeted windows. That smell attaches to clothing, hair, air, your skin. Foster parents know what it is, yet I'd thought I was the only one who noticed. That rush when you open the door, the thing you want to get away from.

The smell of an okay relative's house: cigarette smoke cut with heavy-duty strawberry Air Wick.

It's enough to make me long for the dizzying, hateful, pseudoclean fumes of teen Axe spray cologne.

And should you recognize, you always wonder, the smell of meth? Does it smell like strong dry-cleaner fluid?, you want to ask somebody. And, if not, what in the world does?

A BREATH

In our own household I'm predictably active in the forefront, bossing homework, booking appointments, rehearsing Love and Logic catchphrases—like snappy comebacks, they're never there when you want them. I'm the one making resolutions and taking the kids to have experiences—or, in the nauseating jargon of the TLC reality shows, to "make memories" in the impossible hope that the good memories will crowd out the bad.

Will, who frequently cooks for the boys, is the hugely necessary "kid person," who gets on their wavelength and can be laid back and have fun—or yell at them much more bluntly than I ever would. He is also one of the few healthy, steadily employed male role models they've ever seen up close, as much as they've glorified his opposites. As Will said at the outset, what he really wanted was a long-term relationship rather than short-term care for many kids, and for the most part our connections and intermittent care have been with children in the same extended family. Male or female, toddler or teen, each has shared a great bond with Will, almost instantly. Luckily Will also proved to be much more resigned to Michael and Ryan's comings and goings over the years than I was—for after the long-ago sadness of losing his own son Vince's daily presence through divorce, how much worse could it get for him? This was another way in which we complemented and balanced each other, for as often as I'd tried to demand that he share my sorrow, fear, and outrage, Will's habit of simply rolling with change helped hold our lives steady. I envied his ability to live in the present while my mind leapt ahead to disarm the future by dwelling on the worst it could bring. I'm working on that reflex still (and perhaps it is the most culturally Jewish thing about me), but I doubt I'll ever achieve Will's level of equanimity.

I can't imagine what our life would have been like without these boys—if the water regulations had never changed or if their mother had chosen at any point to close the door, as was fully her right. Adoption or no, custody or not, two days or twelve years, I know indisputably that I, and countless others, can love someone else's child as my own—and, as arrogant as it sounds, perhaps even more, given the accidental, finite, uncanny nature of it all. One missed phone call and it might never have been, or we might have missed extracting the boys on the critical night they needed to get away from the fighting. Our social worker, Gerri, has said for years that things generally work out the way they're supposed to—a notion I've always chalked up as a DSS platitude, handing over to fate all they can't do—but I've also always hoped it might be true.

Like other foster and adoptive parents, I learn again and again that trauma is a never-ending story: even adoption at birth is not a happily-ever-after, and each age and stage resurrects its own reminders and reenactments of fear and loss. This was one of the first lessons I remember learning in our long-ago licensing training, and as clearly as the case studies illustrated this phenomenon, somehow it's still a shock each time trauma reincarnates in a new guise. Resilient as these boys have shown themselves to be, moving bravely forward, if not "moving on" as we might like to believe is possible, they would be far from where they are if not for others' great generosity. We owe their mother a lifetime debt for their presence; we owe their teachers, youth mentors, and church for always building these children up; and we owe DSS and the mostly beloved social workers for their continuous support and advice, as hamstrung as they've often been. While we are always braced for the earthquake and alert to every tremor, having these boys safe within our walls for this long has been unimaginably fulfilling. All I've ever wanted, since Michael's first backward stare at me, was the seemingly unattainable knowledge that he'd stay with us—that we'd have the same illusory sense of security that biological and adoptive parents carry daily.

BUT NOW, at least, I can breathe. We can't adopt the boys, but this is as close as we can get: the legal and physical custody that DSS negotiated a year ago with both parents, granting the boys some permanency and peace of mind after their fraught and terrible winter while sparing the agency the burden of unneeded investigation, ugliness, and taxpayer expense. Will and I had to get a lawyer, go to court, and wait months for the last papers to be signed, but it was uncontested, to our great relief. Legally uncontested, at least—on their first afternoon visit after Will and I gained custody, their mom told them—as a secret—that as soon as she could borrow $1,000 from her mother—meaning never—she would use it to get them back. *I didn't have a choice*, she told them. And who am I, especially now, to say someone shouldn't save face, when that is the last thing she has to save? What parent could actually face that stark truth? Who could actually stare at that sun?

To me, it also matters what the kids believe to be the facts of our situation. While I recognize the subtext—that their mother had not abandoned them—her words also allowed the boys no closure and no way to reckon their losses, however sad, and fully take root in a new life, with no fear of getting ripped away just as they'd sent out exploratory roots. Her whispered words left a box eternally open, something to keep them from throwing all their lots in with us.

All our signatures and that dated, purple court stamp mean the boys are physically safe and can't be taken away to another house or state by a knock on the door and a revving car in the driveway. So they are safe, at least, to start unknotting the tangle of facts, fear, and memories within them. Safer than we ever thought they'd be. I can't speak for Ryan, but for Michael, for Will, and for me, it is really all we need.

AS WE'D always known was the case, things had to get much worse to get better, but that's another story. And once things got better, I gradually got worse in many ways, making up for years of having no control by exerting far too much and becoming more impatient, harsh, and full of lectures about all the baggage the boys carried with them. I just wanted them to say *uncle,* to surrender all their skewed beliefs in one swoop, to give up the hidden knives, the reflexive lying, and the Dixie Classic sweatshirts a relative had bought them. Getting the boys to fold a shirt my way began to seem insanely important; I demanded never to see a bare chest or camo cap inside the house again.

Daily, I resolve to improve myself and read the electronic Post-it slogans on my computer screen from Celebrate Calm and Connected Parenting. Letting go and letting God, if I can do that as a nonbeliever. Trusting in natural consequences instead of the byzantine correctives I might dream up. Daily, I remind myself to be better, but it's a battle I lose each morning when my short patience runs out. I lose it and resolve again to stay calm at any price, to give teen resistance nothing to push against. In wanting so badly to mend my little corner of the world, I do my own damage daily, I fear.

SELFISHLY, AND almost trivially, Will and I are grateful that our long life with these boys has grounded us in the university world. It's so easy to get caught up in academic life, values, arguments about course numbers, and abstract politics—world and office—but our experience through these years tethers us to the very real world outside the university. While I'd be "just a mom" if I could at this point, I can't financially, as is true for most families; yet even when I'm up grading past midnight, I am so lucky to have the flexibility—and credibility—that my teaching schedule and position gives me.

I can also see how the boys' growing up on the perimeter of the university world has seeped into their expectations for themselves. Through the years they've loved nothing more than sitting in my classes on snow days, passing out candy or writing subversive messages to the students on the chalkboard behind me. Their easy familiarity with the cafeteria, the statues, the bookstore, the card-swipe vending machines, the library's DVD shelves, and the year-end celebrations has given them an unquestioning sense of belonging, even ownership, here on our campus. It's almost become their birthright.

THE RELIEF of knowing the boys are here for the long haul strikes me afresh so many mornings when I wake up fearful and forgetting. We are here for them; they can visit and talk with their mom on our turf; their Grandma Irene anchors them with her lifelong love and comfort; their cousins have drawn them into the compassionate family of their church; and we have the further blessed assurance that the boys can nurture their relationship with their biological dad, Luke, from the safety of his imprisonment through their growing years, without the giant eraser of drugs literally wiping him out. The boys can see his caring, Christian baseline self and know him as a loving father who needs their company more than anything and desires their daily health and success. The advice he gives them is always the best, for it is drawn from hard experience and years of regret.

For a decade I'd told people, *I feel like I'm holding my breath.* But the stone on my chest has rolled away; the band of fear around my lungs has been released. I can fully breathe now, and I can let that breath go without losing everything. I have to remind myself: the phone won't ring at midnight again. I can focus on being better, doing better myself. On actually helping them. I have that peace.

MIRROR UNIVERSE

I still get angry on behalf of the kids for the trauma that they've suffered, and furious at myself when I get impatient with them, but when it comes to our relationships and experiences with their family, I forget how much I take for granted and how easily none of it could have happened. I owe it all to Jessica, and to Irene for keeping me tethered to the boys through the early days of their reunification and beyond.

How often do I remember that my life could still be as bleak and sandblasted as it was the day we first had to return two-year-old Michael from foster care? How many times have I wondered if I'd recognize him now, and now, and now—at three, at seven, at eleven and thirteen—in a grocery store or Walmart? Would I have found excuses to go shopping in the next county and hung around gas stations and crummy Dollar Stores, hoping I'd see his sweet little face and that he'd jump down from a grocery cart and come running to me? The one he would have thought had sent him away?

Without Jessica's decision to allow me to stay connected, we wouldn't now have the daily miracle of Michael's and Ryan's presence, to say nothing of our eighteen photo books full of memories. Instead, I would have been on a lifelong search for Michael, seeing flashes in a crowd, as you do of a person recently dead, but he would have been a ghost of the living, floating through the mountain fog and Walmart mobs, forever out of sight and out of reach. If they'd all emigrated permanently to a southernmost state, would I have even sensed it?

The boys' mother didn't have to keep any connection—not with us or DSS—didn't have to say as much as thank you for the half-year of foster care. She was the person whose power I most feared, besides Benny, who often pulled the strings, yet Jessica was the person who gave it all back to me. She didn't have to do any of it. How many mothers would?

SHIMBAREE, SHIMBARAH

Way back at the beginning in 2005, as the official date when Michael would leave our care after six months approached, I couldn't even get through the corny old *Barney* song without dissolving into tears, which I knew better than to inflict on a child. Most parents despised Barney's song, I knew, but nothing was bearable about the looming loss, and Will and I spoke the earnest language of Barney, Dora, Thomas the Tank Engine, Blue, and Scoop, Muck, Bob, and Wendy, using their slogans and sayings to try to implant memories of love and ways to cope with the unimaginable life that lay ahead. Back then we quoted *Bob the Builder* most of all, as two-year-old Michael adored any form of construction and could gleefully identify a backhoe; the glossy, sunny yellow of Scoop, Bob's lead machine, promised a brightness that couldn't be shattered. *Can we fix it?* Bob's crew was prompted at every turn, and, long before Obama took their slogan, the machines always replied in chorus: *Yes, we can.*

In those years every professional adult we met spoke Bob-talk as shorthand to boys, and it was as laden with meaning as the baby sign language that day care providers encourage. As Michael's reunification date approached, everything outside our little bubble seemed more and more broken: the day care director couldn't get the social worker to register alarm that Michael came back from transition weekends talking of belts and spanking; I couldn't get her to worry that his asthma medicine came back only half used, while his weekend's laundry reeked of cigarette smoke. The guardian ad litem, whom the court had appointed to advocate for Michael, never spoke to him or us. Barely two years old, Michael would say no when I forced myself to brightly remind him when he was going home again. *No . . . no . . . you Mommy,* he said more than once, and I despaired of knowing how to prepare him without making it sound like we were willingly giving him up.

When he said those words, though, it seemed like our secret locked into place: I was at once gratified that Michael felt the same truth that I did, but my heart seized with panic that Jessica would hear him say that. It would wound her feelings, but more crucially I knew it would kill the promised chance of our getting to see each other once he went home. And in fact I'd had to deny him when he called me Mommy for a third time—by accident, after a family visit—in front of his sister in the car. "No," I instructed him, "I'm Deborah, remember? Jessica is your mommy." Isabelle had appeared not to be listening, but months later I had these words spoken back to me, more than once, by the grandmother, who was quoting Jessica. Isabelle had told her mother how I'd corrected Michael, and Jessica had told Irene, and it had come back to me, in the circuitous game of telephone we were to play for years. I knew that my words in that moment, as hard as they'd been to say to Michael, were the very reason we could visit. That denial and redirection had been the key that unlocked our future together.

AT THE last doctor visit before Michael went back to live with his mother, the very professional and poker-faced doctor, who'd first examined this child when he came into state custody, looked even more serious than usual when I referred to the upcoming transition. I begged the doctor to be superaware the next time he saw Michael—to listen to how clear his chest sounded now and please to call his social worker if it crackled again later. Our doctor sighed and told me, "It's a hard thing to go through"; coming from him, it meant more than the sympathetic words of all my friends. He didn't condemn Social Services or Jessica or say much else, but he gave Michael a high five and two *Bob the Builder* Band-Aids. Backing out the door—he was so tall his head almost met the frame—he nodded back at Michael and told him, "Yes, we can."

Words I will always hope to believe.

The Questions

WHY DO *they, why don't they, why won't they tell us, how do they, how could they, why can't they, how could they, how could a judge—*

The minute the foster parent experience goes from the theoretical to the tangible, questions erupt.

The questions may change, but the word *they* stays the same. And by *they*, I don't mean a biological family whose children we care for. We're discouraged from viewing any family in "us and them" terms. No, by *they*, I mean Social Services and the officials who work along every strand of the web that extends from its center.

That biofamily, I'm sure, has many more urgent questions than ours and probably more unspoken ones after a lifetime of feeling voiceless. As obvious as their questions might seem, I wouldn't presume to guess what they might be, although I can imagine they feel that they have none of the control for which I actually have envied them: the power to change their family's situation and have their children back again. I've scoured the government *Now What?* guide for bioparents whose children have been removed, as if it contained some secrets, and was amazed at the plain, logical, respectful, direct, and noninflammatory language—in *my* opinion, of course. Like everything about this process, all I can pretend to know is my own narrow perspective. My own questions. And I always have just one more question.

My questions feel urgent with someone else's child in my home—but I also know that I grew up in a home that enabled me to become a foster parent, a home in which I could assume my questions would and should be answered. Not that many foster parents I've met grew up as I did, but if they didn't have social privilege, at least they had the conviction of their faith and church to steel them with the determination to do right by even their seventh, eleventh, or nineteenth foster child. I'm probably even more cowed by authority than they are, wanting as I do to be seen by the agency staff as a compliant and reasonable equal.

Certainly I don't want to be seen as the pesky fly or nervous do-gooder who is always coming back with "just one more thing" to ask—as I compulsively need to. So I write my questions for the workers down and condense and edit them as carefully as I can, often unsure whether I even have the standing to ask about a certain thing. I doubt I'm typical of foster parents, though—and maybe I was just scared off by our children's first social worker and by my lifelong fear of coming across as pushy. That first worker was young and tenacious, but, I think, eager for success; her reticence to explain or respond seems atypical for our agency. I see that now, but back then every time I opened my mouth, I felt like I'd overstepped. In later years, when crises did come, I often heard from our social workers why Social Services couldn't help—but I never got that sense again that I was overstepping the bounds by asking why. Now, however, in reading social media posts of advice from parents fostering with private and public agencies alike nationwide, it appears that the number one complaint and reason for crowdsourcing advice from a Facebook group is frustration with unanswered questions and unreturned phone calls, far beyond anything we experienced.

Rationally, I know strengthening of children's biofamilies must be an agency's first priority since the fundamental goal now is almost always reunification. Reasonably, I know that we foster families are a tool of Social Services uses to achieve that end—or whatever alternative goal may develop—so—in my understanding, when I'm calm enough to think about it—it makes sense that answering foster parents' questions might be not be a top priority. Of course the needs and questions of the children, and then their families, need primary attention. I doubt any agency staff member would put it that way, but that's what I told myself back at the beginning . . . when I was feeling cool and distanced, at least. Because as soon as a real, urgent, needy, happy, rapidly learning child is in front of you—in your home, your hands, your bathtub, your car seat—it's as if the cute wooden Pinocchio of your textbook training manual has suddenly become a real living, breathing, irresistible boy.

And then you're on fire with questions. Everything is new each time you bring a foster child into your home—new and the opposite of natural. And once you're past forty, how many completely new and baffling experiences do you have? The newness also helps you suspend judgment of the biofamily, as you've been trained you must, while repeating the mantra that the parents—usually Mom—was doing the best she could at the time. Certainly that's a mantra you're going to have to learn to use about yourself in the future—and it won't be nearly as easy to suspend judgment of your own mistakes and oversights. But at the start you're ravenous for answers from the workers who control the process, who schedule visits, who give permission for everything from vacations to haircuts, who make recommendations to the judge at every step—who, even more than the biofamilies, seem to hold the keys to the future.

No human, much less a social worker for Child Protective Services, could ever hold still long enough, or repeat themselves enough times or in enough ways, to satisfy the bottomless pit of uncertainty in your gut. When every instruction rushes by and the asthma nebulizer's hose-thing comes loose and sputters aerosolized albuterol everywhere, and you smart at the rebuke when your new child arrives thirty minutes late at his required day care on his very first morning at your house—well, what middle-aged professional likes to make mistakes? And those are just the immediate, critical, get-through-the-day type questions—whole orders of magnitude from the taboo questions, the so-what-would-have-to-happen-to-keep-this-child-with-me-forever type questions. (By the way, figuring out how a nebulizer machine works was my lot in life well before Google, Siri, and the internet provided instant answers.)

Of all the things I continue to learn about our children's lives, past and present, and all the answers I'll never know, and all the questions I still have about how Michael came to us and why the path followed the course it did—and I mean the concrete questions of this world, not the ones I might ask of God or fate or how the stars happened to align just as they did—there persist many questions I have of child welfare policies in general.

And so one day, as I could and should have done all along, I tried to pull back from the tunnel vision of my own experience and simply made an appointment and sat down in a long-time worker's office and asked the questions I needed to ask. I asked my basic, general, burning questions—the why-things-are-the-way-they-are questions that I now can Google and still not comprehend.

INTERVIEW QUESTIONS

"DSS has a lot of power. There's no other government entity that has the power to take a child—even the police can't. Given that, we *have* to have a lot of restrictions on us." That is how Paula Hutchins, an investigative / assessment & treatment social worker, responded to my litany of questions about what a county Social Services agency *can't* do. I trusted everyone at the agency at the time, but Paula is my personal hero, because she was the veteran social worker who inherited the case that helped us negotiate custody of our boys in their teen years. "With so much power," she explained, "it makes sense to me that we have to go by extremely strict rules. Another family might not parent in the way that I would, but people live and express themselves in many different ways, and how they choose to do that is not our call, as long as a child is not a victim of abuse, neglect, or dependency."

For all the media stereotypes of social workers as rushed or jaded, it was reassuring to hear a reaffirmation that the staff members of this agency were true believers. That they were all about the purpose that the state had mandated—reunifying birth families, collaboration between birth and foster parents, multidisciplinary teamwork, and other policies that might give some prospective foster parents pause. As comforting as I might once have found it to believe our social workers were cynics (secretly on "our side"—when sides are not supposed to exist), who were just checking the prescribed case plan boxes under protest, it was clear this staff was all the way on board with the mission.

"What I actually do, people in the community have no idea," Paula told me. "People want to say we should 'take the kids out of those places, and don't send them back,' or they say the opposite—that we take them and don't send them back. The two most common questions we get are 'Why did you remove *this* child?' And 'Why didn't you remove *that* child?' People understand very little of child welfare policies and that very specific laws govern all the moves we can make. And the public doesn't get the finer details, since we can't talk to anyone about these confidential cases. Not a lot of information is shared."

The pendulum of bringing children into foster care has swung, she said. "Twenty-five years ago, it was in the other camp: 'Take 'em all,' 'Get 'em out of these families,' people thought. Yet over time, court cases and legislation have brought change about toward the goal of reunification. Now the process is heavily weighted toward reunification—and I think it's the right place to be. The parent-child bond is still stronger than that child is going to form with any subsequent caregiver. This is the place to be.

"But out in the community," Paula continued, "when people see families where the system recidivism is high—the general perception is often 'Oh, DSS skips harder choices and just hands back the kids.'"

That's exactly what I'd felt myself, I wanted to say, but really wished that Paula had been here then, instead of the very young worker who explained the minimum of Michael's case, in fragments, as if betraying state secrets, so that I wasn't even sure what we were allowed to know. Which, it turns out, was almost everything.

"What reunification *really* is," Paula explained, "is a very intensive, action-oriented process, with comprehensive case plans. Parents may have to engage in therapy, follow a routine, go to court monthly—all while maintaining a job and housing. Best case is six months, but it's usually at the year mark—and then it can stay open another three months or longer, case by case—even two to three years, if the judge sees the parents are still trying."

"But what about when the issue is not just the parent's actions, but who the parent is living *with*?" I ask. That was the central question for us, though it has also been the foster parents' chief concern in any number of cases in which our peers have been involved.

"We're looking at that reunification home, to see if it's safe and appropriate," Paula said. "Whoever is in the home has to do a case plan and criminal background check, if they are an adult, eighteen or older. If they're found in need of services, then they will have to use those services. That includes nonrelatives—it's whoever lives in the home."

Whoever, I think. I'm remembering the studies cited by the *Daily Beast* following the 2015 death of Baby Bella, the unknown toddler who was found in Boston Harbor—the studies show that the greatest risk factor for children is the presence in the home of males with no biological relationship to them, and the presence of the "mother's boyfriend." Within our new family, that was the factor that confounded us most. But statistics mean nothing, case by case, when decisions are about individual families and must be based on evidence.

MORE THAN a decade into this venture, I'm still eaten up with questions; despite all the training workshops I've attended and the short-term and respite care we've provided on our long road with Michael and Ryan, we've really been through the whole start-to-finish process only with them. For years, as the boys came and went, then came for longer and longer periods, we stayed licensed for foster care, never knowing when a quake would open the cracks in their home to chasms visible to even the most optimistic investigator. I can see there is more transparency now than we first experienced, and more deliberate education of foster families about the court process and reasons for children's coming into foster care—and quite likely, there always was. Maybe our original case just had an unfortunate combination of my novice timidity and one young worker's determination to show that her reunification plans could actually succeed.

I ASK about the recent waves of media and online outrage on every side of the controversies about "free-range kids," Baby Bella, Balloon Boy, the Duggars, the Kentucky family of twelve that was living in a tent compound off the grid, back to the removal and return of the prairie-dressed girls from the Texas polygamy cult. The viral stories every American can't help but hear and have a reflexive opinion about, assuming we all know the full story—and that we know best what is happening. That Social Services is either interfering too much or doing nothing. That liberals and/or then-president Barack Obama had built a nanny/police state. The subtext goes on and on.

"So the public perception is often that we're meddling," Paula responded, "when what we're checking for is whether the child's situation meets minimum standards. We're not the parenting police, or the parental militia—it's whether or not the child is a victim of neglect, abuse, or dependence." *Dependence*, she explains, generally means that, for whatever reason, a parent "is unable to provide for care or supervision and lacks an appropriate alternative childcare arrangement."

I asked her about another thing that I know confounds some foster parents. "Why does DSS tell parents when they're coming to their home after receiving a report? Why give them the chance to literally clean up their act?" (To say nothing of a chance to ruminate on, or call around about, the probable source of that anonymous report.)

The number of malicious reports surprises me, but DSS can't decide the caller's motive, Paula said, and even if DSS suspects a report is bogus, it has to "screen it in" if the call meets certain criteria. If a report warrants follow-up, what happens next depends on the allegations in the report. Differential response, a system reform that now operates in a number of states and localities, allows Child Protective Services to follow one of two or more pathways of investigation or assessment for cases that are screened in and accepted. A report of sexual abuse, for example, must follow the investigative track, which probably is what most people imagine to be how Social Services traditionally operates: follow-up is either immediate or within a specified number of hours; the social workers' visit can be unannounced; and workers may interview the children at school and without the parents' knowledge. These are the higher-risk cases, Paula said, the ones in which there is likelihood that children are in immediate danger or are the victims of extensive abuse. The more recent, and otherwise preferred, track is family assessment, which is where the announced and scheduled visits come in. "Family assessment is strength-based, partnering with the parents," Paula said. "DSS is aligning *with* the family—the point is not to surprise them and be the enemy. This is done on purpose to start developing trust with the family, so we're not [seen as] trying to set them up or catch them doing something wrong." This track is intended to be family friendly and to provide a range of services from a variety of sources; its goal is to do what it takes to eliminate risk: when the risk is determined to have been eliminated, then Social Services has done its job.

I strain to imagine the family that welcomes intervention, however family friendly such help may be. Unless a family asks Social Services for help, which does happen, I wonder whether those on the receiving end of a family assessment even realize this is the kinder, gentler approach. I remember how incensed one mother was—she'd shown me the full-page note from a pair of social workers announcing their impending visit, written on steno paper in such girlish pen that I almost expected the *i*'s to have been dotted with hearts. "I showed them I had food in the cupboards—the kids were eating hotdogs when they came back!" she said. "And they asked if I had enough kerosene," she said, outraged, "like I'd let my kids freeze."

I'd never have the diplomacy or guts to do social work, I know. There's a reason I'm in awe of so many social workers, and a reason I could never imagine my college-age self ever exploring this field. I can't negotiate or assert or assure anyone of anything without worrying about mis-speaking, offending, or getting tongue-tied. Maybe that's why I can't imagine how social workers manage to bring anxious, angry parents around to feel that they are truly on the parents' side.

Surely immediately allying with parents whenever possible looks easier on paper than it might prove in real life—or, at least, in my imagination. To say nothing of getting foster and biological parents to ally with each other from the start, as if fear, jealousy, and, unfortunately, judgment did not exist. Our own cooperation, initiated by Michael's mother, had come about informally—and despite my reluctance, which stemmed from my perennial fear of having someone mad at me. In recent years, the process of building that co-parenting relationship has become both more systematic and expected: foster parents often join bioparents in icebreaker meetings and are strongly encouraged to share photos and information, facilitate visits, attend school conferences and medical appointments, arrange phone calls, and most of all adjust their own attitudes to make a given situation work. Increasingly, partnerships between birth and foster parents are seen by social workers and researchers to play a vital role in supporting reunification efforts and in nurturing children's well-being, whatever the ultimate outcome of their case. Given my initial trepidation, despite the reassuring things I'd heard about the children's mother, shared parenting was something I'd never have done voluntarily. Yet it turned out to be the very lifesaver that has brought us to the place we are today.

WHAT DOES Paula find most difficult about her job?

"It's really hard to see the way children love their parents and are just not getting their needs met. Even with extreme physical and sexual abuse, children love their parents and want to be with them," she said. "Regardless of what's happened, seeing that heartbreak is very difficult."

Also: "Kids who get left in the system, floundering. Things snowball once you have to start moving them and disrupting placements, until they've grown up entirely in the system, getting pregnant so they finally have someone to love them, and then it starts all over again.

"It's typical," she says, "if you've been working a long time, that you're going down the court docket, saying, *We had her in care, now we have her children.* 'But I needed somebody to love me,' you'd hear, 'someone who would never leave and would love me unconditionally.'"

All the careful case plans and staggered steps can go only so far, Paula cautioned. "We're already in a field where it's difficult to do the job, but it's near-impossible within a broken system." And she doesn't mean only Social Services; she means the mental health system as well. "It's so inept, so broken. It's failing at a miserable rate. It becomes incarceration. The lack of mental health care has a huge impact on child welfare, on domestic violence. Change has to be a priority to help the parents, but the kids need mental health services as well."

Another huge gap, she said, is in small counties like ours. While I always think it's the bigger cities that must be worst off, according to Paula, it's the midsized to small counties with limited social services budgets that are the hardest hit. And there are never enough foster families—the need has far outpaced the supply, especially in the tough economic times of recent years that seem to presage an increase in the number of children coming into foster care. When the county homes are maxed out, she said, the kids go to other counties or to group homes. More than a dozen times in recent years, Paula said, social workers have spent the night at the office when they had no place to put a child and were waiting for a bed.

OUR FAMILY is technically not in the world of adoption, although our day-to-day experience of having custody feels close, so I'm amazed at how many of our foster-parent friends have adopted—and somehow still continue to foster new children.

As in foster care, the focus of adoption and its practices have changed significantly since the early 1990s and in some cases earlier, from the proliferation and legalization of adoptions by gay parents, to an increasing number of adoptions by single parents, to further acceptance of transracial adoption. Decades ago, preference for same-race placements predominated, arising first from white prejudice and later with the controversy of the early 1970s when the National Association of Black Social Workers famously opposed placement of African American children with white adoptive parents, even if such placements meant that children had long stays in group homes and institutions (a position modified and expanded in 1994 to emphasize "preservation of families of African ancestry" and, when necessary, "the importance of finding culturally grounded options for children of African ancestry before giving consideration to placing our children outside of the community"). Federal legislation in the mid-1990s aimed to eliminate race-related barriers to children's placement in foster and adoptive homes, while also requiring that states make diligent efforts to recruit parents whose racial and ethnic diversity reflects that of the children needing placement in foster and adoptive families. Now, our county's adoption worker told me, "it is definitely not the case that children must go to the same-race family first" and that legally "race is not considered at all" in adoption cases. With both domestic and international transracial adoptions now much more common, parents who adopt transracially are urged to educate themselves to the realities their children will face as they grow up in two worlds, and they are expected to actively work to empower their children through development of racial and cultural identity and pride, while bringing into their lives same-race role models and community experiences. And the infamous earlier practice of removing great numbers of Native American children from reservations to white homes and institutions, which led to the 1978 Indian Child Welfare Act, has since meant that Social Services can't take children off reservations. "Many tribes have their own versions of DSS, and if any child is the child of a tribe member and eligible for membership, even if they're living off the reservation," Paula explained, "the agency still has to reach out to the tribe, which decides if they'll make an allowance" for the local agency to work with a child. That's why determining whether a child is of Indian heritage is a priority item on intake paperwork, she told me.

WITH THE well-known decline in the number of North American infants available for adoption came the huge boom in international adoptions. Commonly assumed motivations for taking on the enormous investment of adopting internationally included a desire to be spared the uncertainty and heartbreak of a birth mother's changing her mind about adoption and to avoid, for better or worse, the complications of an existing, extended North American birth family. Expense, long waiting periods, and agonizing uncertainty nonetheless often have brought their own major stresses to prospective international adoptive parents. Where internationally adoptive families and those who've adopted through American foster care increasingly come together, however, is in dealing with the effects of childhood trauma, whether it be the trauma that led to and resulted from children's removal from American homes or the traumas and attachment disorders resulting from prenatal and orphanage conditions in many countries. These parent communities come together on websites and in Facebook groups in a common search for answers and understanding. The national origin of their children seems to be the least relevant factor.

Still, despite the scarcity of adoptable infants and toddlers, and the growing realization that no child, even a newborn, starts with a blank slate, as I write this more than 100,000 children and sibling groups are waiting to be adopted—they've been completely cleared for no-cost and often subsidized adoption, according to the federal government's AdoptUSKids program. Yet most of these boys and girls will continue to wait many years for adoptive families, while more than twenty thousand children each year "age out" of the foster care system without having been adopted.

INITIAL AND ongoing training for foster and adoptive parents stresses meeting the needs of children, understanding family dynamics, building on strengths, exploring the factors driving complex behaviors, and supporting family visits and reunification or other permanency plans. While the training curriculum that my husband and I and our small group worked through in the early 2000s was thorough, supportive, and taught us ways of interpreting behaviors to find underlying needs, in the years since, that curriculum has become much more comprehensive, and I can't imagine any new foster family in our area will ever feel as confused as we sometimes did.

While my questions and answers are rooted in one small county of one medium-sized state, I know that our family is lucky to be here, in this county, within a child protective services system that, to me and many other foster parents, seems to be as good as it gets. Given the generations of human imperfection that have led to the system's reason for existence, it is a tribute to our agency that at past state training conferences, our local foster parents found that our experiences with our agency were the envy of other parents around the state. While our local workers and judges often don't do what *our* hearts and minds wish they would and could, we nonetheless have a system that strives to support the children and their biological families through the process, and foster parents have the privilege of being supported too. Obviously, I don't speak for the experience of those birth families. But for all the adoptive and foster families whose pleas and protests I've read online, and for the parents I've met across the state and country, I wish the same experience that we have here.

THERE WILL always be questions. Questions about the system or about an individual child or a behavior or an agency or judge's decision; questions about the process and things that don't feel right. Questions others ask of us, indirectly, because they are itching to know why the children are in our care or how Mom is doing, bless her heart. Questions of other foster and adoptive parents, questions of bafflement and despair, and questions about our kids' traumas, which will never be known with certainty and will never stop. We're like Tim O'Brien's young soldiers, marching through Vietnam in his short story "The Things They Carried," where "for all the ambiguities . . . all the mysteries and unknowns, there was at least the single abiding certainty that they would never be at a loss for things to carry." For me, that certainty is the persistence of questions. In the life we've chosen, I'll never be at a loss for questions. I know more than I did when I started, and more, even, than I did last month or last year. But there will always be just one more thing I have to call back about.

II

LEARNING THE ROAD

DSS

Department of Social Services

Sometimes good, sometimes not good.

—a nine-year-old former client

A SUIT-DRESSED couple unloads baby stuff from a minivan—the poufy diaper bag, a big red Grover doll, and finally the child himself, of maybe two, dressed in a plaid shirt, hair combed, and looking as if he could be going to work with them. The woman looks like Annabella Sciorra from *Jungle Fever,* in her early office days, cream heels and all. The man is carrying the child toward the entrance, the boy's face hidden in his shoulder. They are early, of course, probably the story of their calm, efficient lives. Or maybe it's their plan to avoid an awful, squirming parking-lot encounter.

I didn't know them, but right away I recognized them as foster parents, every detail made perfect, bringing the child here, to the Department of Social Services, for a visit. At least, I hoped it was just a visit.

I knew if I sat in my car and waited, I would see the other side of this, and soon I heard a car with no muffler before I saw it: a Ford Pinto, as obsolete as a manual typewriter. A bleached-out young woman, with ringed eyes and a ponytail, was driving; beside her was someone I immediately identified as her mother, who no doubt had come along to balance the numbers in this equation. Mother and daughter were not looking at each other but out the windshield, inhaling enough nicotine to last them the hour.

Or maybe it was more than just a visit. Maybe it was the day this case would close, one way or the other. But if it were closing in the couple's favor, they probably would have been in the courthouse parking lot. So maybe it was the day that perfect toddler would be returned—would transition back—to the home from which he started.

NEAR THE giant granite planters that frame the entrance to DSS, you smell cigarette smoke, whether anyone is actually smoking there or not—enough Basics and Doral 100s get sucked down before the nightly drug- and alcohol-testing session that the smell lingers permanently in the air. In the mornings teens hang around, perching on the rims of the planters and leaning back into the unkillable boxwood bushes: kids too pierced, pale, and black-haired to still be kids, smacking at each other to flirt, the way they did just months ago in school, I'd guess.

Evenings, men come for the substance abuse education sessions they're required to attend between weekends in jail; the lucky ones get dropped off, but a good number are walking, from who knows how far. You can see from their boots that they've come from work, if they're lucky enough to have it. Their faces move under cap bills as they mumble only to each other, cursing the probation officer who patrols the Main Street bars to bust them or wondering if their session will be led by the twenty-year-old intern again. Inside, in class, they can talk or not, but ye shalt never take someone else's Higher Power in vain; outside, afterward, by these planters is the easiest time and place in town to score drugs.

HERE YOU learn that every word has two meanings, the actual and the euphemism.

At DSS, for example, the verb *screen* does not mean to shield for privacy or to separate coarse from fine. It refers to drugs, not doors: "Dad's not seeing the kids this weekend," the children's worker might grumble out of the side of her mouth. "He showed up twenty minutes late and then couldn't screen. After I came in on my day off for this."

Here you learn that social workers, like doctors, will never translate for you—won't think to tell you that "to screen" means to pee in a cup for a drug test or that, in other contexts, it refers to a Child Protective Services report that will allow the agency to intervene in the biological family; that *staffed*, used as a verb in the past tense, means that two or more of the pros discussed your question and you'll never really know what they said; that *appropriate* can mean not getting tearful where kids can see you—smoking is okay, crying is not; and that *transition* actually means abrupt change, as in "transitioning back home": here one day and gone the next, lifetimes apart.

INSIDE THE county building the air is cool, with the calm whir of air-conditioning year-round. Maybe the building is deliberately chilled, the way a crisis waiting room is painted fuchsia, to cool the swarm of furies that has landed people here. The halls have a clean medicinal smell as well, but it's hard to imagine where it comes from—the only clinic here is for mental health. Maybe the scent just emanates from the ground-floor WIC office. From the outside, you never see movement—it looks as still as the rest of the building—because the whole glass-fronted office is screened off for privacy. Tacked to the beige screens are bright cut-outs of apples, oranges, corn, broccoli, grain sheaves, and glasses of bubbled milk, along with cardboard toddlers dressed in overalls, getting healthy exercise by chasing butterflies. It's the bright spot in this building—second to the glowing vending machines and free seed packet rack by the entrance.

The only clue to the building's former life as an old high school, remodeled back when the county consolidated, is the white porcelain water fountains with half-bleached rust rings around the drains. In the basement is a sheltered workshop that fills mail orders and manufactures plastic forms for packaging medical instruments. The workshop clients come and go through their own entrance, where a small circular driveway fills with wheelchair-ready minibuses and group home vans at 9 and 5 each weekday. In an adjoining building, an afterschool program for the county's middle schoolers fills the echoing space that was once the high school cafeteria. Across the street a car lot stretches over the one-time football field.

Entering at the first floor, you see polished floor tiles gleam all the way down the hall. Footsteps echo: the click of low heels, the thunk of motorcycle boots, the squeaking scuff of sneakers here unwillingly.

DO NOT ALLOW CHILDREN TO PLAY ON THE RAILINGS says a sign screwed in below the staircase.

Beyond the stairs are restrooms and between them one of the last pay phones in existence.

HERE, IN a room at the top of these stairs, the evening parenting classes take place, attended by a wary combination of birth parents compelled to participate, worn-out grandmothers with toddler kinship placements, and new foster parents, brightly eager for help, their foster children in the waiting room across the hall, eating Hardee's takeout with the adopted teens who babysit and take turns scrolling through their phones.

The class is called Love and Logic, as if there is any any logic (which perhaps there is) to casually tossing them all into this room to rub together like sandpaper. Those required to be here sit up front carrying attendance papers to be signed; the foster parents line the back tables, as if hoping to remain invisible, although their eager questions will soon get the better of them. The instructor seems completely at ease with all of it, slimly dressed as she is in bohemian chic—a long tan skirt and real Frye boots, tinkly silver earrings beneath her crunchy blond curls.

Like any kind of human services workshop, it starts with the dreaded icebreaker—today it's throwing around a ball with questions on it—you're supposed to answer whatever question lands beneath your left thumb—questions about the standard wishes, hopes, dreams, and quirky revelations . . . but feel free to skip the ones about God, the instructor says. Though, really, God is the least of it.

The ball lands up front first, with a woman in a white tank, vest, and tight black pants. Harshly blonde, she has a tattoo of a man's name on the back of her neck and what must be a monitoring bracelet around her ankle.

"What's a family tradition you'd like to start?" she reads off the ball.

"Not being here," she answers.

"As in *here* here?" the instructor asks.

"Here in this building."

"With all these services." The teacher's earrings glitter.

"Right."

HERE YOU learn how anonymous reporting is really used, as easy revenge. "People fight," the social worker shrugs, "they're owed money, they call up and report their friends." "Her baby's out of formula—she'll only give him Mountain Dew," they'll allege about a friend who won't buy food stamps from them. "That child's ate up with diaper rash; they're giving their toddler rum in Coke to watch him fall down and walk again." Maybe these callers just want to cause their neighbor more trouble than they themselves are in.

"Try not to stress about it," the worker says as you twist your fingers with worry that reporting the parents will sever every fragile tie you've made with them. "With all the crazy friends they have, they'll never guess it was you that shared this."

ACROSS THE hall are mental health clinics you know better than to look into, although you almost reflexively check the faces you can see through the smoked glass. What you can see is a no-firearms decal and a stack of guides outlining complaint procedure; the waiting room lights are low and shadowy, a contrast with the pop Muzak that clouds the air. You've spent plenty of hours in that waiting room with different kids, different parents. The kids could always tell when you were surveying the faces and postures of the waiting clients; made nervous by your unease, they asked you why in loud whispers. When things felt too dicey, the staff let you take them into the kids' waiting room next door, where the toys were surprisingly functional, the Disney puzzles had all their pieces, and the many plastic toddler chairs could be lined up into a train. So the place itself is not entirely grim.

HERE AT DSS you learn it's not illegal for a registered sex offender to live with a child who is related (or, more usually, not), if Mom says she sees no danger.

ON THE front door and bulletin boards hang neon-bright flyers that say NOT EVEN FOR A MINUTE, the answer to the *Jeopardy* question of how long you can leave a baby in a car. Statewide, even nationwide, the number of car-related infant fatalities seems to be cresting, with everything from work stress to intentional negligence and the all-purpose plague of texting getting the blame.

FARTHER DOWN the hall is the multipurpose DSS waiting room, where it's rude to glance around. Anyone could be there for anything—to apply for after-school subsidies, food stamps, Lifeline telephones, Elves' Workshop, work permits, fuel assistance, or any of the myriad reasons a person might need to see a social worker. Not necessarily to see Child Protective Services—*the goblins who'll get you if you open your big, fat mouth. . . .* Nor does anyone look at you or demand to know if their children are in your care, even though your lack of a fast-food uniform and cigarettes, and the presence of your heels and linen jacket, instantly brand you a Foster Parent. In any case, it's best to fix your gaze on the healthy-living infomercials on the wall-mounted TV. DO NOT CHANGE THE CHANNEL, an orange placard says.

The social workers are back beyond the waiting room in their warren of offices, humming with belief in human possibility but, like the mental health staff down the hall, still wisely trusting only to buzzer and key. Behind her window the secretary frowns when you name the worker you need and says, "Oh, they never move their in-out tokens on the board—I'll have to call and see."

A yellow tub of toys and a Little Tikes slide sit in a corner to keep kids busy. The Hot Wheels carwash has no cars and the Dora dollhouse no figurines, but all the stuffed animals have both their eyes, the baby dolls are clothed and clean, and the toy cash register really rings when you hit it. Because this is a government facility, there's no blue pseudo-Bible for kids on a chain, as you find in any hospital or other scary place to wait, ubiquitous as *Highlights for Children.* Keep foster kids long enough, and you'll break down and read it in some other office, only to find it has no actual Bible stories.

YOU SIT here while a Child Protective Services worker, who you think should know better, asks two siblings about the violence in their home, right in front of the person she suspects committed it. Your heart sinks as you see the worker play them—the eight-year-old knows the language of shrugs and silence, knows to surrender only neutral monosyllables, while the four-year-old is talking like the big man, flattered by the attention—"I'm afraid he'll get a knife and kill Mommy"—thinking he's supposed to speak up, just like he does at preschool.

Why talk to everyone all together like this? Is it so the worker won't hear something irrefutably actionable at 4:37 p.m. on a Friday? Maybe in some other place that could be true, but you wouldn't believe it here. Or is the reason some baffling sideways method of shaking up and shaming the parents?

The social worker's takeaway message: Watch what language the children hear because they're little tape recorders—it will come back out when they turn fourteen. (As if it hasn't already, and as if the real worry is their language and not their lives.) Then she asks the kids if they know how to call 911 in a house where she should know no telephone exists.

And yet when asked at last to speak, you walk the same tightrope yourself, careful as the eight-year-old, hating yourself yet afraid to jeopardize whatever future you might have with your children's biofamily. *Don't trust me,* you try to telegraph to the worker, *I'm not your eyes and ears—I can't be.* But this social worker probably was out with a sheriff's deputy at dawn, bringing back an AWOL teen or picking up an infant abandoned at the ER, more of the same old, same old emergency diet of adrenaline. Maybe by quitting time Friday, with someone else on call this weekend, her appetite for danger is sated. Or maybe you're just a novice, with a crippling panic reflex. And/or a lot of nerve to question whether a professional would take the appropriate action no matter what time the clock said. Your fear has turned to sickness. Will that four-year-old ever speak the truth again? You'd imagined all this going a very different way.

Yet here you have already learned that *social worker* is not a term of derision or synonymous with buck-passing bureaucrat, as *20/20* or *Dateline* would have you believe. From the foster parents' side of the equation, social workers are often confusing, sometimes confounding, but just as often flat-out amazing compared with anything you've ever read in a young adult novel or the city news section of a newspaper. The great ones are the rule, not the exception. Here, they know all the children's names and, more important, they know their clothing sizes. Yes, there are frustrations, and your opinions can flip by the week, yet usually the worst to be said is that the women on the Child Protective Services team always seem to be annoyingly slim and stylish, with the perfect toenails no foster parent will ever accomplish in the chaos of drive-and-diaper world. When talking to children—or frustrated adults—the perfect, positively phrased, motivating response seems to flow effortlessly from the worker's lips, whereas I sputter and grasp for the elusive catchphrases I've strained to memorize from the Love and Logic, Celebrate Calm, and Positive Parenting scripts.

There's just a natural tug-of-war tension between social workers and foster parents, for once the county has pulled children out of their birth homes—an unimaginable ordeal—the workers' next job is to put them back, while the foster parents pull as hard as they can in the other direction.

ONE MORNING a month the regional Social Security Administration holds local office hours here in a conference room; one night a week there's Love and Logic; addiction, alcoholism, and anger groups cycle through; and foster parents get trained for relicensing, grazing through dinner on Cheetos and grapes (or pizza during a good budget year) while absorbing everything from human trafficking statistics to first aid in ninety-minute sessions.

At night it's always cold in the meeting rooms; the PowerPoint presentations always fail to work; and in the background you occasionally hear actual laughter, sometimes the strumming of a guitar.

HERE I once was followed out by a young teen boy in tears, his baggy pants sagging, sure his mother was lying about her destination, convinced she was going to a jail from which she'd never return. The only thing that slowed the tears was when I put his huge, messy ferret cage in the back of my car so he could bring it to my home with him.

And here you learn, as social workers everywhere will say, that the universal suitcase for children is not an Elsa valise or Paw Patrol pack on wheels, but a Dollar Store garbage bag that's threatening to split.

But wow, the veteran foster parents will say, how great they brought clothes with them.

Out back is where the staff park; foster parents might park there as well if they fear the eyes of birth parents or think Mom's ex-boyfriend has been following their car. On sunny days the director of the entire Social Services agency is sometimes out in that lot, slacklining between the trees at the perimeter. He keeps an impossible balance, moving with scoots and jumps, three steps forward and one lurch back, arms leaning on the air, before lunchtime ends and he heads back down the hall through the cool echo of footsteps and the hiss of bleach-infused air through the building's ventilation system.

HERE I left the unused gift certificate the agency had given me for a donated spa massage; I rejected the consolation prize because I was so confused by the agency's attempt to fulfill the letter but not the spirit of my foster child's reunification plan. Some social workers don't trust you enough to explain the why or how yet insist you keep no secrets yourself. And once it's all over, once this child is back in his original home, will the agency finally tell you—let alone his biomom—why this child was taken into care to start with?

Here you meet the only people on Earth who make you feel normal—other foster parents, no matter how different you are from their homeschooling, Christian, conservative outlook. Or no matter that they are gay and you are not. Or a sixth-generation county native and you're a suburban transplant. Because all of them know what open-ended grieving means, and the daily grind of uncertainty for a child's basic safety. They wish they *could* sweat the small stuff—what luxury that would be—or simply dwell on the same planet as other school parents, where a plague of kindergarten head lice would feel like the year's low ebb.

Instead, they know what it means for the child you had in hair bows and princess overalls last week to be back home and seen playing alone in the apartment building's parking lot, chasing her bouncy ball in and out of the rows of parked cars. They know what it means to rely on college student tenants to report this. They know why children hoard food or hide steak knife blades inside the heating vents. They know what it means to live with a shadow of panic always over your heart.

The foster parents' advice is the best: cry and pray before the children leave, but after they're gone, just clean and clean mindlessly—keep moving, keep polishing the empty places. "After all," says one, "inside a month, mine came back."

YET HERE you also learn that while you never doubted you'd always do the right thing . . . when the next time comes, you have plenty of doubt, and what the right thing—or the best thing—actually might be isn't at all clear. If you want to keep seeing these children once they're home, how much can you say—if anything—before the birth family permanently cuts you off? How much is cowardice, how much is doubt? To an outsider, to Dr. Laura, to Oprah, and for sure to Jesus, the right thing would be starkly clear. *A cigarette burn,* you hear yourself thinking about a different child, well, *maybe that was a one-time thing.* And what could it mean for a toddler to say, "Daddy shot me with a gun?" before lifting a shirt to show you a tiny, bloodless hole?

Has this child, with his few words, ever told you a lie? Do you start to think of all the other things this could mean?

YOU HAVE doubts about what the right thing to do is, because this time they'd know it was you making the report.

Because he's still alive.

Because who would see it next time?

Because you just don't want it to be true.

Because you know too much, look away, and hope for the best.

HERE AT DSS every word has two definitions: the euphemism and the actual.

And it's here at DSS, be it a steamy June lunch hour or a snapping, blue-skied November morning, that you, a first-time foster parent who can't see life beyond this day, will find out what *transition* truly means.

Dry Creek Drive

The Highway to Hell

—Michael

THE FIRST time I learned to drive, I was five years old. I drove on a road with sharp turns and a big ditch on one side the whole way down the road. (I didn't ride the bus that day, but a school bus once drove off that same road.) My mom's now ex-boyfriend, Benny, asked me, "You wanna help me drive, little man?"

"Sure," I said.

Benny said, "Hop up here."

When I got up there, he said, "You wanna do the pedals or steer?"

I wanted to steer, so I said, "Steer!" I thought that it was a good idea at the time, but now I know that I wasn't able to make good decisions at that age.

This road was made of gravel and it was bumpy. The ditch along the road by our house I have wrecked into often with my four-wheeler. I steered well this time, but I decided to swerve, so the car went left, then right. My mom was scared, and Benny was laughing. Luckily, we made it to the house and no one was hurt.

ON THIS road, Dry Creek Drive, so many things happened. Our landlord stole our guns from us, and there were couches in the ditch, along with stoves, chairs, and tires. People drove fast along the road, with no slowing down for the next curve or children on bikes. Now I realize how scary, even paranormal, the place was. I always heard my name being called, but no one was there. One night, I thought I saw Freddie Krueger, but it may have been an Indian. When I looked back, there was no one there outside the window.

My mom's parents lived close to us, so I would go there all the time. They had a house with a giant brown rat in it. The septic tank overflowed, and you could always smell it. Benny fell in it once because he was drunk. When he drove, Benny was always drinking but not enough to make him drunk. Benny had lost his license, but he drove anyway. Benny has made a lot of bad decisions, especially about cars. That is why I learned to stay away from alcohol and drugs. I also learned to wait until I'm sixteen to drive legally.

At least I got off that road where so many things that were bad happened. Now I'm off that road, metaphorically and physically. I'm on the right road now.

The Poem of Hell on Earth

—Michael

Sirens, lights, cussing
Were all I heard
Police, drugs, fighting
Were all I saw.

Crying, limping, scared
Is what my mother was.
You can't do anything about it except
Scream.

Gliding through the halls
Was smoke.
We knew it wasn't a fire.
Downstairs, in a room, they were
Having a "safety meeting."
A safety meeting—yeah, right, it's more like
Meeting to smoke weed.

Do as I say and not as I do
　　Is the thing they always say,
But they do it all in front of us.
I will try not to follow their way,
But, man, that's almost too hard to do.
One thing I do because of them is
　　Cuss.

They all say you can make a change,
But all I can do is rage.
They lock you up in a big gray cage.
All I can say is, *I won't change.*

Counting Down

Reunification

(Fall 2005)

EACH MINUTE had the weight of hours, and the hours flew like seconds. It was five weeks, a month, a week, three days, and then the counting turned to hours—seventy-two hours sounds so much longer than three days—and then forty-eight, almost a luxury, and the last ten hours, well, if you counted that by minutes, it was six hundred, and even the last hours and minutes expanded to their seconds, and the numbers got bigger and bigger, looming in close-up, each one containing a multitude of kisses, of breaths, as the time outside streamed on. Until my toddler boy would turn back into his mother's boy and go away, perhaps for good.

I had no choice; Social Services had made my irrelevance starkly clear. Let the Nancy Graces of the world rant on: this decision had been preordained at the start. "This child is going home." That's what the family's social worker had said bluntly to the day care director when she called the agency to report her concerns; to me she'd say, "We'll keep an eye on it" or, much worse, "I'll let Mom know" when I'd try to alert her to diaper rash or asthmatic crackling in Michael's chest after the weekend trial visits with his biological mother and siblings at her new boyfriend's home. This half-family reunification was going to be a check in the Win column—a success story, until someday it wasn't anymore.

Success, I gathered from other foster parents, often meant an agonizingly slow and uncertain termination of parental rights, then adoption by us. Not the success of birth family reunification to which we'd pledged allegiance in theory—for the immediacy of real life and real children had a way of making one say "Yes, if" or "Yes, but . . ." After all, we foster parents offered love, limits, clean clothes, and everything from Vacation Bible School to three kinds of therapy, twice-daily nebulizer treatments, new Walmart sneakers, Goldfish, and sanitized sippy cups.

Success, in the agency's view and as mandated by the state and driven by national policy, meant returning foster children to birth families—and however the social workers might have privately felt, it reminded me of when the president orders an unwanted war—everyone in the ranks turns and gets on board. "The best interests of the child?" friends would inquire, suddenly transformed to TV lawyers. My bitter answer: "That's not the standard anymore."

Michael had been with us for six months. Half a year. Almost a quarter of his young life. And the best, most intense, saddest, most loving, most desperate and exhausted months of mine.

"WHY DO you have him?" people asked about his foster placement, with a twist of the mouth or hungry crook of the eyebrow, inviting me to confide.

"Oh, they don't really tell us much," the agency suggests we shrug, saving face and confidentiality. Although in our case, it was true. The social worker had left both the birth mom, Jessica, and me to come up with our own reasons for her children's removal, although the agency must have had to give some basis in court. "Mom's not doing what she's supposed to" was the only explanation I ever received.

BEFORE I continue, let me say that this story has a happy ending—it came twelve years later, when we finalized custody and could feel secure about the boys' safety, but also in the short term, within weeks after reunification. Okay, a semihappy ending that was often fraught with fear, with the messiness of real stories in the non-fairy-tale world, where the ogres can be both kind and drunk, and the witches, good and/or wicked, can as easily be the DSS workers or judges as birth mothers who despise you. But, no, this story has the best ending realistically possible in my view, despite the current of worry that hummed in my heart through those years. Thanks to Jessica's forbearance, Michael and sometimes Ryan, Will, and I got to spend countless days and weekends, vacation weeks, and Tuesday nights at Cub Scouts together. While DSS could encourage but never mandate a postcustody relationship, this happened with the consent of Jessica, who'd first schemed to meet me by prolonging her cigarette out back of the agency, where I always parked to avoid just such a confrontation during Michael's early supervised visits. "He's lost so many people in his life, I don't want him to lose you too," Jessica first said early in the process, months before Michael returned to her new home a whole mountain county away. *How often can I get him?* I'd wanted to ask immediately. *Can we set up a schedule?* But I knew that voicing my compulsive panic would backfire. "She always says what people want to hear," I'd been warned, yet how I longed to hear the promise of a future in Jessica's words.

Trying to wring out some relief, I repeated her promise (was it a promise?) to myself as fall came and the weeks before Michael's return to his mother shrank away. But what if she'd said this only to ease whatever resistance she might wrongly think I could put up? Maybe she hoped I'd mention it to her social worker so she'd add another gold star to Jessica's case? Already, Jessica's family was on track to be a model of compliance and would soon be featured in a newspaper profile as proof the agency worked with motivated parents to successfully reunite families.

Still, my cold gut told me that sharing our darling boy would prove too hard for Jessica. Surely she and Benny would decide to cut this cord or at least to let it fray; surely my visits with Michael would grow fewer and dwindle to never. Plus, they had no phone. The better to disappear with.

COUNTING DOWN. The precious nightmare of those last days, weeks, seconds, hours. In a negotiation as layered as a State Department protocol, it was arranged for Michael to stay one extra day, to spend my Saturday birthday with Will and me, even though it meant the social worker would have to handle our final transition on a Sunday morning, with her own new baby in tow.

Never have I been so present in each ballooning moment as during those last weeks Michael was with us; never had I realized the weight an instant could contain. And still, the hours flew.

"It's like a death," another social worker said, aiming to comfort. "With most great losses, you don't know when they're coming. This one you do."

COUNTING DOWN the days: I was working, teaching, somehow grading through the weekends while Michael was gone on overnight transition visits. Resentfully organizing a documentary film festival set for three days before Michael had to leave us. The Friday of our university's two-day fall break I pulled him out of day care, even though it meant lost reimbursement for the center, to spend a day together, just playing and climbing the rocks around an absent neighbor's pond. I would try to tell him, so brightly, what was coming, and he'd say *no.* Old enough to understand but somehow too young to know I wasn't sending him away, that I'd have happily spent the rest of my life sitting with him in a car or dentist's waiting room or the most boring place imaginable, just to be there or anywhere with him, pressed to the glow of that warm skin.

My husband, still so good to Michael, retreated, as some men do, when a wife's pain seems inevitable and unanswerable. "You're being obsessive," he'd mutter as I packed and folded and raged and drew up asthma treatment charts, but so what? If I couldn't go along with Michael, at least I could make his packing and final days with us perfect.

When I think of that last week, I remember the little photo book I made him to take home, with happy photos of us, though nothing too flashy or possessive. But the actual moments I spent with him? No, that memory is wiped away. What I remember is the ever-aching sinuses of my withheld tears, and the relief when I could climb into the car or fling myself onto the bed and melt into weeping, or the hate I felt when people at work kindly told me they were sorry or gently probed about whether his mom was "doing better," and I'd say, "What *I* think doesn't matter," and glare at the floor, behind the hot mask of my face. All those people, trying to offer solace, yet I just hated them, knowing they'd still be here the next week, when he wasn't.

What I also remember is . . . the packing, which I stashed in a guest room so he wouldn't see it as proof of my complicity. The perfect plastic tubs and flat boxes I'd bought to hold Michael's perfect clothes and his prized toy mower, books, and other toys: all, I feared, would be snatched up quickly by Benny's grandson, who'd already laid claim to Michael's birthday present from my parents. And the clothes—would they survive the lack of a dryer come winter? Clothes had never before mattered to me, but now I prized Michael's OshKosh color schemes and sweet Healthtex overalls, in which he was comfortably himself, in which he was clean. Any foster parent will understand what this means.

For his last morning at day care, Michael wore perfect autumn-orange overalls and a matching lumberjack shirt, cuffs rolled. He knew what was coming, and when I brought the farewell cupcakes that afternoon, he grew so gray and speechless that he couldn't eat even one. The brusque teacher half-hugged me and said, "It's tough, huh?" She stepped outside for me to take their photo together, showing Michael the glossy *Bob the Builder* flap book she'd bought for him. Posing, she grinned for his future memories, yet he wouldn't even look at her, grimly sad or perhaps just stunned by our helpless betrayal in sending him away: those past three Mondays at day care, back from a weekend spent in his new-old life, he'd walked up and down the preschool's indoor slide, warning us of spankings. I knew he knew we'd heard him.

I was exhausted. As Michael slept and Will took refuge in his TV, it took me a week of nights to pack and wipe and fold, to subtract our lives here piece by piece by piece. To try to comfort myself with the thought that Michael would have his clothes, his toys, his things, his Jesus-Loves-Me wind-up lullaby lamb, much as I doubted his possessions would even make it out of their boxes, much as I feared they'd end up in a consignment store, as good as pawned.

ON THAT cold, blue last November morning, the Sunday after my birthday, we woke early, at six, to have the maximum time before the handover at ten. While Will packed Michael's tubs and toys into his pickup, I dragged out the much-craved, hand-me-down construction set Michael had been too young to ever play with: motorized carts, conveyors, and red plastic marbles dropping everywhere. I told him once what would happen in these next hours, as I'd told him each day before, and this morning he didn't say no but stayed dressed in pajamas until the last possible moment and played on and on silently as his boxes went out the door.

Yes, I'm biased—no one needs to tell me. And yes, of course, he also wanted to be with his mother and brother and sister and Benny, who had saved him from drowning on a jet-ski. Michael loved his family and studied their pictures endlessly.

WHEN THE time came, we left early, careful to stay on the right side of every rule yet reluctant to give up a single minute that was still ours. Will drove his packed truck, and Michael came with me. We sang the Barney song, my voice blurring with swallowed sadness, for on this morning of all sad mornings, I could not show a blotched unsmiling face. I could not be the mirror image of his mother the day that Michael had come our way.

But how my last hopes sank when we reached the enormous, empty Social Services parking lot to see their giant borrowed pickup truck roosting there already—how I'd hoped against hope that they would have forgotten or broken down or run out of gas; after my countdown of months, weeks, days, hours, minutes, how I resented having to forfeit those last fifteen minutes. Why hadn't we at least gotten close and then circled the long block? For in this last week, I'd experienced that state that dying people sometimes speak of—of not measuring with the hourglass of disappearing time but of looking instead into the depths of each grain of sand, the quiet pool of each moment opening as I looked into Michael's blue eyes and kissed his little hands and my favorite feet, telling him the toes were grape-flavored or cotton candy–flavored today.

The sadness of the morning was diffuse, the cloudy after-ache I remembered from a long-ago encounter with tear gas. And then it snapped to an end, as I realized that the unloading and transfer operation from the back of my husband's pickup to theirs was swiftly underway, that they were tying the boxes down, that someone was stuffing Michael's beloved toy John Deere weedeater into a crevice, that the truck bed was loaded with more possessions than Jessica and Benny together had owned in the entire length of their childhoods, and all of it in bright, shiny premium colors—the Healthtex pumpkin orange, the yellow and glossy green of John Deere. The boxes of favorite books, which I sent even though I feared they would wind up damp, rippled, and ignored—I sent them and everything else with the faith that they were Michael's. Thinking again of how even his old car seat had once gone through the consignment shop—where I'd bought it not knowing it had been his—and wondering, meanly, if these clothes, these toys for which there was doubtless no room, might similarly disappear for whatever little cigarette money they could bring. And which clothes would go to Benny's already-jealous grandson, to be picked from a jumble of creased and unsorted laundromat laundry, while the best of the construction toys and birthday presents were strong-armed away from Michael.

I drove my car up to meet them and Michael froze in his seat. I can't remember if I carried him out, but there isn't some big handover movie in my head, like something out of a Cold War spy exchange. Maybe

Will did it. I think I might have asked him to, so the memory of what would seem like my giving Michael away wouldn't be in his head. I do remember Michael's shock that his brother and sister weren't there to greet him, although clearly there wasn't room in the front seat of this giant pickup.

The goal of their race to load, I realized—for the transfer seemed polite enough but rushed—was to get done and take off early before their social worker, Kayla—the one who had ignored me and whom they probably liked little more—arrived and followed them back over the mountains for her weekly visit. They'd been hoping to elude her, to have it all done before she arrived to witness the carrying out of the agency's decree.

I SAW the social worker's maroon minivan drive up through the lot, and I was relieved to see at least this plan thwarted. But it soon turned into an argument, with Benny's insisting she should do their home visit a different day, but since she was already here disrupting her weekend, Kayla wanted to go ahead and get it over with—all this went on while her new baby was strapped to her chest. A family birthday party was planned, and Benny took offense at the notion that the social worker would just march in and weave through all the other relatives and friends who also wanted nothing to do with DSS folks—even though Michael's Grandma Irene had already told me that they'd changed the party time in case the worker did follow.

Angry as I was at DSS, I was trying to stay back from the argument and from associating myself with the agency, as if ours was not an inescapable alliance. The wind was freezing my ears and fingertips as I unloaded the last items from my car.

Somehow, when I wasn't looking, Michael had been buckled into a battered car seat in the middle of the truck bench, and he sat there by himself, had been sitting there for lost moments already, as the argument continued thirty parking spaces away. I'd already given him my last kiss and hug, or had I? Yet now I couldn't open this truck door, whether because it was locked or couldn't open on this side or was simply not my territory. The car seat didn't fit the mold of the hard seat, and it was tilted too far back. There he sat, strapped in and tipped back, bundled up in his brown bomber jacket with its little cartoon airplane. He was looking straight through the cracked windshield, a rocket pilot starting the ascent, facing his journey into the blue.

HE WAS all alone. I couldn't stand the thought, and my stomach clutched with the unfairness of all I imagined was to come. I knocked on the window and he looked up at me, not smiling, serious as a ninety-year-old. I blew kisses and he blew them back; I stood there mouthing "I love you, I love you" and wishing I'd taught him the I-love-you sign so I could press it to the glass, unable to reach him but as present as I could be on the other side of the window, aching to signal all I could not say, just standing there to love and be his companion, wanting to promise *I'll squeeze out every moment, I'll be there waiting for you on the other side of my glass wall always, you won't be able to see me, maybe I'll shrink away in your mind to the ghost of someone who left you and then fade to smoke to sky, but please know, please feel, that if they would only not drive you away, I'd spend every last minute of my life here watching you and sending love through this cold glass window, trying to smile yet not look happy, straining with the necessity not to cry.*

My little jumping bunny, my one and only Michael—the whole litany that might rise in your throat if this piercing moment ever came for you. *Just let me stand here forever, let them not drive you away. Just please stamp that on your little mind, that I stood here with you, waving and waving, doing the almost nothing I could do, loving you every last long and still not long-enough hollow second*—until they came back across the parking lot, cursing the social worker who, yes, was going to follow them home, who promised she would not be in the way, undeterred by the idea they might have planned the party to bar her but equally determined to put the seal on her success story, to give them the chance she had told me they deserved, and to let nothing disrupt the outcome she had foreseen from the day she had first raced to get Michael out of day care in the pajamas Grandma Irene had brought him in, to take him away from Jessica, and now to take him away from me.

Jessica stood in front of me, looking tiny and not even half her age, clutching to her wrists the flapping sleeves of Benny's long, gray roofing company T-shirt. I wondered if she hadn't worn a jacket because she couldn't find one or if she'd purposely come without so that our goodbyes could not be drawn out in the blustering autumn chill. "Thank you," she said to me, "for keeping Michael for me. I know he loves you." Words she did not have to say, that there was no one else to hear; words that were the gift every foster parent wants to hear and so seldom does; a gift, but not the one I wanted at that moment.

Still.

The tables were now completely turned, and I swallowed my own words in the hope of seeing him again, again, again.

OUR SOCIAL worker, Gerri, had known how stressed I was and had come up with an easily justified way to ease the transition: both before and after the kids returned to Jessica, she was required to take Gerri's evening parenting class, which she actually enjoyed ("Can't wait till this shit's over," Benny would say, smoking in the car outside). I was to watch Michael, Ryan, and Isabelle, which was like watching crazy billiard balls shooting off in three directions, for the seventy-five minutes the class lasted—not long enough to really go anywhere in the twilight, but we'd drive away nonetheless, just to escape the shadow of the DSS building and the temptation to race through the huge, dark parking lot, dodging headlights and shrieking.

But on the Tuesday two days after Michael returned to Jessica, I'd begged Will to come too, and for some brainless reason we joined the other siblings' foster families at a cacophonous Pizza Hut table for twenty—a terrible idea. My Michael looked completely different: glassy-eyed, his once-round face now pointed and pinched with tension. "He looks different, he looks different," I sobbed back at home, not yet understanding how this could be.

But three weeks later, when his mom decided our break had been long enough to seem final, and Michael saw me arrive to pick him up, Elmo lunchbox and all, the softness broke back over his face and it grew round once again. There in the pale sunlight of a fresh December Friday, we flew to the log fortress of a deserted adventure playground, and he spun on a tire swing and ate his beautiful lunch while I hugged and hugged him, and then he ran and played and vanished and appeared, in and out of the playground hidey-holes, like Peter Pan returned.

FAR FROM the full-stop ending I had feared, after a tenuous start, our lives continued to intertwine. Jessica stayed true to her promise, which led us on to a life I never would have believed possible.

And yet the ten o'clock hour of that Sunday morning in the windy, empty parking lot is the still point in time to which the first half of my life ticked down and the zero hour from which the second half ticks away.

I stood as their truck sputtered and circled, and Will put his arm around my shoulders, the first break in a week of bitter resentments, and we stood there and I waved and waved until the truck's exhaust stream had turned back into clear air.

The Pickup Line

(2009)

IT'S NOT what it sounds like—not the magic words for singles slinking down a bar, blue umbrella drinks clinking. But if you knew that already, it's not just because it's dated, but because we're all too tired and gravity bound to even think of it anymore. No, of course the pickup line is where the car riders are split off from the bus riders, the sheep from the goats, to go home from school. I used to think the pickup line split the hot-house flowers from the tough-enough latchkey kids, until I wound up driving through it myself.

At the boys' old school, the car riders were bafflingly called walkers, as in, they walk to the car line, because no one actually walks to school anymore, or would even dream of running the gauntlet of traffic and candy-baiting kidnappers to cross the entrance road. Back in my elementary school days, when only a killer highway kept us from walking the mile each way, the public address system would daily crackle out, "The walkers may leave please, the walkers may leave." I was all the way to third grade before I figured out that the walkers were not an actual family.

I'm in a good spot today, at the end of the first coil in the long snake of cars—you have to get here twenty minutes early or you will emerge from its slow digestion process twenty minutes late. From here I'm close to the playing field, where signs guilt-trip dog walkers into picking up their pooch's droppings. The kids are still out on the field, which hosts both recess and gym; today, like every day, a great number of kids and teachers are also walking laps—too many and too cheerful to be punishment, so it must be some kind of recess lite, or for the girls, who walk tossing hair and flicking dismissive wrists, a way to ensure that the gossip never stops.

A newly clipped silver terrier is peeking out the window behind me; in the car ahead a grandfather's row of veterans' caps lines the back window. A number of cars, especially those parked in the teachers' aisle, have bumper stickers that say PRAY FOR MR. K, a young and beloved multi-school music teacher whose treatment for Hodgkin lymphoma is regularly supported with car washes and concerts.

Across the parking lot, in the snake's second coil, is the little girl, maybe three, who's always unbelted and climbing around on her mother's lap, head and arms hanging out over the door. I've seen them drive in this way, so maybe it shows how far we are from parental police-state suburbia that everyone just smiles and waves back instead of scolding about seatbelts and boosters. Whereas I feel guilty if I even scoot up a car length in line without reattaching my seatbelt, as if the traffic monitor in her cute capris is going to rap on my window and lecture me over her headset microphone.

More guilt: Should I leave the engine idling after a couple of premature move-ups, when the car line, like a giant accordion, squeezes in? There must be some formula to compute wasted gas and emissions, but like so many other things here, I'm ignorant. And what is the etiquette for, and/or liability of, pulling around someone who seems rooted in place at the pickup point?

We're here in a desirably scenic mountain zone, with this school district one-fourth the regal offspring of doctors and real estate agents, one-fourth professors' kids (the new, politically correct PKs—although the preachers' kids are still there too), one-fourth community-minded church stalwarts, and one-fourth self-proclaimed redneck hillbillies. The hard-won new dress code can't begin to blur those distinctions, although short-shorts and rebel flag T-shirts have gone the way of spaghetti straps. So why, then, between the princess blondes and the arm-punching inciters, is a boy walking the track with a Hare Krishna haircut? And I don't mean just a mohawk—it looks like the real deal, complete with a topknot and orange T-shirt. Maybe I'm showing my age to label it this way—our university campus sees occasional Hare Krishna hauntings, but mellow Wiccan solstice gatherings seem as extreme as this county gets.

I'm of the professor breed, of course—who else would be bothering to divide people into these taxonomies, noting cars and clothing like the markings of birds?

I wonder whether all these cars are encrusted with snack refuse, as mine is, the kind of permanent Kraft-colored orange rind that cannot even be foamed off. I wonder whether other cars have crayons melted into the seatbelt straps and the rubber tubing peeled away from the door. (What else in a car comes off quite so satisfyingly in a child's grip?)

But I doubt it. Most of these are probably real parents, with rules against such things. Perhaps they actually live by the Pearls of Love and Logic wisdom the school sends home every other week, with Stepford children who ruminate balefully on their mistakes, feel bad about failed spelling tests, and actually answer questions about how they think they'll handle mistakes. But I haven't figured all this out, much less the car-cleaning secrets. I'm a part-time, hybrid parent—not a stepmother but the kind teachers call "your second mom" for want of something better. A former foster mother, four years on at this point, lucky enough to remain, as people cautiously say, "regularly involved" in the lives of the boys who visit me. The emotional highs of this life are the very highest, while I try to curb the lows by plunging into the realm of the practical—that is, into the realm of the senses that engulfs all parents, real and otherwise: doing laundry, which is never lacking, and it's more productive and less tearful than meditation; purging the Happy Meal toy trove; and preparing another round of snacks because their next visit is never so distant that it's too soon to do that. Hence, here in my high-mileage car, it's clear that anything goes as far as food and sticky drinks, with the exceptions of Lunchables Mini-Pizzas (shredded cheese) and scrambled eggs that are not cheese-glued to a transfat biscuit.

But whether it's car cleaning (surely no twenty-first-century parent actually forbids food in the car) or how to get the Love and Logic pearl spat back out at you, the real parents in this line must know secrets that I don't: how to make a French braid; which homework help *not* to give; how you know which Friday is Hat Day; or maybe that daily life actually could become mundane, one routine among many, instead of a luxury. But maybe that's another thing the PRAY FOR MR. K. bumper stickers are here to remind us. To remind me, at least, in the slough of self-pity, that I'm hardly the only one to grasp at mere ordinariness, leaping at the chance to bring the kindergarten snack or to find the perfect shirt for spring picture day.

(Not that I can pick the right snack when I get the chance, even after Talmudic fretting over the line between crowd-pleasing and county-mandated "healthy" and individually wrapped snacks. At Michael's old school my best consumer efforts got him only "We hate your snack and we hate you." And this in response to Shrek-shaped Cheez Nips—what more could a kindergartener ask? Apparently, Michael told me, they demanded the girl-consensus favorite food—pizza dipped in ranch dressing—for every lunch, snack, and party.)

These everyday privileges at which I grasp are not so different from the constant envies of my own grade-school years. Back then I longed for the icons that could make me magically complete and normal, from the glittering braces and navy windbreakers of sixth-graders to the perfectly executed cheer routines, three-snap Viceroy jeans, and wet-look boots and purses that seemed so ordinary to most yet just out of reach to me. Now, years later, the markers and mysteries for which I yearn just take a different form—this exhaust-spewing pickup line, for one.

Like everyone, though, homework is the one chore I'd ask for less of, especially when it comes to Ryan, Michael's older brother, who is in third grade this year. Our great homework triumphs were creating Ben Franklin's head out of a too-tight swimming cap and doll hair, and rigging his famous electrocution experiment with a Spiderman kite, and the completion of the monthlong moon journal, first assigned when the moon did not rise before 9:37 at night. And the spelling words are baffling, with a high proportion of tween-consumer brainwashing words, especially in the prefix unit: *Preshrunk? preorder? prepaid?* What third-grader needs to know that? Of course that became clear when the cookie dough sale came up. Then the near-obsolete *rewind* and *resume,* which I could explain only in terms of old VCR tapes and DVD players. Next came *splotch* and *plunk* and then even *drunk.*

"Back up, back up," a gym teacher shouts to the kids on the field, not the cars. "Y'all are missing playtime." She's wearing black bike shorts and a white V-neck tee, sunglasses—a far cry from the droopy sweatpants of the phys ed teachers of my youth but fairly close to the polished professional moms who have stepped out to take a few power strides around the track while their parked cars hold their places. "Two outs, pressure's on," she hollers.

The outdoor PA system muffles some commands and kids start to shuffle into a line, although the jump rope continues to *hit, hit, hit* the asphalt walkway.

No bell sounds or needs to, but the starting of engines is a chain reaction—the way one neighbor will fire up a lawn mower on a lazy Saturday and the unseen neighbor behind the fence succumbs to the pressure and fires up too, and so on down the block and beyond.

FROM WHAT I've read, the fashion is to be an alienated mom: to revile the perfectionists of the PTA, if they actually exist; to forget to dress your kindergartener in the requisite red, white, or blue on patriotic holidays; to despise SpongeBob on one end and organic algae puffs on the other; and to blindly assume that the homeschooling church families, bless their hearts, are narrow-minded. So that's the fashion, I hear, but having been granted this unstable half-life, I purely want to *belong,* no cool points for alienation needed. I just want the kindergarten canister of Lysol wipes to be the one I sent, and to contribute to Box Tops for Education the correct number of staticky cellophane box tops, which stick to my sleeve as I try to scrape them into the classroom box bank.

And because I'm lucky, because Jessica has a big heart and has seen enough loss, I believe in this hybrid life, even as I pinch myself to make sure it still exists. Because even four years after the boys' stint in foster care, their real mother still includes us. Yes, *real mother*—there's as un-PC a term as you'll find, one you'll never hear in a training class. But anytime you want to know the actual words for things, just listen to the kids—they'll tell you what you need to hear, whether it's on the spelling list or not.

THE MIX of cars here is much different than it was at the boys' old school in the next county, which has fewer scenic views and the toxic choice of work, if one can get it, in either paper mill or prisons. The cars are driven by as many grandmothers as mothers, and I recognize the grandmothers more by exhaustion than age; they leave their sunken Chevy Novas empty in line like the Rapture has struck, as the bumper stickers say, to go pull a flush-faced grandchild out of school and beat the rush. And here, as at the old school, I see a few dads tipped back in their seats, unashamed to nap in public view. But there are half as many work trucks and twice as many forest-green Subarus like mine (apparently the only color they ship up here), and several more gold

SUVs and, of course, minivans. So far here, in this county, I've seen not one car with airbrushed flames.

This school must have printed out the placards that so many people have in their front windows—last names on laminated black-bordered certificates, disturbingly like something you'd see in a funeral parlor. But sign or no sign, the teachers seem to know whose car is whose by this time of year and can even distinguish among the army of green Subarus halfway down the lot. Today's traffic-duty teacher walks down the row of cars and back up again, calling names into a microphone headset, like some middle-aged pop star doing a sound check.

There's nothing like the slow transition from foster parenting, with its black-and-white decrees, abrupt reversals of plans and schedules, and judgment-free language, to a new family rewoven each day with strands of silk. There's nothing like it to make every sappy platitude you've ever gagged on seem suddenly and totally true: I want the ordinary, want to *be* the ordinary. Five spare minutes and a clean car are the last things I would ever wish for; even hours lost to science journal observations of a fogged-out moon and spats about how to compare fractions are far better than an empty afternoon. And so it still seems miraculous that, ordinary of ordinaries, I can give just the names—Ryan M., Michael M.—and pull up to the curb beside the school's awning, and there the boys I could have lost forever—the boys for whom I could have long since faded to a shadow—are, instead—beyond a miracle—standing on the pavement, backpacks jiggling with impatience, just waiting to climb in.

Gel Pens

WHEN NINE-YEAR-OLD Ryan asked the drugstore clerk for "jail pens," I cringed. "No, *gel* pens," I interrupted. "It's *gel*." And we needed a padded envelope too. We were sending them to his dad.

Did Ryan really think I'd make him go and ask for such a thing? No wonder he'd looked a little odd. But after all the Love-and-Logic drills, he was oddly unresistant. (I make him do so many things against his wishes: Brush his teeth in front of me. Read out loud instead of skimming silently. Take off the T-shirt he's hiding beneath his long-sleeved decoy shirt in January. Walk straight across a street instead of diagonally.)

So why wouldn't Ryan think that I'd ask him to comply with one more humiliating request? Why wouldn't I make him march up to the front of a drugstore and ask the teenage slacker clerk for "jail pens," right there in the middle of a knot of church ladies?

"I don't know," the teen at the register shrugged. "If we got 'em, they'd be on aisle 3."

Ryan's dad had made this special request, after all, and he made so few, other than for us to accept the collect call to his kids every week or three that he had to place through the prison-industrial complex Evercom, the country's biggest rip-off phone company.

So Ryan's dad, Luke, could have gel pens, and even glitter pens, to draw his cartoons, now that he was out of county jail and in a real prison, albeit minimum security. The list of permitted items had changed with each move. Gel pens were permissible now, although surely their bright ink could be used to make tattoos. But this prison allowed no postage stamps, only account money with which to buy them. You could send stamps to the county jail but not newspaper clippings, which supposedly could be used to roll cigarettes. There, a five-photo limit. Here, all the photos you could convince someone to send you. Drawings in colored pencil but not crayon. (Years later, in medium security, drawings could be only black pencil.) With such arbitrary restrictions it's no wonder Ryan thought the jail required special pens.

Photos, stick drawings, play programs, and nontoxic school glue all were acceptable, so we'd send them. It was indeed the thought that counted, so jail pens it would be.

THANKS TO the vending machines, the children don't seem to mind the prison visits on alternate Sundays. When else are they allowed to feed five dollars' worth of quarters into slots, as manically as any casino gambler? A regular attention-deficit cocktail of Starbursts, Bugles, and Mountain Dews clunks out of the machines, sending Ryan's six-year-old brother, Michael, spiraling off into his superhero plans to pull the stainless steel table up off its bolts, crash it through the iron mesh cafeteria window, and bust his dad outta here.

The boys ask only once why all the men are wearing the same white T-shirts and green twill pants, or about the laminated posters, YOUR VICTIM'S RIGHTS, side by side in English and Spanish. The boys seem not to notice the guards up above in their glass control booth, or how a guard in latex gloves opens the back door when an inmate leaves early, or that the faded Santa, shamrock, or cornucopia cutout decorations look like they've been there since my elementary school years. The kids do like the fake Christmas tree, devoid of all dangerous ornaments. And they really like to hear about betting on TV football with packets of instant coffee. They love that their dad's won the limit of twenty in one week. He uses them to stain his crafts, not for drinking.

What the kids don't like is waiting out in the car or staying perched on the parking lot curb or getting yelled at for playing on the crumbling concrete steps to the lower lot. That's how we have to spend one of the two visiting hours in these gray wintry months, since there's a three-visitor limit with no unsupervised kids. Three kids requires two adults, which means two separate hour-long visits, plus you can't pass a kid on from one adult to the next, since a minor can't remain in there alone, and no one can go back in after leaving.

WHAT *I* don't like is the drive back, when all the pent-up anger, jealousy, frustration, and unacknowledged wrongness of the whole place and situation burst through a high flood wall of denial. These emotions, of course, do not appear as themselves but have alchemized into other angers and actions: touching, pinching, squawking, angry elbows, litanies of wrongs recounted. None of these wrongs, of course, has been committed by Luke, their dad, who's the hero-in-waiting, but by any sibling or front-seat adult who cares to speak up. Somehow these raw, jagged, gray feelings seem perfectly matched to the road construction zones we climb through. The blasted-out mountain slopes themselves even mirror the mood, imprisoned as they are with chain-link netting to prevent falling rocks and landslides.

The long ride down there is not so bad. I'm glad not to be the one who drives it, with my useful reputation for going too slowly. It's full of good moods and anticipation—of the cascade of junk food quarters more than anything. We do Mad Libs and play Twenty Questions or What Am I Wearing? with the only answers variously "SpongeBob," "'Rick' Obama," "Peter Pan," and "Hillary," who, like the tooth fairy, is known to be "good to kids." Ryan and Michael's sister, Isabelle, makes numerous pretend cell phone calls to herself, ringtones and all, demonstrating her popularity with a cutely pink but minuteless phone.

I'm glad to go, glad to do any practical thing to slightly blunt the losses for these children, even though I see the class grading work I could be doing passing by my eyes and hear the excuses I'll make back in class on Monday. This trip doesn't have the feeling of duty but just of cheerfully participating in something mildly wrong, like visiting a funeral parlor for someone you didn't know well, where everyone is chatting about tire chains and snow removal. You can't really be happy on a prison visit, obviously, but you're not supposed to speak of the gloom and intensity either, as some of the couples around us will do, gripping each other's shoulders and leaning in. There's the veneer of small talk over something gaping and insoluble, yet it's small talk you're grateful to pull from the air—the mere sound of speaking eases things. Our light conversation with Luke about dogs, learning Letterland characters, and drought seems so much more valuable than the actual words exchanged.

I HAVEN'T had to go each time. But why do I have to go at all? When three kids and a grandmother are going, someone else has to go to make the adult-kid ratio fit. Most often, that someone is me. I knew that Luke had cussed me at times, before this prison term, for getting weekend visits with Michael that he thought should have come his way, and he sent messages through the children to make sure I knew this was the case. I was relieved I didn't have to deal with his resentment face to face, and I knew he was not in his right mind—and it wasn't until he was in prison that I would see him sober.

I care about the children's father in the abstract and as the person he became, or was revealed to have been all along, as the forced sobriety chipped away, month by month, at the granite block that so long encased him. I care that he succeeds for the children's sake and for his own, yet I know the statistics. If he ultimately makes it, month by month, week by week, hour by hour, minute by minute, everyone would marvel, and it would truly be a miracle in his life and the life of these kids. Yet if he backslides, I won't be the one who takes it personally or feels rejected or deceived; I'll just feel sad and fearful of whatever destruction might lie ahead, wondering how wide a swath it will cut. I respect Luke for all he's now done and written to us, and for all he's thanked and apologized for while he's been imprisoned; I like him as the person he is at this very moment, stepped out of history.

ARMORED BY neutrality, and knowing it's Jessica, his estranged wife and the boys' mother, whom Luke would rather see than me, I did my best to make these prison visits work, and he never failed to thank me. There was always a thin line between standing back and letting the visiting hour deteriorate into Michael's escape fantasies and my intrusively tiresome prompting of tales of school, Santa visits, and gymnastic feats. I didn't want my familiarity with Michael's daily life and its monumentally important details to sound like I was showing off a closer bond than his father shared with him, but I also didn't want to sound like I presumed they needed a ventriloquist to bridge the space between them: *Tell Daddy about your magic tricks, the Shrek piñata, what two plus four makes, how you saw Peter Pan fly through a window, now show him the place where your tooth used to be.* But the right balance of prompting and silence eluded me. After all, Luke told me, it was not like he had much to share, since his own day-in, day-out life didn't vary.

I'm still amazed that the visits were nowhere near what I had first dreaded. The kids could touch, hug, sit on laps, and predictably spill sodas and get paper towels to wipe them up. The staff were perfectly courteous to us, and the entrance walk was lined with rows of red impatiens, aptly called, and the name of the institution was spelled out in stones beneath the clanging flagpole. Most important, we could use the staff bathroom during visits, which was no small consideration with wound-up kids.

My detachment wasn't simple but rather relief at climbing off the roller-coaster of all the drama that led up to his imprisonment. The enforced ordinariness of these visits was new, and it was a blessing. The first time I met Luke, after he had been freed from a summer in county jail, I was shocked by his pale vampire skin, the profusion of guitar string and safety pin tattoos, and most of all by the soft, damp grip of his hand as I shook it. Later I'd see him at his mother's home, sleeping or gazing at old westerns on TV while the kids squabbled over plastic toys on the floor; I grew wary of those rare times I saw him talkative and outgoing, realizing later that those were the highest times, that only drugs cranked him back to the semblance of normality. After six months of incarceration he looked like a different person, as though inflated with a bicycle pump. His exercise program had filled him out, plus he had color in his face and a real but slightly awkward smile that made me glad to shake his hand but embarrassed to meet his eye. Luke no longer talked in a whisper or sent harsh accusations; instead he seemed to be caring, focused, loving. He was everything you'd like a dad to be.

From prison he drew the kids amazing cartoons on their letters and envelopes. They proudly showed off a Scooby Doo head with glittering green eyes or PJ from *Family Circus*. And he made meticulous frontier miniatures, staining them wood color with the coffee packets he'd won. From paper straws, newspaper, soap, and toothpicks he built rocking chairs and cabins; tiny wooden rifles and blocky cars; a minister's lectern with a miniature Bible open to John 3:16; and even a tray-sized log cabin that lights up inside. All the end product of a massive dose of boredom and the rechanneled ingenuity of a meth cooker, who when cranked could turn lamps into pipes and take a computer apart with the certainty he could put it back together better.

ON THE way home we would slow down to see the drought-yellowed yard of a bungalow three miles from the prison. It was crammed with Christmas inflatables, lined up from front step to sidewalk like a line of kids playing Mother May I. There were blowing snow globes, bobbing Santas, puffy snowmen—a whole Kmart section blown up and packed in. I wondered if the owners thought much about living three miles from a multifacility state prison complex. Perhaps the bungalow's owners worked there, as Ryan's former Cub Scout leader did, or perhaps they simply blocked out its existence, like a nuclear plant looming up behind the back fence. But did these homeowners know their decorations made the day less drudgery (to say nothing of even more surreal) for the children coming and going from prison visits? Surely, we were not the only ones to pull over.

McDonald's was another bright spot, continuing in the surreal/mundane vein. Budgeted for carefully by their grandmother all week, this treat was punctuated with time-outs from the play equipment and bargaining with the disdainful preteen Isabelle, who showed her disgust with the world by gagging on McNuggets. The clashing colors of this Play Place—a jangling combination of orange, yellow, purple, and navy—seemed as useless a gesture of cheer as the faded Norman Rockwell holiday decorations on the walls of the prison cafeteria.

FOR ME these visits were easy, just another type A–foster-parent task I wanted to do crazily well, but for others around us, they looked like life or death every time. I instinctively looked away from other families' tables, my blurred gaze conjuring curtains of privacy. Still, I couldn't help but see the fifty-year-old man with crutches and a flushed face who was always leaning toward his wife, her face in her hands, long hair puffed out behind her. A younger man held his daughter on his lap in her stiff Sunday tulle dress; his other arm circled the hips of his wife, whose jeans looked tight enough to cut her in half.

But the familiar routine of these visits was almost a blessing, compared with the blaring TV visits of the past at Grandma Irene's home, the birthday parties when strangers suddenly walked in, jagged switchblades that appeared between the sofa cushions or cylinders of foil that peeked out behind Strawberry Shortcake bedroom curtains, and Sundays on the couch as Dad, coming down from his high, snored on the sofa while cars pulled into the driveway, idled, and then pulled out when he did not emerge. Still, the kids flew to the window each time they heard a car drive in.

BUT NOWADAYS the kids are the ones who might or might not show up for a visit, might or might not be too giddy to talk. They have a choice whether to spend half a day visiting prison or not, and an opportunity for fishing, a cousin's birthday, a Simpsons marathon, or basic anger-tainted apathy might prevail. They don't seem to feel shame about going or to recognize how much they make or break their father's week. The kids have the power to visit or not, and to actually talk or spout nonsense through an eighteen-dollar phone call. For once they have the power to disappoint instead of to be constantly disappointed themselves.

WHEN MICHAEL was six years old, he said he wanted first to be a police officer, then a "lorrer," which sounds like a parakeet species but actually means *lawyer*, a word he learned from the Lynyrd Skynyrd song "Red, White, and Blue." Sometimes he wanted to be a lawyer because he knew lawyers help get people out of jail—"like my daddy!" he announced—other times, he wanted to be a lawyer because he'd been told he likes to argue. Being a judge would be his next career move. "A judge!" he'd proclaim. "Judge Michael! And Judge Joe Brown will be my best friend." At that age he asked me if what happened on *Judge Judy* was real and why the people on the show kept arguing if it wasn't real. But while all his awareness of these professions stemmed from his father's being in prison, it seemed to me they were a definite and pragmatic step forward from a career as a superhero who could break the iron mesh off the prison windows and fly free.

Every few weeks Michael asked to read a book called *Daddy, Will You Miss Me?* about a boy whose father has to go to Africa to help wildlife for a month that feels like a century to the child. I'm curious to know whether the author meant it for lives like those of Luke's children or was thinking only of kids whose dads go off on corporate field trips. The watercolors are pretty and the child's doubts are so real. He even looks like Michael, gazing out the window as a car with a light on top takes his daddy away, and in the world of this fantasy, that light is a taxi's. I keep wondering whether anyone else is reading this book for the same reason and in the same way. Because with all the places the Berenstain Bears and Little Critter go, with all the problems they tackle and close, I have yet to see *The Berenstain Bears and Too Much Prison,* which would have been truly useful to me.

At the time I realized the prison visits might be as good as it got, for all of them, as far as having a father-child relationship went. I truly hoped not. Almost two years into that sentence, Luke told his mother he'd stopped having meth dreams, which I had heard others say was a key step in recovery. But I wondered then, as I wonder again now, how he would ever step out of prison and magically across a gaping moat into a new world of real job and home and routine, when the numbers of jobs and rentals open even to the most enterprising ex-inmates and addicts were few. Was it even possible for Luke to walk back through these towns like a half-visible ghost, unseen and undrawn to the people who still dwelled in meth world—the ones who would reach their sticky hands out to pull him back like the damned in the pit of hell in some medieval painting, clamoring and waving for their old companions? Or would he leap down into that fire first?

THE ANSWER became clear a few years after Luke's release and it didn't surprise me: he went back to prison. Same incorrigible drug, different drug-related crimes, different and longer sentence, but ironically, after a circuitous path through medium security, he's back in the same minimum-security prison again. Now, with the boys in their teens, their father-son bonds seem stronger than ever. And for the same reason—those Sunday prison visits.

I'd like to say there were a few good years between these two prison terms, but I can't. I can say Luke had a few years of freedom. He found places to stay, so the boys' visits didn't happen at Grandma Irene's anymore, except for holidays, but once again we were back to accusations that I was getting the visits with Michael that should have been Luke's, and maybe that was true. True and necessary, for from what I saw and heard, Luke often seemed paranoid, short-tempered, and preoccupied with cell phone calls—all signs that his drug use had returned. But Luke did not want to come visit at our house or Benny's or have his mother go on visits with him. Although Jessica dodged Luke's phone calls or left messages that Michael already had plans with me—and he always did—she still sent Ryan to stay with his dad. Perhaps she thought Ryan and his dad were closer, or that Ryan could handle more, being older, or maybe that he needed a break from Benny.

Luke didn't accuse me of being an FBI agent this time, but we did have one long yelling fight on the phone about a friend he'd had drive Ryan back to our house alone after Jessica and Benny had gone south and left the boys with us. I tried then to declare strict new rules for Ryan's visits with Luke, but we were all in limbo legally. Trying to say no to a bioparent was hard enough, but only Jessica had custody and while she backed me up long-distance, it was a miserable issue to negotiate when I had no authority myself.

IF LUKE had been willing to check into a halfway house to start with and yoke himself to another regimen and routine, I'd have had more hope for him after his first release. He'd made considerable effort to go through a treatment program while he served time, but a halfway house would have been just one more prison to him, and beds were scarce for even the most willing. Then, as now, although he wants to live sober, he craves being free—free of rules, of crowds, of debts, of drug screens, of noise, of set hours and expectations, in prison or out.

AFTER ALMOST a year back in jail and months in the processing prison, Luke was transferred to a medium-security prison—one with a more stunningly scenic view, beyond the wire, than most people could afford. There, the children's visits got back on track and felt very familiar, with a normalcy that had been lacking in real-life visits earlier. Since everyone was older, they had more opportunities for actual two-way conversations, both during monthly visits and weekly over the phone. In this prison hugs were allowed only at a visit's beginning and end and there were no tables, just clusters of dusty green plastic deck chairs, which made it a little awkward to know where to put your hands and elbows for two hours. But these new conversations were real and peppered with good advice from Luke—even the Bible talk had more specifics and fewer slogans. The boys too had some perspective on all they had experienced, and hearing their dad take responsibility and detail his regrets over and over again seemed to sink in.

After two years in the medium-security prison, Luke qualified to go down to minimum security and even for limited work release. He was returned to the same prison in which he'd served his previous term, and he remains there, where the boys, their sister, grandmother, and other family members still visit him regularly. Luke reads a lot but no longer makes or draws things now that he's back where he can; his conversations with the boys have deepened, and his good advice to them has more credibility than when Will or I or a counselor might suggest the same thing. Aside from the ungraspable loss of their childhoods, the most useful thing I think Luke has shown them about prison is just how infinitely boring it is.

He won't be released until Ryan is nearing real adulthood and Michael graduates high school, but I have more hope this time, if only because of his age, and the ever more pressing sense of all the time lost.

My wish for Luke's next release is just what it was before—that he will stay drug-free, find work, and have a full life and continued healthy relationships with his children and family. If he'll only somehow power through the days and months after prison, fueled by these visits, these photos, these news clippings with the children's names and praises, then there can be a flicker of hope, at least. But with a single dad who's basically been married to meth, the here and now could be the high point for these kids. These two-hour Sunday visits could actually prove to be the best of times—years from now, that is—when they look back through the foggy rearview mirror. These visits, these letters, the old cartoon-decorated envelopes, are the deposits, small but steady, into their bank of future memory. They're seeing the dad he could be, might be, is, as his most true, most decent, most predictable, most caring self. They see that he loves them more than a drug, even if it's currently out of reach.

THERE'S NO veil over Luke now, no Sunday fog, because he's already come down to earth hard and stayed there. Still, if prison were the bottom (and, really, it isn't, if you consider his year indoors and the black-mold showers of the county jail while awaiting trial), it's a lucky place to be. A blessing, even. For Luke, the addict, it could just be a lifesaver, literally and spiritually, however temporary its shore against his ruin. It's kept him alive while his children were growing, and prevented an even more unbearable loss than that of his company. So let's keep those jail pens, letters, quarters, news clippings, cartoons, collect calls, straw houses, Bugles, Starbursts, coffee crystals, and winning bets coming. Because for Ryan and Michael, the dad they have come to know these prison Sundays might be the best dad they'll ever see.

In a Prison

—Michael

EVERY TIME I walk into a prison, I feel happy. I do not think I should feel happy, but I am. Do I feel sad or mad? No, that comes later, when I have to leave. My dad has been in the system since he was a teen, but the first time I remember him being in jail was when I was in foster care before I was two years old. The first time I remember actually going to visit a jail was when I was about five. Since that first time I visited my father, I have been to see him at a minimum-security prison about fifteen times, the county jail in our town about thirty times, and the medium-security prison my father is in now eight times. I have seen my mother in the county jail, and my daddy in the same jail and in prisons. I do not want anyone to assume that I am like my parents, but I still love them both and I have gone to visit them in jails and prisons to make them happy.

Nobody I know at school understands the difference between a jail and a prison, but I do. A jail is temporary, and visiting is done using a phone to talk to an inmate who is behind a plexiglass window, so there is less security. In a prison a visitor is allowed to sit face to face with the inmate, but multiple guards are standing around and the visitor has to be put through a metal detector before going through the gates.

The prison my father is in now is a medium-security prison a long way from where I live. Even though he hasn't much freedom in there, drugs and alcohol still go around in the prison. Inmates use stamps as money to buy coffee and other things. I have heard people say that prison food is bad. Well, that is true and not true. On an inmate's birthday the other inmates make something called steak cakes. A steak cake is a honey bun with ground-up peanut butter crackers microwaved into a liquid glaze. They make taffy out of coffee creamer and fruit punch. The inmates make these things because they can't buy the real ones.

When we visit, the adults have to give the guards their IDs. On the other side of the fence, a guard puts a stamp on my hand that is invisible except under a black light. This stamp would let the guards know if an inmate was trying to escape with the visitors as they were leaving. Next, another guard guides us through the gates. When I walk into the visiting room, I immediately look for my dad. He is never there first, but I do it anyway.

When my dad walks in, we all smile at each other. He sits down and we all start talking. We begin discussing his life in prison so far. He complains and tells us about how his job of cleaning trash off the roads is going. He tells us about riding in a bus for half of the day to get to the place they will clean trash, even though it is not that far away, and how the backs of the seats on the bus have been ripped off so the inmates have to sit on the bus floor or benches. I talk about school. My brother talks about football. My dad tells us how he survives in the prison.

Prison gives my dad a lot of time to learn. Prison can help people become street smart and book smart. My dad learned to light his cigarette with the smoke detector batteries and a staple. Last time he was in prison, he could make us art. My dad made us a house of rolled-up newspaper, and the fireplace lit up with a tiny LED light bulb. He once drew me a Scooby Doo card. Now, in this medium-security prison, he cannot do art, probably because the guards might think someone would stab somebody else with a crayon. My dad also reads a lot in there. He gets books from the prison library and when we send them right from the publisher. My dad reads dystopian novels, and he read *The Hunger Games* trilogy along with me. This made me happy because we were doing something together even though we were not with each other while we read the novels.

If anyone ever goes to prison, they should make sure to read a lot or they will get bored, because the inmates don't have the freedom to leave . . . but no one should try to go to prison in the first place.

As I leave, I get sad that I will not see my dad for another few weeks. I will miss my father, but at least I will see him again soon. The view in the parking lot is of orange cones, other people laughing or crying as they walk away to their cars, the blue buses my daddy rides in to work, the gray-blue mountains in the orange sunset, and, behind us, the ugly brick prison and coils of razor-sharp barbed wire. I wish that my daddy were not in prison, but he is, and there is nothing I can do about it but cry and visit him again.

What's in Your Toolbox?

—Michael

I always was used as a tool.
For my mother, I was a screwdriver,
Unscrewing my father's bolts,
Making all my father's screws loose.

And for my father, I was a hammer,
Smashing back at my mother,
Always trying to fix things,
But usually splitting the wood.

For Benny, I was a gun.
A silenced gun with blanks, no ammo.
He made threats but never did anything.
Every time he fired, I'd be the one to make noise,

But no one thought it was real.
I always felt like Jesus was my Power Tool,
Who tried to fix everything,
But everyone else unplugged His cord

And took Him out of my life.
But when I was in the prison
Visiting my dad today,
I felt that someone plugged

The Power Tool back in again,
And now I feel like "the Builder,"
Screwing back in my father's bolts,
And I also take the nails back out of my mother's hands.

I also take the silencer off the gun,
But the blanks are still in the chamber
And then everyone hears the shot
And knows something has happened.

I throw the gun into the river.

A Fork in the Road

—Michael

NEAR THE greeting card section of the local drugstore, I crouched down and looked at the glass case. It had been unlocked with its door partly open for weeks. I had noticed this every time I had gone into the drugstore to get a prescription refilled. This standing glass case could spin around when you wanted to look in the other side. I was peering into the glass case to see what I could see, because anything in a glass case looks valuable because it is guarded by walls of mirrors. There were shiny gold, silver, and bronze pens in the glass case. I am attracted to metallic objects, and they seemed to hypnotize me. The pens seemed to be whispering in a creepy, demonic voice, *Michael, I know you want to write with me . . . Michael, we want to be free, Michael.* At that moment, I started thinking about stealing them.

Looking back, I stole the pens because I believed I might look rich to other kids if I stole expensive items, and this seemed like a good idea because I was poor. My stomach was bouncing around in my body like a pinball machine. I felt excited but also guilty. I knew my dad was in prison for drugs, and I wondered if this was how his criminal life had started out, with minor thefts. While Deborah, my foster mom, sat in a chair, waiting for my prescription to be filled, I searched around to make sure no one was looking. Deborah had trusted me to be alone because I had promised not to steal ever again after I stole some candy from the gas station two months earlier. I stole only when I was with Deborah because I wasn't scared of her. If she caught me, she'd just make me go back and give the stolen item to the manager, but with my mom, I would have gotten a spanking. I peered around the aisle to make sure no one was around, and then I snatched the pens. I slipped them into my shoes and back pockets.

I didn't think I would be caught. I didn't think I would end up in juvenile hall, like the warnings I'd heard from Deborah and other adults. I had seen the inside of a prison but only as a visitor. I loved visiting my dad in prison, where we got to eat chips and drink soda. Our attention was always on the snack machines, instead of on my dad, so he never got to tell me what *not* to do to so I could stay out of trouble. It did not seem like I would ever go to prison for breaking the law, so I thought I could steal and get away with it. I knew I would steal again if no one was watching, and I felt scared.

WHEN I got in the car, I stashed the pens under the seat. We drove to the library from the drug store. I felt full of adrenaline, like I feel when I hear the *Batman* song. Deborah stayed in the car to clean the trash out, but I went into the library ahead of her.

Deborah came in while I was reading *Horton Hears a Who.* "Where did these come from?" she asked sternly. She was holding the pens in her hand, showing them to me. Light reflected off the gold and silver pens.

I was mad, sad, and afraid at the same time. I felt angry, like the Joker does when Batman catches him. I despised myself because Deborah had discovered my secret pen stash, and I was disappointed that I hadn't hidden the pens better. I felt a rush of vengeance against Deborah for discovering my stolen pens. I wanted to steal more of anything, just to get back at her. I didn't know then that people were serious when they said I could get into trouble. I didn't know what my dad would tell me if he found out. Would he say, "Why did you steal?" or "You'll end up in prison like me"? I knew he wouldn't be happy I had stolen.

Deborah's phone rang, and it was my mother, who had asked Deborah to pick her up and take her somewhere. We picked up my mom, and Deborah told her that we would have to go back to the drugstore.

Deborah told my mother what had happened, and I acted like I was not the one who had stolen the pens. I shrugged my shoulders, but my mother did not believe me. This story feels now like a *Curious George* story because I was getting into trouble. I did know what was going on, though, unlike Curious George, who is a monkey and doesn't know for real how he is supposed to live his life, but I did.

My mother told me that she could see I was lying and that I should just stop and go confess to the manager. That's when Deborah told her that we were going back to the store to return the pens and that I would go and tell what I had done. I was kicking the car seat and looking at the floor. The car seat was filled with M&M's, loose peanuts, cracker crumbs, melted crayons, and coloring books. I peeled the paper off of a crayon and threw it on the floor. I hoped it would melt all over the floor because I was mad and embarrassed. We drove back to the drugstore without talking about anything else.

I walked in and returned the pens. Pointing at the glass case, I said to the clerk, "I got these pens from over there." I was trembling. I tried to make my story sound harmless. "I wanted to give them to you," I said.

"Uh, I think you stole them," Deborah said. She was standing next to me, watching me and pointing at me.

"How did you get them out?" the store clerk asked.

I explained that the glass case had been unlocked and cracked open for weeks. I would watch it when I came in to see if it was still unlocked and plan to open it.

The clerk said that she would ask her manager what should happen. Then we left the store. I felt guilty.

A FEW hours later, the phone rang. Deborah said it was the drugstore manager. "They said you are banned and cannot go in again," she told me.

I pictured my father covering his face, showing how disappointed he would be to hear that I had been stealing. He would have to think about my theft until I could see him again. He would probably be worried that one day I might go to prison like him. My father wants me to have a good life and stay out of trouble.

I have not been in that drugstore in six years. Now you may see me standing in the vestibule like a statue, doing nothing. If I had gotten away with it, I would have been happy but more of a criminal. But I got caught, and I could have gone to court and juvenile jail. Deborah made me go see a juvenile delinquent probation officer. I was scared of her because she was so stern and I knew I had to listen. That is why I did not steal again for four years because I knew people were serious about stealing. I know now that anyone can go to jail, even as a kid, if they steal.

Cleaning Up for DSS

Clean up, clean up,
Everybody do your share

IT WAS the opposite of a barn raising: a stab at deconstructing the trash and junk pile that reached as high as the trailer's back window, like one of those dump mountains you hear about in the Philippines. It contained two, possibly three, years' worth of spoiled food, coffee grounds, torn-up tires, used diapers rolled up like hedgehogs, naked GI Joes with limbs splayed sideways, and this year's Salvation Army Christmas boxes, smashed and waterlogged. Most of it had to be rebagged, as a winter's worth of snow, ice, and rain had worn holes in the always impossible Dollar General trash sacks—and that was only the top layer. There was no trash pickup out here in the county; plus this particular "Mom" and "Dad" (as Social Services seems to call every parent at risk) had no vehicle to haul it away. Besides, some of it could have proved useful someday. But someday would never come, and on this day all the wheels, parts, gears, springs, and bits of projects would bite the dust. Almost everything had to go. DSS was coming back soon and the landlord was evicting this family, sparking a perfect storm of urgency.

MOST FITTINGLY, this cleanup was being done in heavy rain; nonetheless, everybody pitched in somewhere and did their share, whether it was watching the babies ride circles around the side of the trailer, boiling hot dogs on the heater, heaving these bags over the back of the pickup with a broken tailgate, or cradling the sacks as they threatened to split open and erupt nastiness. A near-ritualized necessity, the cleanup brought out every friend and relation during the weekend, after the social workers had posted a notebook-paper summons on the door, requesting a phone call and giving notice that they'd be back. "Surely DSS won't come on a weekend?" Mom said, and I said, "Right," thinking *if only.* But my best role here was to echo and agree.

So everyone came out of the woodwork for this, even the near-deaf grandmother, scavenging uncle, and long-lost half brother back from Florida, who was making up for years of absence by offering the use of a rare road-legal pickup truck. For an hour, Jessica and Benny too stopped by as the mom was a second cousin and Jessica had tried to help her children out with hand-me-downs and old riding toys that were getting tossed out now. All manner of supposed friends last seen with tallboy beer cans tucked inside their jackets, and even I, the bringer of Halloween pumpkins and weatherizing applications, the past foster parent to cousins, were now offering carefully phrased advice and rubber gloves. It was anyone's guess who might have dropped the dime to DSS—out of spite, because one of the parents owed them money, or—least likely—out of concern.

Only the landlord stayed away, as conspicuously absent as Judas. Having caught wind of what was going on, he probably was afraid DSS would nail him for umpteen housing code violations, to say nothing of the lack of a working stove in this trailer. Nail him for not allowing Mom to pay the contract trash-haulers to come, just out of meanness, or a church to donate a rent check, because the payment might be found in an IRS audit and he openly admitted that he declared no income from any of his rentals.

SO THERE I was—trying sincerely, yet not too hard, to offer Mom the best arguments to make to the social workers so everything would look good.

Good but not too good.

I didn't want to be the hero for either side, neither for silence nor for speaking up about past terrors whose signs had now melted away. I wanted things to go well for Mom and even for Dad; I knew that they really did care, and I knew how fast room temperature can reach a boil. I wanted to believe that the worst was behind them or Mom wouldn't have told me about the worst. Yet I wanted doubt to linger when the social workers finally returned; I wanted that doubt to be the grit in the oyster that might keep the social workers checking in.

So even with a Little Tikes playhouse full of beer cans sitting ten feet away, I couldn't bring myself to remove a Miller bottle, perched on its side at eye level and sandwiched between bags in the trash mountain. Bag after hauled bag, I pretended not to see it, because I was unwilling to be the one who, in helping, hid it, as if that one glass beer bottle could be the key that unlocked everything, the chink that would cause this whole mountain of trash, this house of cards, this fire trap of a life to collapse right in the social workers' sight.

What if this one empty bottle had the potential to change these kids' lives? (Yes, I've seen too many movies, too many zoom-in close-ups.) And although I knew how improbable it was, the bottle still felt radioactive—and that throwing it away, erasing it from the picture, would make me entirely complicit. So I pretended not to see it for long enough that Mom finally got it herself and threw it into the black Hefty lawn bag I'd brought over.

HALF THE trash mountain's content still waited to be shoveled into bags: faded Easter baskets; a beer stein with a triangle of glass broken out; the shiny silver trigger stock of what must have been a toy gun (I couldn't help but weigh it in my hand to be sure); stray Duplo blocks—unscathed, but who had the energy to retrieve and wash them?; the glass mice from Mom's childhood that Dad had pulverized in drunken anger; and, of course, dirty diapers—the eternal diapers. There are always more diapers.

And then there was the pile of jagged car parts and trike tires—all potential money in the pocket, if the rust held off. This was a family that could rig a spaceship from spare parts, or at least Frankenstein together a backroad transport out of a wonky wheelchair and defunct Lawnboy, then haul a trove of crushed Busch Lite cans to that Big Rock Candy Mountain where they buy aluminum scrap and collect the thousands of pop-tops that are rumored to fund cancer cures.

"Hey, Mom, I found a lighter," Big Brother called in triumph.

It was the heaviest trash in the universe, weighted with dirty rainwater. Even if they had been dry, hoisting these bags to shoulder level and pitching them over the broken tailgate into the pickup truck would have been difficult.

THE RAIN picked up, and I couldn't get the drone of that preschool "Clean up, clean up" song out of my head. I decided to sacrifice the front seat of my car and wrestle one more trash bag onto the passenger side. I looked back at the trash pile. The morning's work hadn't made a bit of difference.

Now I thought of a Girl Scout camp song about the little bird in the Land of Odin that sharpens its beak on a mountain, eroding it by crumbs every million years. Here too it seemed, eternity would arrive, and the social workers with it, before this whole mountain could be hauled away.

THE CATALYST for this DSS summons was surely the burn on the back of four-year-old Big Brother's hand, the yellow parts now scabbed over. "I got mad and punched the heater," he told everyone without prompting. Working through her exhaustion, Mom said, "What do they think, that I got mad and held his hand there?"

"They were taking pictures," she confided, talking about when DSS first showed up recently and she wouldn't answer the door. "Do you think it was the trash, or was there something they were looking for?"

Part of me sighed with relief—so at least they'd seen this rot, recorded it.

THE SPAGHETTI stain down the side of Baby Sister's face looked like blood—how did she even manage that when she appeared to be eating pineapple? I could see how it would look to the social workers, and I wondered why everyone else didn't too. "Hold still," I told her and scrubbed the stain with my rain-soaked sleeve, wiping more dirt on her as I erased it.

But what of the backyard tent full of more leaking trash bags and the playhouse full of half-crushed beer cans that Dad had saved to sell? They were worth a nickel per pound as scrap, and he'd never give them up just to make the yard look nice. I hoped he'd scavenged at least a few of those cans along the road.

AND WHY was it always Busch: regular, Light, Ice? Is that the only cheap beer left? Is the alcohol content higher? Is it the alpine mountains on the box? At any place DSS investigators might alight, I'd bet they find a litter of those death-blue cans and could follow them like crumbs to another half-shed, half-trailer, broken-down dwelling. I can't walk past a blue Busch display in the grocery store, coolly stacked on an end cap for every upcoming holiday, without feeling my heart tighten and my anger surge. That steely shade of Busch blue, a beacon to pissed-off men, has become the color of my dread.

WHO CALLED DSS this time?

That's the question in the air.

Because it was always the *who,* never the *why,* when the group was obsessing about these anonymous reports to Child Protective Services. Who called, who betrayed you, and why were they mad? But the *what*—the actual content, the percentage of truth in the report that might need to be dealt with—that was never up for discussion.

It became a weekend-long game of Clue: find the *who,* forget the *what,* and know that the *why* was an impure motive. The *weapon* was always the phone. The *where,* today, was this crumbling trailer, where even the smoke alarm batteries were a decade out of date. And then there was the *when. When* will the social workers drive up? And *when* will they leave us alone? *How* can Mom ever trust anyone again?

But most important was the *who.* So if I did leave at last—to do my own grocery shopping, shower off the stickiness, put on dry clothes, clean my own house, tend my own garden, lie on the couch, and read my own mountain of magazines—then how long until the speculation turned to me? (I wasn't the *who* this time, as I was anonymously in the past and would be again.)

I didn't know the particular social workers whose names were on the note, thank God, but I suspected they were the same people who talked to me so nicely when we were introduced at the Adoption Day pool party. DSS must speak one way to foster parents, who have actual first names—and another way entirely to them, Mom and Dad, when Dad, as they like to say, is in the picture. Printed perfectly, even cutely, it was not the words themselves—"Please call us right away. This concerns the children"—but the imperative voice that rang through as Mom read the note aloud. That is, I could hear the resentment of that imperative, built up from all her previous encounters with DSS, from her childhood on.

"Yeah, well, fuck them," she told me, her eyes tearing up as she refolded the note. "Sorry for my language, but can't they see I'm doing my best?"

EVERYONE WAS volunteering to speak for the family: "Tell them to call me, I'll tell them what a great mom you are." But the only person DSS might have believed was me. So why didn't I join in this chorus of advocates instead of slinking back to the trash pile and hoping no one would notice my silence?

There was no balance in my balancing act. I had been trusted with much more than I wanted to know, and once I'd crossed the line from helper to surrogate aunt for this family, I lost my balance. I had too much to lose by speaking and too much to lose by silence. The secrets were worse than what DSS might have uncovered, yet this knowledge was entrusted to me as a gift, and I couldn't bring myself to blow that cover. And there wouldn't even be any appreciable result if I did. The DSS standards are not what most people imagine. While I fantasized about hearing these outrages spouted by Nancy Grace, they were all things DSS might gloss over with a platitude, unless they were happening right in the moment—measurably, reportably—right in front of the social workers.

BESIDES, MOM had to talk, to vent, to someone. I sometimes wished that someone wasn't me, but just as it had been with Jessica, I was the one driving her up and down the highway to the store, the food bank, the WIC appointments I'd made for her. And I should have been grateful that she trusted me. It was not so much sharing her burden as spilling it before it burst and contaminated everything. How clear would this picture have been to Dr. Laura, to Dr. Phil, to even empathetic Oprah? How starkly would it have broken down into headlines? I kept secret upon toxic secret. Yet I wanted to pretend their fate rode on a stupid beer bottle I was too pure to hide away.

THE TRASH pile was around back, but out front, facing the road, hung the giant rebel flag of a living room curtain and the broken window, repatched with red electric tape. Surely that flag broadcast the message "Hey, come and get me. Here I am. Bring it on," to DSS, to police ("I hate cops," Big Brother said whenever we drove through the four-lane highway crossover where police liked to stake out speeders), and to any other authorities Mom and Dad would not want to summon.

I WAS dressed for a fund-raising breakfast. But the event was over, my name tag was on the dashboard, and I was resigned to getting mud on my black pants and leather clogs. If only I'd had a giant, stained T-shirt in the trunk instead of having to carry these garbage bags clutched to my shimmery green top.

I'd arrived with rubber dish gloves that I would leave behind for Mom, even though both gloves were right-handers. Even these would have made her day fractionally easier. But while driving to the county dump, I discovered that, despite the gloves, I had still gotten coffee grounds under my fingernails.

AT THE dump the bags seemed even heavier. The dumpsters at this site opened over my head; there was no way to heave these bags into the dumpster without getting them on my shoulder, against my chest, and smearing the dirty rain all over me.

As I left for the dump, there'd been another round of people clamoring to speak up on Mom's behalf, to give DSS a piece of their mind. I remained silent, unable to lie to DSS and sure I'd spill the secrets I'd foolishly promised Mom I'd keep. Was it all truly coming down? By now, even I couldn't say what would be best, tempting as it was to imagine the children with me or in one of my friends' foster homes, in toy-filled baths, preschool, new clothes, and real beds. Yet I couldn't forget the first time I picked Big Brother up and just the two of us went to see the movie *Kung Fu Panda.* A hundred times he turned to me and asked, "Where's my mama?" Even with popcorn and gummies, all he'd wanted was to go home again.

WHO KNEW when the DSS workers would return, traveling in pairs like Will Smith and Tommy Lee Jones in *Men in Black,* but I froze at the approaching rumble of every car. I needed to get out before the social workers appeared—out of that picture and all the myriad things wrong with it. DSS could do its job without quizzing me.

It was *their* job, after all; I couldn't help what others chose to tell me. When I was first starting out as a teacher teasing apart the classic short stories about guilt and betrayal, I insisted that the line between right and wrong was pure black and white, uncrossably clear. Right was hard and good; wrong was clear and selfish. My brain never got caught in these loops of endless calculation, trying to balance out the good, bad, and possible in ever-changing gray equations.

DURING THE summer a year before the cleanup, Will and I stopped at a waterfall park in the middle of a long trip—the only time I ever traveled out of range of Michael and Ryan. The park had immense cascades of water and rock, and a railed overlook that jutted from the cliff on stilts several stories above the falls. It looked like Niagara Falls, from the videos I'd seen, powering on and on.

I was waiting on the overlook for Will to return from walking the dizzying trail to the bottom, and it was taking a lot longer than we expected. A teenage boy, looking disturbed, burst onto the overlook, cursing to himself; behind him was a younger girl with perfect pigtails and a woman I supposed was his mother, breathlessly calling for him to slow down in a voice that said she knew he wouldn't. "God, can we just go now?" he said, flinging himself about the broad platform while his mother and sister peered over the edge. His mother called him to come see the thundering water, but I could tell she had been ignored too many times to believe he would. All this I recognized well from my fostering life, from the weariness in her voice.

I saw the stains covering the boy's white T-shirt, which was far too big for even his newly adolescent body. I sat at the hillside end of the platform, afraid to walk up to the edge myself, as if those giant stilts would give way or the waters would hypnotize me into throwing myself over the edge. So I sat, wishing I'd brought a book from the car, when I saw the boy climb over the side of the railing where it joined the cliffside, which was steep and wooded, then dropped away. A trash can was lashed by bungee cords to the side of the overlook railing, and at first I thought the boy was climbing out to throw something in the trash or even to fish something out of it.

This wasn't your regular teenage daredevil; I knew something was really wrong with this kid. If I said anything, he would surely cuss me—not that it should matter. He clutched one of the skinny trees, but the drop below was lethal. I figured I should yell at him, "Hey, get back here over that railing," just to get his mother to look back and shriek. Yet I just watched the clouds, silently imploring Mom to turn around. Maybe she wouldn't think anything of it—just another piece of the craziness that she was used to. Maybe I was seeing danger where there wasn't any—my depth perception is a little screwy. Maybe I didn't want to be the bad guy or the interfering supermom or to suggest the kid was lacking sense. Maybe I didn't want to be cussed at. Maybe I felt I was on vacation from the life where I always had to be the one to see death lurking.

Almost six years into foster parenting at that point, I could tell as I sat there that I was living through a big, fat metaphor for my life back home, for being the one to see the danger, weigh my options, and look away, hoping for the best. Hoping someone else would raise the alarm and bring the family hate down on them. But here at the waterfall, the stakes were immediate and real. If this kid fell, I would always carry that weight. And if he didn't? Well, I'd always know that he could have. And still I turned my gaze away and started cleaning out my purse.

THE PRE-EVICTION, pre-DSS cleanup was yet one more glaring metaphor, start to finish. One more test. I wanted to think I was helping, but I was hiding. Without me, the precarious mountain might have collapsed, yet surely that was what needed to happen. But no—it might have collapsed all over these kids, with no one to drive them to twice-weekly preschool and the dentist and no one to notice what was still invisible to DSS.

I ALWAYS thought the path would be clear; I never thought I'd become this person. I would be the one who'd make a scene and pull that kid off the side of the cliff, snatch out that keystone beer bottle, drop that dime, not look away.

For a while I was stunned that Mom's answer to Big Brother's alarms ("Daddy killed the baby deer; Daddy hit Mama in face; Daddy shot me with his gun") was never "What happened? Let's get to the bottom of this," but always, "Oh, don't say that—you'll get your daddy in trouble."

"You stupid whore," Big Brother said, parroting echoes from some past fight. "Goddamn it."

But the secrets I had gotten so mad at everyone else for keeping, I now had swallowed entirely.

MY PRECIOUS help was like a half-course of antibiotics, scammed from someone in exchange for two pain pills—just enough to hide the symptoms from prying eyes but not enough to kill the underlying infection, which will grow and rage and come back forever, always worse.

Clean up, clean up,
Everybody, everywhere,
Clean up, clean up,
Everybody do your share.

She Said Yes

I DON'T know why I lied when the smiling pastor came into Cooper's Garage with a wobbling axle and a question. "Now where do y'all go to church?" he said to the waiting room in general. I didn't know he was a pastor—he looked more like a retired, long-ago football player. He was as jovial as a politician, with blow-dried white hair and a face flushed with enthusiasm. I'd just taken Michael to his aunt's little church for the third Sunday that summer, and I still wondered what I'd done that had caused his grandmother to ask what I'd been raised as. So, when the other two customers in that plastic-paned greenhouse of a garage waiting room full of scrap carpeting, lawn furniture, and free cookies answered, and the pastor made booming small talk with them about their churches, I took the "where do you go to church" question literally and said the name of the area and not the name of the aunt's church itself.

"Oh, a beautiful place, I went to a wedding there once," the man said, assuming that I meant the Episcopal church, probably because of the university look about me, and not the aunt's Independent Baptist, which was small enough that most of the congregation was related. Related, and Christian enough to both donate new packages of Fruit of the Loom on foster care month Underwear Sundays and funeral expenses to the family of a drunk driver killed in a crash. And the Sunday school teacher for women, I'd been amazed to discover, was the same university bakery staffer who had taught me cake decorating. I was even worse at piping those darned icing roses than I was at trying to pass for a Christian.

I didn't lie to my favorite foster parent, a woman who is a cross between Joan Rivers and Christian Homeschooler of the Year, when she asked me with sincere curiosity what it is that Jews don't believe.

I wish I had asked this pastor why the meek are supposed to inherit the Earth (the chief fallacy of Christianity, according to one old Hebrew school teacher of mine)—and, more important, *how*—but I kept it to myself and bowed my head with the others when he offered to pray with us. I was curious what one would pray for in a mechanics' garage, but basically it was a nice, protective charm of a prayer—"Lord, we just ask you"—about safe trips and brake work.

No doubt he would have said something welcoming if I'd said I was Jewish—*grew up Jewish* is the actual hedge, which sounds like you couldn't really help it and might still see the light, but please don't invite me to dishonor my parents by coming to a specific service. I don't think for a minute he would have said something awful, even coated in southern well-meaning (and many steps removed from my old sun-leathered neighbor who was distressed he wouldn't see me in heaven, presumably so he would keep trying to grab me in the afterlife). But I knew that whatever followed would be an ordeal, and we all had at least another forty-five minutes to wait at that garage together. It was that and, I guess, just good southern manners. Why splinter when we can all go together? If some of my students, especially the rebellious locals, had been there, they'd have delighted in telling the man they were pagans and Satanists, and thirty years earlier, I'd probably have done the same.

But at that time I'd lived eleven years in this Appalachian mountain town, with three years on the edge of a reunified foster family, and I still wanted badly to fit in. I thought about Cassie Bernall, the martyred Columbine High School student who supposedly had professed her belief in God when the killers had confronted her about her faith (the story turned out to be a misunderstanding). I had nothing more lethal than embarrassment pointed my way and still, when the question of Jesus Christ came up, I smiled back at the preacher, took the meek way out, and lied. I ducked my head for his prayer and then gratefully retreated, disguise intact, to the pages of my magazine.

Shepherd's Way

—Michael

SHEPHERD'S WAY was an out-of-the-way church that my family and I went to when I was five and six years old. This church was supposed to help people in poverty, but they did not really try very hard. Shepherd's Way always had a service that was way too long, with a lot of singing. At the end of the service, they would give us boxes of free food. The food that they gave us was always expired, and once they gave my grandmother some old flour, and when she opened it, moths flew out. The church had a cable TV show about how they helped poor people in the Appalachian Mountains. They also posted these episodes on their website, where anyone could see them. They broadcast these shows to try to get people to send money to Shepherd's Way.

One day the pastor, his wife, and three others came to record my family for the show. When they walked up the driveway carrying cameras, I was excited. They started recording right away, with a shot of me waving out the window at them. They asked us to pray in a circle, holding hands in the living room. In our bedroom they made my brother and me tell them about the stuffed animals on my top bunk. Then the pastor asked me to go outside for a shot, but I could not find my shoes. The pastor said he would just carry me, so he held me in his arms outside in the yard while the crew took the shot. It turned out later that they had hidden my shoes to make us look poor. Even though we were poor, they made us look even more poor than we were. Now I am mad at the film crew for making us look helpless.

Two months later, when my mom and I watched the video on the internet, the first scene showed the film crew trying to find our house. The crew made it look like we were just a bunch of hillbillies that lived way back in the woods. The video showed me looking out of a window that had been broken by a rock. The crew had told us not to smile, so I looked depressed. In all the scenes that showed my stepdad, Benny, they had tried to cut him out to make it look like my mom was single and was supporting two kids alone. I did not like how they made everything look worse than it already was, just so they could receive money from people who felt bad for the family in the video.

The video made by Shepherd's Way made my mom and me so angry that she forced them to take it off their website, but they had already shown the video on TV here in town. The worst part of it was that they had filmed the bad parts of our house after my mother and aunt had cleaned up the house for three days to make it look better. My mother had even dressed us nicely for the episode. I think that filming in a way that made us look bad was a cruel thing to do. We did not get any of the money that Shepherd's Way made off of the episode about my family. A few years later, Shepherd's Way got a bad reputation for misspending money and closed down. Now they won't be able to make anybody believe in Appalachian stereotypes anymore, just to make money for themselves. I have learned not to believe everything I see on television, because I know from these past experiences that it might be a scam.

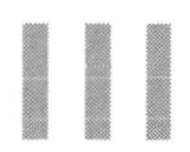

READING AROUND THE CURVES

Cody

WHAT EVERYONE knows about Cody is this: He is what used to be called retarded.

But "you can't tell by looking at him. Not at first." That's what everyone says, glossing over what that *would* look like.

He's "low IQ," or severely learning disabled, or some muttered something, plus maybe bipolar—"Son, I'm *highly* bipolar," he'll correct you—and, of course, he has the pandemic ADHD, right off the charts.

"You can't tell," they say, "not at first." And now, even though I know better, it's what I say too.

Because it's not until Cody says that his brother plays quarterback for the Steelers or the Saints or whatever team jersey you might be wearing, or until the matter of what year it is, or what month his birthday falls in, or until he insists that the speed limit is 100 outside town limits that you start to notice.

And then it's like—*oh, yeah.*

THAT'S WHAT everyone knows. But what I know is this.

He loves to move. Hard. Fast and furious. He loves to fly. A bike ride isn't a bike ride unless he's popped a tire in the process. And *tire* means a $14 reinforced, unpuncturable-tube tire, the toughest Walmart has to offer.

Cody wants to show you the scabs along his shins—biking battle scars, trophies of recklessness, the larger and longer the better. And he'll pick them off, bit by bit, because he likes to see fresh pink-red wound there. And he wants you to admire it too.

WHAT ELSE I know . . .

That he may have a low IQ, but he can steal a cheap watch from right in front of the cash registers at Roses, and he'll do it even though you've already promised him five dollars to buy whatever he chooses. "You don't have to follow me through the store," he snarls, "my mom never does" (because she'll no longer take him into a store, I soon found out). Too late, I realized Cody's protest should have been my cue to do the opposite—he'll always tell you what he's up to, if you can read around the curves.

Just as he'll announce later, revealing what he means to conceal: "Look, my brother gave me this watch. Those Indian knives. That pack of cigarettes." Or, "Guess what? I took my medication by myself. Mom didn't even have to make me." That's a sure sign he sold it for two bucks to whatever pillhead on the trailer park's third row wanted to buy it. He's sneaky enough and good enough that these announcements are the only way you'd know.

He can't tell you how to use a dollar sign with a number, but he'll never misuse a cuss word.

So Cody can steal from under the cashier's eyes or find Brick, an older neighbor, to get him alcohol—"Oh, that vodka bottle's just for decoration," Cody will say of the empty blueberry Absolut bottle on top of his pictureless TV. "It's up there because it looks cool—don't you think it looks pretty?" Well, not as pretty as his lava lamp but prettier than the holes he's punched in the Sheetrock walls of his room.

I KNOW all this because his mom, Risa, works thirty-seven hours a week at a job she feels twenty years too old for and has no car or phone, so I help drive her and Cody around and get to school events, having gotten to know them through one of the many agencies that weave through their lives, offering Christmas help here and a week of groceries there, and more for anyone who has a phone or computer and knows where to look, as I do, because it's infinitely easier to ask when you're not looking for yourself. And when his mom had to be gone for two weeks after her only cousin lost half a leg to diabetes, we were Cody's temporary foster parents, daily trying to persuade him that it wasn't all a lie, that his mom wasn't actually in jail somewhere for trying to reconnect the power or borrowing their neighbor's unregistered car. Risa had to put a nurse's aide on the phone to convince Cody of this, which he accepted with great relief, as if that could not be faked, although he'd doubted every word I'd said. But once his mom returned and Cody had gone home, the memory of his stay with us faded quickly. He was back to the present, busy fighting to lose this day's homework sheets before the Afterschool staff could make him do them.

"How did you get tangled up in my life?" Cody asks me now, always with disgust, and I always say, "Because I like you so much," and he never believes that is the truth.

CODY CAN make the connections to tell the most elaborate lies but to read he can only tap out one-syllable, short-vowel words, huffing the sounds, and he can't or won't understand the link between brushing his teeth and getting braces—braces he craved because you'd swear he has twice the usual number of teeth crammed into his head. Medicaid will actually pay, but he can't seem to digest the dentist's warning that "your teeth will rot out if you get braces without brushing."

"So we'll see how you're doing six months from now," the dentist said.

But he might as well have said "by two o'clock today," for all Cody understands time or finds it remotely useful.

"Girls don't like boys without teeth" is the one mantra that sticks with Cody. It's the one slogan he can repeat, even as he sneaks Gatorade and Skittles candy into the periodontist's office to snack on as he waits to get his gum disease checked.

WHAT HE loves, when he visits my house, is to work—to split wood, to haul it out of a pasture, to push a heavy manure cart around and around the yard, if there's nothing left to do that's productive. Will will dream up chores and pay Cody to do them, but that doesn't even matter—half the time Cody will leave the crumpled dollars on the kitchen table. And he loves to take apart and rewire our dusty old stereos and speakers, hooking up four, even eight, together. He somehow does it by instinct, branching wires off like veins—what's more, he does it right, although he could no more decipher a direction or diagram than I could, if he even had the patience we both lack. "Come on up and listen now," he'll holler down our staircase when he's finished a new configuration. "It'll blow out your mind." But he loves nothing more than playing with Matchbox cars outside in the dirt, carrying whole convoys outdoors, then leaving them out there until it rains, of course.

WHAT EVERYONE knows is that Cody always claims to have three girlfriends, their identities changing daily—and when I pick him up from camp, I do see they're after him.

But what I know is that he never remembers their names, and although they have their dramas, he's never kissed even one of them. "I know I don't want to be a father now," he says. Wise enough, since he is fourteen. I can tell he is repeating the words of a teacher or counselor, yet he sounds a bit flattered by the thought that he could be.

And what I know is that no one says no to him when it counts. At school, yes, and at Afterschool, and with hateful me on those days when he wants to go home sick to watch *The Simpsons Movie* but not to the doctor's office. But not at home. Not in the drug den of the trailer park when it's 8:30 at night, which is his curfew—and it shouldn't be even as late as six. He hears "no" only when he punches through yet another wall in rage, cracking the drywall or making a hole in a closet door; the expense of repair means they'll never be able to leave this rental trailer and crime-ridden trailer park. Otherwise, when it comes to no, he doesn't even stick around to hear it. "Cody," his mother will groan as the screen door slams behind him, "there are so many people trying to help you."

I know why she hardly ever says no to him—I can feel the weight of her undeserved guilt and hear the years of neighbors telling her to just beat some brains into that young'un, back before anyone knew or cared what ADHD was. And I can see how he's learned to wield that guilt too: When he has nothing, how can you deny him, how can you bear up under the rage he spouts, how can you let him hate you?

I CAN see the good path—a great path, even—for Cody, if he were dropped down in a middle-class, regular-neighborhood, rule-bound situation, where his mom didn't have to scrabble every day for the county bus or put off paying the light bill, where they had a kitchen with fuses that worked, where he couldn't just bulldoze through a single mom's guilt and exhaustion. In such a place he could learn to read, tell time, write on a calendar once and for all, then go on through the special-ed track of the high school and start stockpiling vocational skills—he loves to be useful, after all—then start working afternoons at the sheltered workshop, learn how to punch in and take breaks, and finally graduate and get a community job and job shadow, live in an adult group home and play Special Olympics volleyball and have a clean and decent life and save his money for the sheltered workshop cruises, and, and, and . . .

It's so easy to see all that when you come from my world, where every problem has a strategy and every need an agency application.

In his world, there's only luck and whatever catastrophe veers into view, popping up like hazards on a video game raceway.

WHAT I fear is the path that really awaits him, once he's old enough to drop out and freely roam. ("Just don't tell him it's his birthday," said his teacher, "you know he never learns it.") Even now, as a juvenile, friends set him up to break the window or steal the scrap metal or scope out the cars in the junkyards and always, always be the one to take the fall.

What I know is that any fix is only temporary in Cody's world.

And what I know is that if all teachers gave students one-tenth the attention and devotion that Cody's special-ed teachers and Afterschool counselors give him—working with him, buying him sneakers, cutting his hair, paying installments on his eighth-grade Disney World trip—those other kids would be in Harvard by ninth grade.

"Maybe," his mother says, "in high school, they won't be all over us about every little thing. In high school I don't think they're in everyone's business, the way they are here." And, with regret, I shudder to agree.

WHAT I know is that any fix in Cody's world isn't even a Band-Aid but mere scabbing over.

"Good news," his mom says, greeting me as I struggle to get the screen door to open. "His friend, Brick, that older man he runs with? He's in jail, and maybe Cody will stay home nights. I heard Brick might do fifteen years. Things are looking up, finally."

Somehow Brick's back out just a weekend later.

THIS YEAR two things seem to have made a dent—first, an amazing one-on-one worker who does counseling with Cody while playing basketball. The state keeps trying to cut community counselors, but somehow the agency keeps loopholing this one through.

And, second, the luckiest unlucky break of all—Cody stole ten dollars off his best friend, Dale, the same one who convinced Cody to steal construction scrap, which started a cascade of trouble. Cody stole ten dollars from Dale's bookbag in front of the teen's sister and then was jumped by the 7-11 parking lot kids, who ran him over with a bike and then beat the crap out of him.

Luckily, nothing was broken. Luckily, the threat of greater retaliation has done more to rein Cody in than all the exhortations, pleas, and juvenile officer's random checks combined.

WHAT EVERYONE knows is that for now there's some kind of protective charm around Cody and that he'll charm you back and make you glad to see him.

What I know is that his life hangs on luck—the barely missed crash, the right teacher, the wrong budget cut, the right meds, an adult friend who is—thank God—back in jail again instead of taking Cody on the bus again to buy pot behind Walgreen's —

That's what I know, and here's what I wish I didn't: that no matter how much I or anyone else might wish, pray, practice jump shots, prescribe, cajole, or yell, it all comes down to luck and chance, and you can't tell by looking just how long that luck will hold.

The Fast and the Furious, *or Other* Visions of Cody

Have you ever seen anyone like Cody Pomeray?

—Jack Kerouac, *Visions of Cody*

I SEE him crying, tears cascading down in frustration, his face crumbling. He's fourteen, then fifteen, and still the tears erupt, spontaneously and unashamed. He doesn't even think to hide his crying or stifle his gulping sobs. Today he stands behind a column in his white graduation shirt and slams his fist into the bricks. He's angry that he can't cut out and go home right now, as he knows so many other graduating eighth-graders will do. But this could be any day, and the reason for fury could be anything.

By tomorrow he'll be back to popping wheelies up and down his driveway, determined to flatten the superthick, indestructible inner tubes we've bought for his eight-dollar thrift store bike. "Hey, son, watch this," he'll call out to me, his one-time foster mom. He'll screech around, imitating a brake squeal, then race off down the dirt, past the empty slab where the haunted trailer used to sit, and rear back straight off the ground, front wheel to the sky.

"THERE'S JUNKIES," he'll say, "and then there's dirty junkies. Clean junkies change their needles. Dirty junkies use any needles they can find or steal. They pull over by the side of the road and shoot up in a van." He glares at the ground when he says this, and I'm sure he's seen someone do this firsthand.

BUT HE'LL also carry armfuls of toy cars, jeeps, and tanks outside, then lie on his stomach and line them up, or sit hunched over his knees and make car sounds and wheel them around for hours. This is as content as you'll ever see him, fourteen and running a Hot Wheels car around and around a dirt track beside the house or swinging it crazily to the sky.

This is going to be the complete Cody.

—*Visions of Cody*

"HOW DID you get tangled up in my life?" he'll still peer around and say to me.

Fifteen now, but unable to read a clock or calendar, he still knows too much time has passed—that it's been a year since he stayed with Will and me. Why haven't I disappeared already, with all my busy notions of what he should be doing and when? Why am I stuck to him like an unwanted shadow?

"Because you're so cool," I try to tell him, like the dorky adult I am. Because your mom doesn't have a phone or a car or daytime hours free for your appointments, and I do. Because what takes me twenty minutes would take her all evening otherwise, and she's already stuck riding the bus three hours a day so she can work seven-hour shifts with college student managers who write her up for taking a school nurse's phone call.

"Oh, right," he says. "Then can you take me to get a milkshake?"

Any normal teenager would ask me instead, "Why don't you get a life?"

FAKE IT till you make it is a lesson he has absorbed since birth. The faking, I understand—why should Cody say, "I can't read that, I've never done that, I just don't understand"? Then he might as well wear a visible target on the school bus or while weaving through the trailer park rows;

he might as well give up that dollar in his pocket than wait around for somebody to snatch it away. So, instead, Cody's reflexive answer to anything—from hiking up the Grand Canyon to having his tonsils out to landing a helicopter on the roof of an office building—is "Yeah, I did that, no big deal. It was boring."

He'll always answer with something definite, out of habit—saying, "Oh, Mom's out at the store" when she hasn't come home from work or she's dared to slip out to a friend's house on the next row. Or he'll claim his brother was a stunt driver for *The Fast and the Furious*, but the next day it was for *Gone in 60 Seconds*. He'll tell even doctors that he's a year older, a grade ahead—and how long till he tries to impress a cop that way? "Done it," he'll answer like a robot, no matter the subject. You could talk about your cousin going into labor—"Did it last year," he'll interrupt and turn the music up.

The faking it I get used to, although his teachers say to confront it. No, it's the making it part that worries me—will making it ever be part of the bargain? Really reading, for example?

HE'S BENDING the Brain Quest cards I keep in the pocket of the car door for Michael and Ryan to use during office waits. Picture questions are on one card and the answers are on the next. It's all held together by one white tack, and I picture it disintegrating in his hands, as so many solid objects do. "Give it to me," I say. "*Now*—you're going to break it."

"I just want to ask you some questions," he says, and I can't resist, of course.

He pretends to read what the card says: "How many weeks in a year?"

"Fifty-two."

"Wrong," he says, "it's seventy."

"No, it's fifty-two."

"Wrong—seventy. How many cards in a deck?"

"Fifty-two?" Surely these can't both be true.

"Right. Don't play fifty-two pickup—my uncle's girlfriend got me there."

"Okay," I say, "now give that game back." It'll be only a matter of seconds before he takes the whole stack apart and leaves it useless.

"Just one more question." He flips through a few more cards, which ask questions like which sport Ryan the Lion is playing, or how many balloons are clutched in his paw. "If Jesus had a son, what would his name be?"

"Jesus, Junior?"

"Right—high five. No, actually, Son of Satan." He hands the cards back, miraculously intact. "Okay, let's go now."

CAN I blame him for always wanting to be the one to know? For stringing things together his own way? When nothing in his life has ever been explained to him, much less made sense? From why all his teeth rotted when he was a baby to how the dead man he found in the closet could be revived to why his medication gets stolen to why a sex offender will soon move in and all the authorities that usually tell Cody what to do are powerless to stop it to why, even later, another man will blacken his eyes and throw him out of his own home? (Not that I can make any sense of this either—or of why his teacher could get nowhere when she tried to make reports.)

So of course he supplies his own answer to everything.

We're walking through the county recreation center, and I'm starting to explain the difference between the lap pool and the square, heated therapy pool, where my friend went to work on his shattered knee.

"The therapy pool," I say, "it's for—"

"—anger issues, I know," Cody says, dismissing me.

IF YOU don't mind being cussed in public, then Cody is the teen for you. If you don't mind it on playgrounds, in libraries, at Burger Kings, Walmart, or other family zones, so much the better. You have to not mind, you have to ignore, because he's learned it gets results.

And if you don't mind his pounding the ceiling of your car, punching your dashboard buttons, running your windshield-wiper fluid dry, blocking your automatic windows with a wrist, then Cody's for you too. If you don't mind a fifteen-year-old in size 18 pants and a rage to sag; if you don't mind watching scabs peeled ("Did you know that if you swallow your blood, it goes right back into your body?"); if you don't mind ruining someone's summer by being "a demon queen"; if you don't mind being told how to drive by someone who will never earn a license; if you don't mind hearing *Gone in 60 Seconds* and *The Fast and the Furious: Tokyo Drift* fifty times over on a car DVD player; if you don't mind being female, three-plus decades older, and routinely being called "son"; and if you don't mind making half a giant Bunny Bread loaf of peanut butter and Marshmallow Fluff sandwiches, then Cody is definitely the one.

Of course it's easier when you don't have to live with him.

His constant refrain: "I'm so fucking tired of getting blamed for breaking things. It's really starting to piss me off."

You might start to wonder if you should mind more, and what you'd even do if you did, but once you finally grasp that Love and Logic tricks don't compute for someone whose mind, rattled by trauma, can't hook a cause to a consequence, then you're probably back in the kitchen, making him just one more mallow whip sandwich to eat in the car on the way to the dentist.

Yes, I waited, to see if his mom's patience might give out. But after that first, voluntary placement with us, Cody never came into official foster care, much less became free for adoption.

Actually living with him, though, day to day, how crazy would I have become? How many times a day would I have pointed my finger, gotten in his face, torn closets apart, screamed? Would I have understood then why his mom lets him just curse her and bang out the screen door, while she murmurs an unheard curfew to save face?

Given all my own challenges and deep flaws in dealing with teens that I've discovered in the interim, it was a preposterously smug and comfortable fantasy to imagine that we might have adopted Cody and given him the very ordinary life he deserved—a life with all the speakers, wires, and Matchbox cars he desired; a life without what actually was soon to follow—the jail, cigarettes, alcohol, beatings, babies, the walking along the highway with the day's new best friend, and all the rest I didn't see. It was easy to believe I could have fixed so much, and so calmly, as long as it was all in daydream theory. How arrogant to think I could even have postponed these things.

My biggest real-life mistake with Cody, I've come to see, was not that I got him the summer landscaping job I thought he'd love but then had to bully him to go to—a job he would have done fine with, had he actually taken his daily medication. No, my mistake was doing all that paperwork, and all that legwork, to get him approved for disability payments, with a monthly check coming in. The very thing that was meant to bring relief to his mom and provide for his needs—to buy him a belt and a pair of pants that would fit and to help with his part of the rent—instead became a permanent shackle for him. Mom's new boyfriend after new boyfriend might throw Cody out, but now, with that monthly free money attached, would never release him.

"BE HERE Now": Hasn't everyone from Baba Ram Dass to Dr. Oz to the trauma-informed school counselors espoused this?

Who could be more in the eternal Now than Cody? The place that we all aspired to be back in the 1970s. Maybe the prototype was Kerouac's Cassady-Dean-Cody, the embodiment of impulse, but is this redneck teen Cody all that different? So rooted in the Now that he can't tell you where he's just been or what's coming next? Being the beatific, speed-talking, forever gone Cody looks a lot prettier on the page than it does in practice. It's nice for a literary figure but in real life pretty damn inconvenient.

BACK IN eleventh grade, I envied Kerouac's Cody. Back when sleep deprivation and instant coffee were my drugs, inducing shakes and urgency, I longed to silence the ever-present narration of my thoughts, longed to pierce reality's veil without the potential nightmare of LSD, to lose myself in the hypnotic depths of *Siddhartha* and *Steppenwolf,* and to see the sky split open on whatever mythical midnight of the Jewish year that happens; I marveled at my Camel-smoking friends whose crypto-cynical Zen mutterings spilled from their lips. It was the '70s, after all, and Kerouac's Cody was finally edging into the mainstream, coming into his own. Cultivating insomnia, I'd stay up all night rereading the library's paperback *On the Road*, with its glowing orange ball of western sun. I'd try to picture that wild American dawn breaking outside my own yellow curtains, to the sound of clashing trash cans as the county garbage trucks thundered up to the curb.

I felt myself pulled after the fictional Dean/Cody/Neal, just as Sal Paradise did, knowing myself to be the dull overthinker, like Sal, awed by the all-night talk and the go-go-go, the girls, the highway unscrolling west, and the dream of the electric night ahead. I tore through the rest of Kerouac, name-dropping titles to my friends, who named their dogs Japhy, Ryder, and Cody in tribute; finally sobering up with *Visions of Cody*, which stripped the golden glow from it all and cast a harsh, buzzing fluorescent light down on boyhood nights spent on crazy-springed cots in the missions and the alleys, dumpsters, curbs, and rest stops that were also part of the rough road life; all shocking to me then, but closer to the jagged spirit and suffering of this teenage Cody I know here, now, today.

EVEN THE jaded libertarian Medicaid dentist loves Cody Price, and the hygienist brings him bags of still-good jeans and sweatshirts from her own grown son. They know this real-life Cody as well as anybody, after the dozen dental visits to which he's been eager to go, hoping to be able to chew real food again. He's not a picky eater, but if he sees something crunchy or chewy—steak, bread sticks, Doritos—he turns away from it in pain. "You're doing great there, pardner," the dentist will tell him. "You've come a real long way," although Cody still has to squeeze my fingers with his own glue-crusted hand when he gets a shot of novocaine.

"Now if you'd just brush your teeth, you wouldn't have to come here so often," the dentist tells him. "You wouldn't need all these shots and fillings."

"It's okay," Cody will say with a shrug. "I've had worse—much worse—done. I've knocked all my own teeth out, twice."

But they've saved him, the dentist tells us, from losing all his teeth at age twenty, and for once, outside his own mind, Cody is someone's success story.

CODY WON'T brush his teeth except at school, but he loves mouthwash—the harsher the better—even the dreaded Peridex. He'll toast you with a cup of Listerine in his hand; he keeps stealing supersized bottles from home and carrying them in his bookbag, which gets him in trouble at school for suspected drinking—of Listerine itself, if not as a cover for something else.

As for flossing, which the hygienist teaches him every time—to Cody that means flossing on the way to the dentist, and in the waiting room, a practice that quickly deteriorates to chewing and ripping more floss off the roll, until he's chomping a golf ball–sized wad of cinnamon-flavored floss like gum.

> There are some young men you look at who seem completely safe, maybe just because of a Scandinavian ski sweater, angelic, saved; on a Cody Pomeray it immediately becomes a dirty stolen sweater worn in wild sweats.
>
> —*Visions of Cody*

CODY'S HELL on clothes—if he's not tearing them up in skateboard accidents, he's staining them with substances you never even see. Food leaps off the plate when Cody's near, and ketchup spurts from the bottle, permanently smearing his shirts. His hands, too, are always filthy, stained dark with industrial glue, vacant lot dirt, and motor oil that survives any washing you can talk him into.

Dirt aside, he cares about his image, and he'll spray himself head to foot with Axe deodorant until everyone around him chokes. He loves enormous, gold-embossed South Pole T-shirts, and somehow he keeps finding pants two sizes too large, which his teacher pleads with his mother to just throw out: new belts vanish within a day, and the choke collars he hangs off the empty belt loops sag his jeans down further still. His backward caps are crushed and bent from being slept in, but he can always find one, unlike any other accessory. Every T-shirt must have an always unraveling wife-beater tank showing beneath it; his favorite shoes are hightop zip-ups patterned like bowling shoes—they once pumped up but now peel tricolored vinyl. Like the jeans, these shoes are two sizes too large since he's taken them from his mostly-absent older brother, Logan.

Buy Cody new school shoes and he'll spend twenty minutes changing the fat laces and getting them to sit just right; then he'll love them so much that he'll wear them all night and then off to work on cars with his cousin, and you'll never see them again in school condition, just scuffs and shreds, the rubber toe shields gaping open. "One day," his mother begs him. "Just keep those shoes nice for one day of school, just for the first day, please, couldn't you?"

> The only people for me are the mad ones, the ones who are mad to live, mad to talk, mad to be saved, desirous of everything at the same time, the ones who never yawn or say a commonplace thing, but burn, burn, burn, like fabulous yellow roman candles exploding like spiders across the stars and in the middle you see the blue centerlight pop and everybody goes "Awww!"
>
> —Kerouac, *On the Road*

CODY'S MOM brings me along to his monthly school conferences—really, so she'll have a ride to work afterward but also, my vanity suggests, as advocate, buffer, and interpreter. At Cody's school, though, a family advocate hardly seems needed—the teachers are so often the ones advocating with the parents on behalf of the kids, begging Mom or Dad to sign homework folders and come to meetings at any time of day that might suit them. The teachers round up Christmas help before they're even asked, slip Chef Boyardee cans into kids' bookbags, and buy sneakers for kids who wear last year's snow boots in gym class. Cody's mom appreciates their help with Christmas—most other school interventions, though, are just nosy people being "all up in your business." And "when," she asks, "are these meetings going to end?"

We meet once a month in the guidance counselor's blue cement-block office, or sometimes in the classroom, scooting metal desks into a cluster. Even though I teach, my students are at the local university, so I'm as lost as any novice parent here in the world of the individualized education plan (IEP), with its profusion of unexplained acronyms and relentless focus on the physical, concrete, and measurable. At first I mistakenly took *exceptional children* to mean *gifted and talented*, then learned it's possible to be both—you just have to memorize the meanings of terms, I've realized, since the words themselves don't tell you.

I'm in awe of these special education teachers and staff, not only for their deft control but also for their generous hours; I'm in awe of the teachers' ability to talk the learning theory talk yet still cheerfully corral these kids into compliance in a way that Cody's mom and I never manage. The teachers want Cody telling time by half-hours by March, whereas I would be happy if he'd simply put on a swimsuit, even if he just stands beside the water, when I drive him over to the county pool on Special Olympics practice days.

Still, these meetings are a welcome change for me from the university world of excruciating abstraction, for dealing with Cody means dwelling in the world of the immediate, feeling the brunt of the physical, and marveling at the connections he makes. Actual connections, much of the time, with actual electricity, as he dissects and reconfigures the Swap Shop appliances I bring back for him. And while he can't decipher a traditional clock face, he can identify more makes and models of cars as we drive down the road than I could bird species—what's more, he's mystified that everyone doesn't know them. When I say that, he thinks I'm pretending.

WHEN HE first stayed with us, I realized how reflexive Cody's lies were: "Oh, I can't go to bed now. Your husband wants me to come upstairs and connect his internet to Carcrash.com." Or, caught smoking in the bathroom: "My mom *gave* me these cigarettes, to calm me down while she's gone."

After a day I could tell the tall tales from the lies—they are related but distinct, like eastern and western blue jays. There are lies—the claims that keep him out of trouble—and then there are tall tales—"Been there, done that, son" . . . "I flipped that car down the hill ten times"—that give him a place in the game. A two-digit math sum might take him forever, yet the logic of a plausible lie can instantly flash through his mind. People have grown rich on less.

HERE'S AN example of a typical, effort-saving lie when he doesn't want to wait.

We're walking through some kind of safety fair at the mall, and I want to stop and get his mom a free smoke detector. Naturally, there's paperwork involved, and Cody's impatient.

CODY: Nah, we don't need one. We got one, we're good.

DEBORAH: But I've seen your smoke alarm, Cody [or rather, I've seen its ripped-out mounting and wires reaching out from the wall, something Cody probably did]. If a candle falls over, your place would go up. That's how trailers are.

CODY: We don't never burn candles.

DEBORAH: There's candles lit every time I go in—your mom loves candles [after being on her feet all day, who could blame her for wanting a little relaxation—and with few working electrical outlets, you see just the glow of the TV screen, lava lamp, and pillar candles if you go in after dusk]. If one gets knocked over—?

"We-don't-never-burn-candles." Cody pounds the display table, inches from the woman with the volunteer fire department's auxiliary.

That's the downside of "you can't tell by looking at him"—"What fifteen-year-old would do this?" the volunteer must think. Or, more obviously, "What kind of adult would let him?" Trying to save face, I lean down and squint at the papers, shaking ink into my pen, as he strides off toward the Game Village to steal something.

> These are the pitiful few dreams of Cody I have—is that all?
>
> —*Visions of Cody*

MY OWN adrenaline surges as I simply look at the walls of his room—when it *is* his room and not taken over by his randomly returning brother—which are full of fist-sized holes.

Says his mother, "Here's the difference between my two sons: Logan's first sentence was 'It's hot.' Cody's was 'Mom, it's broken.'"

"Oh, I could tell you stories," his mom says. "Four years old and that young'un set my *makeup* on fire."

Medication is a challenge, to say the least—getting it; keeping it when their front door won't latch and they live at Ground Zero for pill sales; and picking up monthly prescription slips in person as government regulations require—those prescription slips alone are worth money in themselves. But Cody's own apathy about taking meds is the biggest challenge—he likes the way he is and the way he feels, as distressed as this can make him.

"'This is your antidemon vitamin,'" Cody says the doctor told him, promising peaceful sleep when he finally got an emergency appointment after a three-month wait. "'So take it every day.'"

"He's a whole different kid," the teacher says a mere afternoon later.

ALL OF a sudden it's like that hard teen mask has crumbled away, and the child face has hatched out beneath. Cody has slowed way down—to normal speed, that is—and I hear no lies or cursing, no pounding on walls or car. He watches TV now, which might seem an unlikely triumph. He sleeps. It's like he's back to the real kid he probably never was, instead of chattering around like a wind-up beetle.

But then, four days later: "No fucking way I'm taking it."

Because the night medication makes Cody too tired to go out and get in trouble, his mom tells me, and by six in the evening, he's pretty much ready to pack it in and go to bed.

To her, that sounds ideal, but to him—

"You just have to get used to it," I plead with Cody and his mother. "After all this time we've waited for the doctor, you've got to give it a try."

We, I say, like I'm not just the driver—like anyone cares what I think, like I have any actual say in this.

SO, YES, I've become Nurse Ratched, preferring the dialed-down version of Cody to the real, roaring one. But a powerless Nurse Ratched, even so, left begging his own mother to just *make* him take the meds. But if she won't make him wear a belt with oversized jeans or wash his dirty hands when he resists, what are the chances? My throat stings with angry, swallowed, exhausted tears: how stupid to think that a whole summer of driving him around to dull appointments, trying to get him moved up on the doctor's waiting list, and placating Cody with milkshakes might have given me some right to insist? When all that was by my hopeful choice, and I'm not even the one who has to live with this?

And why am I so uselessly sold on medication? Not just to forestall juvenile delinquency and its certain results but in sincere hope that Cody might now pass his nights without seeing bathroom mirror faces with their eyes turned white, then red. He told me about those one day at the dental clinic, alarming the kid across from us whose mother cradled his ears, as if her own pierced chin wasn't scary.

CODY'S UNDEAD entourage, though, isn't always eerie, but sometimes, like all adult women, simply inconvenient and bitchy. About his uncle's old girlfriend—

CODY: She looks like a hooker.

DEBORAH: You don't say that about anyone, not about any woman—

CODY: Oh, she's passed away.

DEBORAH: Well, you especially don't say bad things about people that have passed away.

CODY: Well, not totally passed away.

DEBORAH: Huh?

CODY: Her spirit's still around. You drop a glass of milk, she'll smack you.

STILL, AT night, his zombies are real and vicious. Isn't Cody's real life hard enough? Must even the spirit world torment him?

SO THAT'S the end of medication, outside of school, at least. "Felt like I broke my butt for a week and a half," Cody says. I'm unashamedly angry, as if it's my place to be anything: Would it really be so bad for Cody to turn into a zombie himself every evening until he's, say, nineteen? To sleep in a haze in front of the TV, instead of wandering the trailer park, loitering behind the bowling alley, or drinking the neighbor's vodka and committing ever worse acts of vandalism?

Would it kill him to sleep through a night, at least?

SO IS he all that different from Kerouac's real Cody—the on-the-road, premedication-era archetype? Is this Cody not equally in the moment, of the moment? Not equally mad with desire to be driving down a mountain road at 200 miles an hour, accosted by girls whose names he never recalls, fevered with passions and urgent needs—like for a cherry slushie—before the world ends around him? Would either Cody see a rocky, muddy, near-sheer bluff without swerving in order to ride a bike straight off the edge and celebrate his wounds at the bottom?

Between this Cody and that one, would a few dozen IQ points and milligrams of chemistry really make that much difference?

BUT ALL that came after.

Now the before. As he lingers all summer on a waiting list, living at home but spending a week of daytimes with me before the start of adventure camp and half-days of community service, as well as staying with me on Fridays when there is no camp. This was my idea, but his mother seemed relieved: her work schedule can't change, so anything that makes it harder for Cody to set another mattress on fire in the weeds or otherwise draw the cops' or rental company's attention has got to make life easier for her.

So Cody's stuck with these tiresome days with me and my delusions that I can improve him, or at least allow him some peace, between his watching reruns of *The Simpsons Movie* and moving wheelbarrows of rocks and logs around the yard. It's not a chore or even helpful—he just finds it relaxing to push heavy stuff around. If he'd ever heard of the myth of Sisyphus, he'd think what Sisyphus was going through was a privilege and not punishment.

There is no one else for him to stay with, anyway; his father is out of the picture. "Got it," the school staff says if you so much as twitch an eyebrow when the blank for father appears on paper. "Gotcha—out of the picture." There's probably even a special acronym for these dads—OTP—that covers a multitude of sins. Actual sins, not figurative ones.

Cody's content enough to spend his mother's workdays with me, during my great stretch of summer freedom from the university when I'm supposed to be productive and not frittering my days away in free babysitting and trying to finagle ways to see Michael and Ryan. Maybe it's my form of procrastination, yet I can't help feeling that each hour Cody spends with us somehow melts an hour of stress off him. Or at least confirms that he is worth someone's time, but that's probably just my own projection—it probably would never dawn on him that he wasn't worth the world. Or, as the social workers say to frustrated foster parents, "at least you're showing the kids there's another way to live." And they don't mean the middle-class way, although that's how it sounds. They just mean a way where people sleep with the TV off, expect to hear the basic truth from each other, don't get high in front of their kids—or with them—and don't scream at each other all the time. Although I'm too often failing at the last one.

But at night, once we pick his mom up from her nursing home job and I take them back home, Cody's first words are "I'm going out, Mom." He pushes past the screen door and vanishes for hours.

I watched him all day for this? I fume in tongue-biting silence, itching to give his mother some of my stubborn resolve, but how could I, really? I don't have her load of guilt for working and leaving him with her mom as a toddler, then more guilt for living too long with his dad's abuse. Guilt that now weighs down and shrinks her to calling out the door, "Don't forget about your curfew, okay?" although what kind of curfew is 11 p.m.? And Cody couldn't read a watch if he had one, or even *keep* one for an hour—the best he can do with a watch is to pry the back off to watch the tiny gears work.

For the moment I manage to mind my own business. Because who even asked me?

DURING THE days I'll let Cody get mad and bloody his own fist on bricks; I'll take him to see donkeys and eat fries, and I'll print out the million-page state drivers' manual in the hope it will inspire him to read. "Start by memorizing the road signs," I suggest. "Hell, I already know what they mean," he says, but what he knows is always things like "stripes ahead."

He's with us for weeks, as it turns out, and I can never stop paying attention. God only knows what will break, explode, get dismantled, or disappear if I do.

> Cody is the brother I lost; he's the brother I had, too.
>
> —*Visions of Cody*

HE DOES seem to feel better when his adult brother, Logan, returns home: Logan can make Cody stay in nights and owns larger saggy jeans that Cody borrows and hides from his mother. I also suspect that Logan scares off the zombies lurking in the mirror and closets. Logan was the smart one, his mother says, who tested off the scale but just got too bored to stay in school. Usually, though, he lives in another town, and when he appears, it's with a new girlfriend who fights with an old one, runs up the light bill, dirties dishes, takes Cody's bed, and, worse, brings three dogs, which leads to fines from the otherwise unreachable landlord, further delaying when Risa can catch up on the rent and ask again for the kitchen fuses to be fixed.

I've seen a blue bandanna, folded flat and ready to be tied around Logan's head. Maybe I've heard too many secondhand versions of school lectures to kids about gangs, but I wouldn't be surprised to hear him claim to be a gang member, even in this mountain town. Cody believes it. Sheriff cars regularly cruise this trailer park, and sometimes the deputies have men lined up and sitting on the ground by the road, hands locked behind their heads. Really, though, gangs here, in the dull Appalachian wonderland?

Also, Logan's had fights with some of the Mexican men in the trailer park, and I wouldn't begin to ask about those confrontations. "Oh, he ain't a racist," Cody says in defense of Logan. "He barely likes white people—and he is one. He just don't like *people,* is Logan's problem."

THE ESSENCE of the summer: We've been to the library and are going home with the limit of five DVDs and two portable DVD players. Car trips are one way of slipping in educational shows kids would never watch at my house, where they can watch cable. In the backseat Michael and Ryan are watching *Bill Nye, the Science Guy* on evolution, while Cody's up front, watching a film based on completely different beliefs: *Another Creation Ark Adventure,* which purports to show how dinosaurs and people coexisted. It's a direct creationist rip-off of the cool Bill Nye features, combined with Indiana Jones graphics and the word *ark* thrown in for good measure, which is what made Cody pick it.

"Animals just don't change that much!" the narrator proclaims. "There is no record of one kind of animal turning into another kind of animal—it *just can't happen!*"

And that's just what I'm afraid of, where Cody's concerned, despite everyone's best efforts to jump-start his transformation.

Cody's going home, going home.

—*Visions of Cody*

WHEN CODY is not out where he shouldn't be, the comfort zone is where this Cody prefers to dwell, held by the gravitational pull of his dim living room, smoky couch, blankets, game controllers, and the glow of an oversized TV screen that gets only a few distorted colors. More than he fears zombies, Cody fears the demanding, draining world outside his door. Haircuts, Special Olympics, and school disturb, of course, but so does everything fun that a week earlier he said he wants to try—car shows, the Marshall Tucker Band, county fair rides, birthday parties—it's always "Ah, yeah, thanks, I mean, I *did* want to go, I did say get me a ticket, but I got plans now, not today—"

Plans to roost in the curtained living room and doze the day away. . . . It takes a whole strategy meeting at school and then practically kidnapping him for the celebratory eighth-grade Disney World trip for which his teacher and I and the school's scholarship fund have paid $700 in installments, with his beloved assistant teacher even going along for Cody's sake. Once he's there, he loves it, the teacher says.

And he's enrolled in Mission: Explore, with its soul-building Saturday outings and rock-face challenges that most other boys would kill for. So far he has yet to go on a single day trip. Community service—picking up bottles from the park—he does without complaint but to go on an all-day bike trip or cave crawl? *No fuckin' way.*

His teacher tries to encourage him to go on the next Mission: Explore backpacking trip, telling him he'll learn to start fires with rocks, dry grass, and sticks.

"I do that now," he says.

And, for once, I believe him.

PISSED THAT it's Labor Day and Special Olympics hasn't canceled swimming practice, Cody's pounding the roof of my car through the window; then he gets out and protests by trying to lift it by the open door frame and rocking it—"God, that won't fucking hurt this car." (The same words he says when he puts his hand on the emergency brake and begs to try *The Fast and the Furious: Tokyo Drift*. "Don't you want to see Subaru Drift?" he always offers.)

Whatever meds he will or won't take, there's no pill for defiance, the doctor always reminds us. "It might just be the hard way that you learn," Cody's mom tells him. "Might very easily be the hard way." Which can mean only one thing, at this point. My other kids aren't sure if juvie, or "kid jail," is real or just something Cody has dreamed up to scare them.

"Oh, it's more than real," Cody's mom tells me: it's Reynolds Camp, down in the humid flatlands. In fact, Cody's former best-friend-till-Cody-stole-ten-dollars-off-his-dresser is already in his seventh week there.

It's dusk and Cody shoves the broken storm door, no doubt going to seek Brick, the adult pal responsible for the empty vodka bottle that adorns the top of Cody's broken bedroom TV.

A hard sidewalk's looming up below, and there's not that far for Cody to fall.

> I not only accept loss forever, I am made of loss—I am made of Cody, too.
>
> —*Visions of Cody*

RISA AND I go to a workshop that dangles the key to solving severe defiance. If medication and the threat of Reynolds Camp can't do it, maybe some new mantras will. It's hard to believe, but Jude, the legendary trainer, promises that 90 percent of changing behavior is "catching them doing it right." No matter what—anything—"strong sitting"; "I like how you crunch those potato chips"; "Awesome—you waited to start speaking until I was done." Nothing is too inane, apparently—just catch them doing it right, Jude swears. Although you're supposed to say *strong,* instead of *good,* since they want to be bad.

"And no sarcasm," she adds, which is pretty hard to pull off. You can believe this works for Jude—she has those ex-Marine assistant principal eyes that cut you short, and that math teacher saunter that makes you think she's going to glance down at your feeble notes. When she puts her hand on your shoulder and says, "Interesting," you wonder what you've done wrong. It's no wonder kids obey when she tells them to fold a pile of dish towels.

So I try this, his mom tries it, glad no one else is around to hear these crazy affirmations. "Great job fastening your seat belt, Cody—I could hear it click and I never even asked you!" "Strong tying your shoelaces—I like how you knot them at the holes." The amazing thing is that Cody doesn't find it at all odd to be commended on minutiae. He agrees—he is indeed awesome. He loves to get a high five for these things and will smack your hand so hard it stings to the middle of next week.

I EVEN hear his guidance counselor grasping for positive straws as I do but with professional grace. "South Pole?" Miss Leila asks as she invites him in from the hallway, trying to make conversation about his T-shirt. "Cool—is that about Christmas?"

Cody doesn't get it, as he probably has never thought about where the South Pole is, or the North Pole either, beyond being home to Santa. But he's crazy about the South Pole clothing label, as are all the other males in his grade. His assistant teacher knows this and buys armloads of these clothes for him from JCPenney's, out of her own school system paycheck.

AND THANK God as well for the few state-allotted hours Cody gets with his basketball-playing community counselor, Blaine, who knows how to make anger management and crucial messages (respect, homework, cutting out the cussing) somehow subliminal. And it's not just that Blaine is a male and can skateboard and free throw that make him an instant authority in Cody's eyes.

"Blaine," Cody says, "yeah, Blaine's cool. He doesn't have as many rules as you. [Blaine's whole job, of course, is to instill some rules.] Hey, me and Blaine, we were driving 110 miles an hour down this road the other day. You don't need to go so slow."

But then the state's or region's priorities shift and the program that employed Blaine and others like him is gone abruptly.

FORGET THE romance, forget the Beat ideals. Cody may be their millennial embodiment, but the goal with this Cody is to get him out of the celebrated Here and Now. To think back, to think ahead, to be jolted from the sound and fury of the moment and into a time line of past and future, cause and effect, act and consequence. For Cody to live inside of time, rooted to the linear, freed from the endless Now.

THE THINGS Cody does know surprise me: that Zippies are things you can run through strands of hair to fill it with color streaks; that he doesn't want to become a father yet; that there is something different and wrong with him but not remotely as different and wrong as the people he constantly gets grouped with. He can see for himself that he doesn't have Down syndrome, just as he can see that he can fix car engines and jump a bike over a picnic table. So why, he must wonder, do none of us, the people so bent on making all his decisions for him, seem to grasp that difference?

MY VISIONS of Cody flash up in frames, like one of his scratched DVDs, freezing in one shot, then jerking to some future scene:

—Running a Matchbox car around a Hot Wheels track, then leaping it over a line of tanks and trucks.

—While helping clean out the foster families' clothing resource room, finding a football helmet and wearing it all night as he totes bags and boxes, then sits on the stairs, hunched over my portable DVD player, watching *The Fast and the Furious 3* for the twentieth time, looking like Atom Ant.

—Hanging out with me at work on quiet summer days, watching Carcrash.com's "funny" crash videos in my husband's office while I type up requisition forms and schedules for the coming year. Still, Cody calls me over every three minutes:

"Hey . . . hey, what's your name—come in here and look at this one."

"Deborah," I say.

"Yeah, I know," Cody says, "I just forgot. But look at this one here, it rocks—"

There's every kind of crash category you could imagine—fiery, funny, under tractor-trailer—I'm surprised there's not one for "fatal," although maybe I just don't want to look that far.

—"I've lost my voice," I tell him one morning as he gets into my car, suspicious about where I'm spiriting him today. "I've lost my voice," I say, "I can't talk."

"Then sing—just sing to me," he says encouragingly.

—And in the front row of a nearly empty movie theater, we're watching *Kung Fu Panda 2,* blasted by air conditioning meant to keep a crowd cool. I keep turning to see a rare and continuous grin on Cody's face, where it's tipped back in the reflected cartoon light beneath his cap.

Kung Fu Panda 2 he likes, and *The Fast and the Furious 4*, of course, but the new *Harry Potter*?

Uh-uh.

"Why not?" I prompt, "too scary?" I'm thinking sympathetically of the white snake face of Voldemort, wondering if he looks like Cody's closet zombies.

"Agh, too geeky," Cody corrects me—"those glasses?"

This from someone who refuses to get a haircut but has straightened his bangs with his mom's curling iron so they jut straight out from his forehead.

ONE OF those summer days at my office, when college prep programs take over the otherwise deserted college building, is a day Cody can't forget. We're out in the hall, on a brief break from Cody's YouTube crash video binges, and he's helping me pick staples out of a bulletin board, when a college prep class troops past. It takes a minute to realize what's off: their line is made up of basic high school boys and girls in drag—smock tops and shorts, bad makeup and circles of blush patched over five o'clock shadow, broad shoulders coming out of tube tops; then a girl in drooping jeans, unmistakably Cody's female double, her jeans sagged and boxers and butt crack showing; another guy dressed up like an office worker in a shiny dotted dress. An entire class worth of cross-dressed teens—some teacher's idea of consciousness raising—and they're entirely silent as they proceed down the hall and stairs and out onto the sidewalk. No hint of giggling.

I try to think of something wise and enlightened to say, but the right words elude me. Not that he'd listen anyway.

Of all the boundaries he sees crossed in his daily life, this is the one he fixates on, and it becomes the memory of our shared time that Cody refers to most often. "Why did they *do* that?" he asks each time he remembers.

EIGHT MONTHS later we're driving through the college and Cody sees a group of parents and teens strung out along the sidewalk. "What's that?" he asks suspiciously, and I chirp, "Oh, just high school seniors on a college tour. They want to see what it's like here." But I can feel his unhappy silence building. "Well, look," I say, "they're all wearing their own clothes. Nobody's switched."

"Oh, good." He sighs and says, "Son, that was just *wrong.*"

My colleagues would rip me for not having a corrective comeback. But for Cody too much else is wrong and I still don't have an answer.

DESPITE HIS own love of scabs and wrecks, when six-year-old Michael gets a bloody nose from falling off his scooter at the park, Cody snaps into emergency mode and pumps his bike double time over to the restroom. We're sitting on the grass, the bottom of my T-shirt to Michael's nose, as Cody races up on his bike and hops off to kneel on the grass, offering up handfuls of wet towels. The crazy thing is, he keeps calling Michael by my own, almost outgrown, pet name for him.

"Don't cry, little bunny, it'll be okay in just a minute," Cody says to comfort Michael as he presses dripping paper towels to staunch the blood and screaming.

AND THEN in Walmart, one frenetic afternoon, he knows the lost boy. We come through the register line, and Cody sees him sitting on the plastic seats up front with the lady who's found him—Cody knows the boy from his class at school and sees right away that this woman's not his mom. She has her arm around the boy, her glossy manicure patting his shoulder. "Man, that's Jimmy Knox," Cody says and makes a beeline over to him.

"We'll find your mom, honey," the woman is saying. "She'll be right here to get you. Can you just tell me what your name is?"

"Cody knows him," I tell her as the crying boy's glasses slip down his nose, and the woman tells us that she used to be an elementary school teacher. When Cody tells her the boy's name, she goes off to find the manager, then comes back, and says, "We'll wait with you, honey."

Cody has his arm around the boy's other side, saying, "Hey, don't worry," and I wonder where the Cody who punches walls and hourly threatens to fuckin' break his teacher's face has gone. But the lost boy keeps staring down, nose dripping.

We hear the lost child announcement—*Attention, shoppers*—coming over the speakers. We're late to pick up Cody's mother, but I know she'll wait and be proud her son tried to take care of this kid.

Then Jimmy's mom materializes in a black T-shirt; she has Brillo-stiff copper hair and a sister in fraying braids and flip-flops. She yanks the boy up by the elbow—"I told you to meet me in Crafts—that means *yarn*"—and drags him back through the register line to her cart. She doesn't look at the rest of us.

"See ya, Jimmy," Cody calls.

Jimmy's made his mom look bad, probably for the hundredth time, I try to think charitably. But clearly she wasn't even searching for him.

The kind ex-teacher gives me a look as we get up to go. "His mom didn't even say thank you," she says, twice.

For all Cody's troubles and trampled boundaries, at least for now there's tangible love at home. I remember the first time Cody came to stay with me and how Cody and his mother huddled together weeping when it was time for Risa to leave. And I've seen them flopped out on the couch, their heads leaned in together, his mom dozing off after work, as *Friday the 13th* plays on the TV. In two years a new boyfriend will arrive and pound a wedge between mother and son—and between them and everybody else.

As we're leaving the store, walking past the gum machines, Cody repeats the teacher's words: "Jimmy's mom didn't even say thank you."

"WORD OF the day," Cody tells me, is "Don't Ask."

There's a big notch on the left side of his bangs.

And, "I fell asleep four times today—first in silent lunch—don't ask"—and "I'll probably go to sleep in the water" if I take him to Special Olympics swimming practice instead of driving him straight home.

I've never known anyone to fall asleep when they're swimming, I tell him.

"Oh, yeah," he insists reflexively, "I've done it before. One night I slept the whole night in a bathtub and when I woke up, my fingers were like, you know—"

This weekly Special Olympics swim practice is another stalemate in the battle of his inertia versus my stubborn desire that he succeed at something. For at the annual spring competition, practice or not, Cody always wins all the gold medals. Just think how far he'd get if he actually practiced, traveled to regionals, or even simply blew off that much steam. About one practice in four, he'll get in the pool after ten minutes of watching and blow everyone away with some record-setting lap, and then the next week nothing. He wonders why we keep trying to shunt him into Special Olympics when he can see for himself that he could be the captain of the high school football team. So I offer to take him to football practice too—at his high school, he could join the team tomorrow.

OUR DEAL is that if he actually participates in swim practice three times, he can quit. Sitting and watching doesn't count. There are incentives—cones of frozen yogurt for the Wednesdays when he actually swims—but we've come to this pool six times, and I'm still waiting for him to swim the third time, if only so it can all be over for me and I'll have kept my word, however pointlessly. But the more the coaches try to tempt Cody with the promise of travel to state meets and medals, the scarier it seems to become for him. The coaches must think I'm crazy to put us both through this—swimming practice is a highlight of the week for these other disabled kids, and they're all just dying to be here.

CODY AND I are sitting on the bench in the lobby because he won't practice today, and I won't leave until practice is over, our usual standoff. (Way too much Love and Logic on my part, I see with years of hindsight, now that I've learned more about trauma and all its indirect effects; in being so determined to rouse Cody from his tightly circumscribed comfort zone and my hunger for him to feel success, I must have triggered so much pain and panic.) I'm listening to the coaches in the pool lobby and ignoring his requests to "go sit in the goddamn car." "It takes a village to put on a swim cap," one coach says, as she and another teacher try to stuff her daughter's long hair into a cap without causing a severe headache.

I keep hearing them talk about "our kids" and wonder if they mean the kids here today or in their school's special education program, but then one starts to describe a camp that was a great success for someone. "The camp's at a college," the coach explains, "but it's all our kids." It finally dawns on me that they don't mean their own particular team, but that "our kids" means all kids with disabilities, as if they've herded them under a big, bright, sheltering umbrella. But I don't have much chance to get sentimental in this chlorine-funked air.

"Jesus fucking Christ," Cody says, "it's practically over. Can't we just leave now?"

FLASH-FORWARD TO eighth-grade graduation again, back before the tears explode. "You'll be so proud of how he looks up there," Cody's teacher brags to his mom. Cody is wearing a white collared shirt with a grimy macrame necklace underneath, black pants, shiny gray belt, the usual bowling shoe sneakers. We wouldn't let him so much as try this outfit on, or even see it before this morning, out of fear these clothes would spontaneously unravel. He does indeed look great, but somehow smaller than ever from our perch up on the bleachers.

Standing in line, then making his quick walk around the gym floor, he's a speck through the eye of my crummy camera. He looks up at us, embarrassed as we wave when he takes his cardboard diploma tube. He stands frozen as he allows the guidance counselors to hug him. The flash of triumph that his mom, teachers, Afterschool counselor, my husband, and I all feel—that same surge of triumph he's supposed to feel—is lost on Cody, although he's heard rumors of graduation cards with money.

AFTERWARD, MOST graduates are cutting out for home with their parents, but Cody's Afterschool program has planned a cookout to celebrate the three graduating middle-schoolers, including Cody. He just has to get through two more hours to the end of school. "We've got a fun day planned," his teacher told me, knowing, as I do, that Cody will be raging to leave.

If he's furiously sad enough, he's sure his mom will make me give in.

My stubbornness rises up again to meet his: I don't know then that eighth-grade graduation will be the pinnacle of his academic success, as he will indeed go on to drop out of high school the moment he is able, but I do know they've planned this cookout to celebrate him, and I want him to feel what an end point is. If I even were to take him home and come back to pick him up for the cookout later, I know he'd be long vanished, so staying at school is the only option. I can see his mom is wavering. I can feel how ridiculously wrong she thinks I am, how much she can't bear his stormy unhappiness, but this time I'm bulldozing over everything: "Sorry, it's my car, Cody, and I'm not taking you in it." Let him be mad at me, let them both be mad at me and my middle-class maneuvering, let him rage that I've ruined his entire summer already. He'll be over it once he gets to the cookout—one of the few blessings of ADHD.

I insist again that we won't take him home, even though his mom has muttered, "We'll think about it," and he knows that should mean yes; he's in tears and punching the brick pillar as the other families stream past, the smart kids' medals clinking. "I hate Afterschool, I fucking hate it."

"We'll take care of it," his teachers assure us, but his mom is afraid he'll turn on them too. "Go while he's getting changed," they urge, and I practically pull Risa and the weight of her guilt back out the school door, abandoning Cody's thirty-four dollars of dress clothes.

What happens with Cody after that, I don't really know, but it isn't good, and somehow my graduation card with fifteen lousy dollars gets lost in the scuffle before he even sees it.

But at least he gets some closure to grade school, and Afterschool gets a chance to celebrate the years they devoted to him, and I feel stupid but still resolved to be the hateful brick wall he can throw himself against. Or lean on, should he ever choose to.

JUST DAYS before, I saw Cody in the library, on an Afterschool outing. I waved and he gave me his usual greeting—"You're not here to get me, are you?" He was hoarse and sounded like he had a bad cold, but he looked almost cheerful, with a new and unstained long-sleeved shirt, his hair newly cut and blonded in the front with stolen Sun-In, and a wire hoop earring.

"You look great," I said, thumping his shoulder. "So cool—who pierced your ear?" I remembered the workshop's exhortation to search out any crumb of anything to praise. "Who pierced your ear—your brother?" I said.

"I did," Cody said. "With a nail."

He turns back to his friend, and I thank the lord he has one.

"Bye—see ya—" he says to me. "Tell the little bunny I said 'hey.'"

BETWEEN SALT Lake and Denver lies the mystery of the soul of Kerouac's Cody, and in the mile between the late-night lights of Woody's Gas 'n Go and the burning mattress above the town's bike path lies this one.

Kerouac's Cody and this one, generations apart, rage by like flaming meteors. They're confounded by the cage of workweek/school-week hours and by the total absurdity of speed limits, dress codes, private property, absence notes, hall passes, gym clothes, drivers' licenses, insurance, sleep cycles, food pyramids, rent, life and death, laws of gravity, laws of physics, and the constant pressure to conform to the dullest, most soul-killing standards.

Why shouldn't they follow a railroad track at dawn, in wet jeans and a T-shirt, straight into some other future?

Their shared threat, at a half-century's distance: Don't fence me in.

AND HERE I am, limping along behind like old Jack, blind to the mad vision, always too conscious of what's going on and my futile attempts to fix it, just watching, dazed, amazed, as Cody streaks past.

A MOMENTARILY HAPPY ENDING

One day during that postgraduation summer—light-years before the first jail time and first baby he'll claim as his—he pulls up on his bike and tells me the bad dreams have stopped. Because his brother's moved back home? Because his days are calmer? Because his night terrors are finally fading? Because he's finally on some steady medication?

"No," Cody says, "because of the dreamcatchers. Mom put one on the wall of my room, and it's done caught my dreams in it. I don't have them no more."

All along, was it just that easy?

He pops a wheelie and swerves away, screeching off into the dust in a perfect Tokyo drift.

> All the mornings you suffer and all for nothing and forgetfulness and the necessary natural blankness of men—and Cody is blank at last.
>
> —*Visions of Cody*

IV

DOOR TO DOOR, HOUSE TO HOUSE

Halloween

—Michael

ON THE first Halloween in two years that my mother went trick-or-treating with me, she was caught by the cops. I had missed my mom while she was doing who knows what down south for the last eight months, and I was looking forward to seeing her now. Trick-or-treating is a time for kids to be joyful, but this night, it was the opposite. This is how I remember it.

First I should tell you about the university Halloween celebration we liked to go to. Several dorms at the local campus have an annual community trick-or-treat night before Halloween. Families can go door to door with no cars to dodge, no dark streets, and no hills to climb, unless you count the staircases connecting the dorms, which were built one above or beside another, going up the long, steep hillside.

It was about 5 p.m. and still light outside. Spooky witches, wretched zombies, a bloody ballerina, bumblebees with antennas, and a mustard and ketchup pair flooded onto the sidewalk, all carrying pumpkin buckets. My cousin and her best friend were dressed as Frankie Stein and Draculaura from Monster High. I decided to go on into the dorms with them because my mom had not shown up as she had promised. I wasn't surprised, but still I was hoping she would come.

When I started toward the dorm, I heard my Poppa's truck—each old car or truck my mom's dad has owned has had its own kind of rattle. I turned and saw my mom in in the back of the truck. I was relieved. She got out and we hugged and went inside.

While my mom and I walked through the halls of the crowded dorms, we ate most of the candy to make room in our buckets for more. My mother was going through our candy, eating all the candy corn and Tootsie Rolls. I saw more friends from my school in the halls. We ate about twenty-five packs of Sour Patch Kids that night. Kids were crying because they'd lost their pumpkin-shaped balloon. At one room the college kids ran out of candy, so they gave me a slice of pizza. My cousin was getting tired, so we all went back to our vehicles and left.

We were done trick-or-treating, so I had to be taken to my Grandma Irene's (my dad's mom's) house. My mother, my sister, my sister's boyfriend, and his friends were all in the back of the truck. My younger cousins sat in the truck with me. Then my mom's dad, Poppa, dropped me off, and my Grandma Irene walked up her driveway to meet me. I don't think my Poppa's been inside her house once. A few minutes later Poppa called on the phone. "They ran out of gas down the road at Roy's Tires," Grandma Irene told me. We got into her car and arrived at the closest gas station to find my brother walking back to the truck with a can of gas.

We drove him back to Poppa's truck. We saw blue flashing lights and knew what was happening, but we passed them. I was crying slightly. We got a call to come back. We went back to Roy's Tires, and I saw my mom talking to the cops. I smelled tobacco burning and saw she was smoking. She came over to hug me. When we were trick-or-treating earlier, she had looked fine, but now she was looking sloppy and scratching her frizzy, messed-up hair. "I'm going to jail again," she said calmly. About to sob, she said, "I'll be fine."

My mother wasn't arrested for something that had happened that night. It was because of a court date that she had missed the previous spring.

WE VISITED her every week with my sister, brother, her parents (my MeMa and Poppa), and sometimes my cousins. It was too many people and the room echoed like a swimming pool with all the voices. Talking on the phone to her on the other side of the window, I could barely hear even myself. My mom called me at home four times a month for ten minutes. After she got out, my real dad, Luke, was arrested about one month later, and my mom's ex-boyfriend, Benny, was also arrested. It was all too awful. Now I can't decide whether I should go to trick-or-treat at the university again. I don't need anymore memories like these.

Hallowtide

Allhallowtide, Hallowtide, Allsaintstide, or the Hallowmas season, is the triduum encompassing the Western Christian observances of All Hallows' Eve (Hallowe'en), All Saints' Day (All Hallows') and All Souls' Day, and runs from October 31 to November 2. Allhallowtide is primarily a time to remember the dead. The present date of Hallowmas (All Saints' Day) and thus also of its vigil (Hallowe'en) was established by Pope Gregory III (731–741) and was made a time of obligation throughout the Frankish Empire by Louis the Pious in 835.

—Juan Bosque, "Allhallowtide," *Book of Days Tales* (blog), October 31, 2015

PUMPKIN HOUSE

The most celebrated day of the children's calendar was coming. The annual festival of candy hauls, steamy masks, skittering leaves, sugar jitters, meltdowns, lost fillings, Bible-costume-only harvest celebrations, razorblade paranoia, and the fresh smell of goopy pumpkin guts on your hands. The time when, for the cost of a Walmart unisuit costume, you could have bought three toddler shirts and a pair of jeans. But this year, 2005—my first Halloween experience since two costumed adults had thrown dog crap all over my duplex door two decades earlier—was going to be a true festival of innocence and delight. It was going to be my first and best shot at the trick-or-treat business as a foster parent. And my two-year-old foster son, Michael, would have it as one of our best nights to remember. And as one of our last nights, as well.

For all the "shared parenting" experiences I'd later grasp at so greedily, I jealously hoarded my anticipation of what would be the first and perhaps only Halloween night I'd get to spend with Michael. I did not want to share it with anybody, even my husband, Will. This was the first Halloween Michael might remember, and I wanted to keep his delight and amazement all to myself. Unlike the Fourth of July, with its terrifying booms, I wanted this holiday to be all sweetness, no fear. All whispered thank-yous. All treats. A plastic pumpkin full of joy to sustain him through the shock of his transition to his mother's new home in the days ahead.

TWO WEEKS shy of his reunification date, I bought Michael the most expensive costume I probably ever would: a $22 *Bob the Builder* suit. I knew he'd be ecstatic as "'struction" was the central obsession of his early life, with trains a close second. I had strollered him as a toddler all over the university campus, at the start of its megaboom in construction, so he could convulse with glee and shout encouragement to the steamrollers, cranes, wrecking balls, and graders as they leveled old buildings and dug the foundations for the new. He was still too wiggly to watch much more than background TV (which vexed his grandmother during those weekends she'd care for all three siblings so they could spend time together), but he could sit transfixed in his stroller for as long as I would stand behind the chainlink construction site barriers. He stared at photos of heavy equipment and tools in library books—a look I'd recognize years later when he'd fall down the shaft of the mesmerizing video game Minecraft—and he could call out the different kinds of vehicles and earthmovers as well any accomplished birder could spot and name a species.

Backhoes were his favorite, and Scoop, Bob's big-eyed yellow backhoe, was his hero. The whole *Bob the Builder* crew had a simple cheer reminiscent of the old 1970s yellow smiley faces, back when those had seemed novel; in the world of Bob and his business partner, Wendy, life's obstacles were purely physical, from hay bales to restack after a storm to the disruptions of the rascally onion-head inexplicably named Spud—but with persistence, everything could be set right. And Bob never cursed or sulked or yelled at Wendy on his plot point–connecting cell phone, even though he usually had his phone upside down and, like most adults, Michael points out now, didn't know how to work it. Bob's glossy orange, red, blue, and yellow village was a good world to live in.

Naturally, Michael loved "Bob-Builder" and the show's theme song; Michael absorbed the eight-minute episodes as lunch or snacks kept him anchored. I was hooked myself, wishing that all the trouble he'd face in his childhood years could be no more challenging than baby porcupines stopping traffic in the road ahead. He loved Bob's stop-motion construction team with a passion matched only by his devotion to Thomas the Tank Engine. To the construction workers Michael enviously ogled in passing, I wanted to say, "I know all boys love this stuff, but he really does—he wants to do what you do." I imagined Michael to be one of the baby geniuses he adored in the eponymous movie series, capable of getting up out of his stroller, picking up a hard hat, and taking his place on the job site. Still, the stumbling block of his shyness was so huge that he even shrank back from one worker's invitation to climb onto the seat of a backhoe and help him back it up. I knew Michael thought he could do it himself, if they'd just hand over the magical key and let him at it; I knew it was his dream.

THE BOB costume didn't come with a mask, and Michael always recoiled from face paint, yet he seemed stunned when adults inquired, "So who are you?" Wasn't it obvious? Hadn't he transmogrified? The costume came with Bob's coveted yellow hard hat, though, and a brick patchwork jumpsuit, a flat felt tool belt with an unsticky stick-on wrench and hammer, and fake boots that bell-bottomed over Michael's real sneakers. Michael loved the costume, and I let him wear it all he wanted leading up to Halloween; I even invited his Grandma Irene over to admire how perfectly it suited him.

His return date—my private phrase for family reunification—was approaching rapidly. I knew only that the future so easily, and legally, could hold nothing at all for me. This could well be the end. At least I'd had Michael's second birthday party and the Fourth of July parade, but this Halloween was another major kid holiday I'd selfishly thought I would get. We would get. Alone together.

"THEY'RE GOING to be at the mall with the other kids," was the message Grandma Irene relayed. "They" always meant Jessica and her boyfriend, Benny—although *boyfriend* seemed like the wrong word for someone even older than I was. "The other kids" were Michael's siblings, Isabelle and Ryan, who had already been returned to Jessica's physical custody in order to stagger the reunification process. Neither Irene nor I ever had to explain our pronouns—she, they, he—we knew what they meant, and all the layers they implied. A few churches and the library had non-Satanic holiday celebrations, but the local mall was the hub of Halloween night activity in our county. "They want you to bring Michael over to the mall about eight tonight," Irene explained, her voice a tense sigh, "so they can see him in his costume."

In hindsight I see my hypocrisy, for in the months and years to follow, when Michael's family held custody, I'd leap at their offer to share any holiday, from Thanksgiving to birthday mornings to the days leading up to Christmas to New Year's Eve countdowns and Easter egg hunts. Often we'd all be together, adults and kids of our mingled families, for parties, visits with Santa and the Easter Bunny, and shared meals; but right now, this one Halloween night, a week before Michael might be gone from my life forever, before I knew any of what was to come, I wanted everything to be memorably, imprintably perfect.

And still I wanted Michael to myself, without the spinning-top, sugar-jangled siblings who'd distract Michael into giddiness, and without having to watch Benny line up in the mall's adult costume contest in glue-shiny work jeans and a $20 zombie skull mask. Undead or alive, Benny was the last person I wanted to see just a week after I'd reported him for drinking and then driving the two older kids—a harrowing decision on my part that had had zero effect on slowing the reunification process but had made Benny angry enough not to talk to me.

Michael would be spending the weekend with his family anyway—so why couldn't I just have this night, when they'd soon have all other nights? My throat was closing up with unfair tears: I was losing everything, just as I'd knowingly signed on to do when I became a foster parent. In the unseeable future reality, we actually would share Halloweens for years to come, thanks to Michael's mother, and I'd be immensely grateful, leaping to buy the slick costumes the kids would not have had otherwise, including a full-out Glinda the Good Witch outfit for the theatrical Isabelle. Now I just felt tears prick the corners of my eyes as Irene passed along the message. Conveniently, Jessica had no phone, so there was no way to discuss, negotiate, or wiggle out of this. And in just over a week, she and Benny would hold all the cards. Jessica would have every right to close me out for good. I didn't want to piss them off any further.

THAT FIRST Halloween night Michael refused to climb down from my arms into the dimly lit, echoing mall mayhem, so I carried him from store to store, waiting for his face to light up at the miracle of free candy clattering into his pumpkin bucket. He was so shy then, and still so scared of women, especially in sultry witch costumes with raccoon-black eyes. He clutched at me as I held him out along with the plastic pumpkin, ventriloquizing talk: "Say, 'Thank you, I'm Bob-Builder.'" We went into the rec department's Dollar Pumpkin House and found little more than a bunch of black curtains tied over pipe frames, but at least there I could be sure his family wasn't watching us from down the mall, scrutinizing our affection. Inside the Pumpkin House, I hugged him through the toddler-height games while he won glow-in-the-dark skeletons and temporary tattoos. I longed to stay for days within this primitively screened black hole and hide out from everyone and everything.

I heard later that Michael's family had stopped to trick-or-treat at the home of Irene's landlord and around a cul-de-sac of new homes behind the university where business professors were rumored to give out full-sized candy bars; maybe they arrived at the mall after we left and the event was closing down—or maybe they'd simply spotted a state trooper on the way into town and turned around. One way or another, though, we didn't see Michael's family there at the mall after all. It was a huge relief, for I'd looked over my shoulder, stomach clenching, the whole time: as would become my habit, I'd let their expected presence cast a cool shadow over everything. My generic Halloween nostalgia had been replaced by my actual childhood memories—of hearing dogs bark at hollering late into the night, then waking up to smashed pumpkins in the street every morning after, wondering who could have been mean enough to do that.

Michael, at fourteen, does not remember that first Halloween night beyond the costume itself: he likes to hear about his refusal to wear the hard hat that was the one clue to his disguise, and the way his knees and heels dug into my waist as he shrank back from whatever sugar-bearing, fish-netted vampirella might have been reaching out to take him. I tell him how hard I held onto him too, as if I could inoculate him with safety. He didn't even want the candy, beyond hearing its rattle and counting the currency of its bright wrappings. Seven days later, I knew, I'd have to pry him loose and hand him back to his mother, sending a plastic pumpkin full of sour and sweetness with him, as I receded into the darkness of his toddler memory, soon to be no more than a sputtering candle flame.

HALLOWMAS

Devolved from the age-old Roman-Celtic-Catholic triduum, or three-day progressive observance, into a two-week extravaganza that rivals the twelve days of Christmas in the outlay of spending, calories, and plastic, Halloween is the holiday that every parent or parent substitute can't wait to relive. And for those parents who never really got to be kids themselves, which would describe the bioparents of most kids in foster care, experiencing Halloween seems pretty close to what foster parent training calls an unmet need. Whatever our American pasts, Halloween is loaded with nostalgic weight, spare UNICEF pennies, and justified candy consumption, without all the family baggage and bondage of Christmas and Thanksgiving.

For me, looking through the lens of Halloween focuses the whole blurred panorama of our extended, blended family's past decade, capturing the highs and lows, horror, cravings, control and loss, craziness, all-night lights and morning darkness, and the desire to see and feel pure childish joy. As if it could ever be pure. Maybe *haunted* childhood joy is what fits children like Michael who believe they see ghostly creatures outside their broken window but who actually see a real-life shape-shifting, howling werewolf within their walls when the lunar cycle peaks.

Our Halloweens also epitomize both how I made everything happen through the shared years—buying the costumes and the pre-trick-or-treating dinner at McDonald's so that everyone could be part of it, and everyone could be happy—and how I then wouldn't like the particular way the children or adults *were* acting happy in my controlled little world, which was often full of outside friends and professionals whose opinions felt hugely important to me. Most emblematic, though, was the way Halloween was something ostensibly intended for kids but taken over for the purposes of adults. Maybe to make up for the childhood they missed; maybe for the sugar they needed when alcohol got depleted. I longed for Halloween myself, wanting it to be perfect. Yet, like a fantastically good dream, it felt always on the verge of turning to horror, with the shadow of the future sweeping in.

ALL HOLIDAYS through those years felt fraught, for Valentine's Day, birthdays, Christmas, Mother's Day, Veterans' Day—especially when celebrated at school or built up on TV—first offered welcome structure to a chaotic year and a brief chance to live in the same world as the other kids. Yet for adult family members who'd grown up through their own forms of trauma, holidays brought up old grief and fear, while offering another reason to drink or self-tranquilize, compounded by the pressure of who would pay for it all.

For the boys and their many cousins, Halloween was something reliable they could look forward to—an unbudgeable calendar date. To me, though, it became the most fearful, fearsome holiday—truly a time, as Houdini's widow said, that the veil between this world and the spirit realm, whatever that might be, was worn most thin. (The Fourth of July felt almost as dangerous, with Michael and Ryan's extended family camping on isolated private hilltops amid a long-anticipated frenzy of alcohol, firecrackers, artillery shells, four-wheelers, pot, and the combustion of temper with all the above.)

Dentists nowadays tell children to eat all their candy in one night, to concentrate all that tooth decay instead of spreading out the assault and rot. That's how the whole Halloween holiday came to feel to me—like one long binge of desire, fear, thrills, terror, longing, and craving. Halloween was the vortex—the eye of a tornado that funneled up everything in its path, all that should have been joyful with everything that was too crazy, frenetic, frantic, and over the line, then hurling it back to earth like Dorothy's sideways house. Hallowtide swept in the perfect storm of a holiday for all the thirty-, forty-, and fifty-year-old souls who had grown up so stressed that they'd missed their first chance to be kids.

TRICK-OR-TREAT 4 KIDZ

Everyone came out for the Halloween celebration on campus, so it was where we saw everyone we knew in one place—the growing children

Michael and Ryan had gone to preschool with, along with other foster families, DSS-connected birth parents, university colleagues, community nonprofit staff, and even the Child Protective Services staff. (Seeing those social workers out in public always gave me the same weird feeling I used to get as a kid when I saw teachers out of school, when those almost mythic figures suddenly appeared as parents themselves, and with a life outside the classroom or, now, outside their offices, stark visiting room, and court.) I knew that Jessica, Benny, and I always looked like the very model of cooperative parenting, and we all went out of our way to say hi to the director and staff of Child Protective Services, garnering their familiar beams of approval, while a little voice in the back of my head tried to warn them, *Don't believe it—danger, Will Robinson, danger!*

EACH YEAR, after a round of afternoon errands, I'd race back to campus for Trick or Treat night with the boys' store-bought costumes and pumpkin buckets, and often with the boys themselves and Isabelle, to meet Jessica, Benny, and whoever had come with them at the dorm parking lot. I was usually late, but they arrived on the dot, aware the candy would run out if we started even half an hour behind the crowd. Another set of young cousins, Levi and Joel, would often come along because their mother could not bear the crowds, tight halls, and jammed stairways; in the happiest photo I have of them, they are perched on a retaining wall, with Joel in Ryan's old Spiderman outfit and Levi in a strange assemblage of a yard-sale Ninja Turtle suit, colonial tricorn hat, and buccaneer sword.

The Halloween visitors were directed to start at each dorm's top floor and spiral their way down. From floor to floor of the dorms would come parades of perfect little costumes—whiskered mice, Tinkerbells, an army of Minions, and characters from Nick Jr. The first year we went, we saw a kid dressed as a little pirate and his dad dressed as a big pirate, velvet jacket and all, complete with a real parrot on his shoulder. The poor bird must have been terrorized by the echoing hallways, kids, and noise, but it held on and the dad got all the happy stares and praise.

Somewhere along the way, we'd be joined by Jonah, Jessica's rowdy Prince Hal of a brother, his more grounded wife, and two more cousins and their friends. Since the university was my workplace, they would include me and wait for me to lead the way from dorm to dorm, but once we actually got on the floors, I would ease my way to the back of our group, while Benny would go up front, holding whichever child was youngest and cutest—Michael or a younger cousin or grandchild—presenting the toddler to the young college women with his *let's party* smile and suggestive laugh, then winking back at preteen Ryan when, among the wholesome Dorothys and Pokemons, a college student's devil-cat costume, Renaissance Faire cleavage, or too-tight Peter Pan tunic came into view.

Clearly, Benny loved that combination of party spirit and doing something to make the kids smile; while I should have been happy that this did not involve pyrotechnics, shotguns, or tipping four-wheelers, I hated how loud our voices were, with the rasping edge of Benny and Jonah's laughter echoing off the walls of the stairwells as we trooped down. Did the other parents catch that familiar whiff of whiskey? Yes, even here and now—at Trick-or-Treat 4 KIDZ? I prayed our chaos would be swallowed up in the larger carnival.

The smell of liquor or weed-infused denim made me cringe, yet far more stressful was waiting to see which cap or T-shirt Benny would turn up in—most had a Confederate flag front and center, and he'd think less than nothing of it. The worst, which he wore at least once through the dorms, was a dark blue Lynyrd Skynyrd shirt bearing a nearly naked woman entwined with a rebel flag, as they always called the Confederate battle flag—on other occasions, he'd even let little Michael wear that T-shirt. My stomach would be in knots all day: Which of my students would see Benny, see his flags, and connect him with me? Who would see through my double act: all awkwardly PC in the classroom and a complicit coward here, lurking behind in apology?

I imagined a blustering Dr. Phil (if he actually cared about such things) asking why the hell I didn't just ask Benny not to wear his rebel gear there on my turf. I don't have a good answer, except for the certainty that it would have erupted into a furious, intractable parking lot argument that would have torpedoed the whole event and caused Benny to lay out every other wrong thing about me. He knew what he knew and, apparently, there was so much I didn't—one confrontation had already proved his invincibility to both of us. Southern white rebel-racist was Benny's one proud identity: his four-wheeler was plastered with Heritage Not Hate flag bumper stickers, never mind that he hated plenty. Burning bridges was Benny's specialty, and he didn't have to spell out that, parent or not, he could always keep Michael away from me.

On our car rides Jessica would half-apologize for Benny's racism, blaming it on his time in prison, and she swore, unasked, that she didn't talk that way, although the kids rolled their eyes when she'd say this. Once Jessica was out of sight, I'd find brown paper towels and restroom soap and try to scrub away whatever flag design Ryan or Michael had drawn in markers that day on their forearms or notebook covers. At least Jessica cared enough to say what she thought I wanted to hear about this, whereas Benny was flat-out convinced of his white superiority.

The best I could do those trick-or-treat nights was shrink back and keep some queasy distance—*it's Michael and Ryan and Isabelle that matter,* I kept telling myself—how could I be the PC police when these kids needed my vigilance, as futile as it might be? All the while certain that my fine tangle of worries hardly mattered if I wasn't going to have the guts to confront Benny.

Worse, when we met up with the boys' uncle Jonah and his family, before they split over his addictions, his wife was always reassuringly decked out in the same green witch greasepaint, hat, broom, and cloak, while Jonah—who played electric guitar with a group of guys in the shed—every year went as some version of Jimi Hendrix, with a giant Afro wig, rainbow headband, black leather jacket, and sagging American flag tank top. Most adults wore no costumes anyway, and in or out of my anxious university world, I didn't want to be trailing a clownish Jimi Hendrix. So I just let them all walk ahead and waited for Benny to push Michael or his grandson or whichever cousin up to the dorm hall doorways as Jessica called out "Just take one piece" and instructed the boys to "say 'Thank you, ma'am,'" to the students in their Hermione robes, Harry Potter drag, or vixen leotards.

After the first hour, the dorm hallways and elevators were steamy; we'd burst out the glass exit doors, craving the bite of late fall air as we walked between buildings through near-dusk. When I wasn't fretting about the Confederate emblems on Benny's cap or whether anyone recognized Jimi Hendrix, I'd silently stew about the oldest cousin's perennial *Scream* outfit, the cowled costume from a horror movie Michael had watched at the age of three. The mask was a white, skeletal version of the Edvard Munch face and coursed with liver-dark blood at the squeeze of a handheld plastic heart pump. Every year I fumed at how scary this costume was for the little kids but nonetheless caved to Michael's own desperate longings when he turned twelve and bought the same terrifying costume because it was the only teen-sized get-up in all of Walmart that wasn't for a childish superhero. As had happened years earlier when his cousin wore the costume, I saw children brace, expressions crumpling, and was aghast when Michael refused to lift the mask to show the toddlers his real, human face.

AT EACH dorm the kids scoped out the games and crafts in the lobby, racing each other to eat apples that dangled from strings and decorating mini-pumpkins with paint markers and plastic googly eyes that wouldn't stick. Then we'd take the elevator to the top floor with a bouncy guide and wind our way down the stairs, floor by floor. Those residents welcoming trick-or-treaters put cutout paper pumpkins beside their door; when they ran out of candy, they'd either shut the door or start giving out random items like microwave popcorn, Pop-Tarts, hair ties, or little cereal boxes they'd taken from the cafeteria. I'd hang back and read the floor bulletin boards, which changed with the year's most pressing issues: in one dorm a bulletin board scripted out what did and did not constitute consent, while a second board suggested ways to prompt a friend to get counseling help; another had colorful condom packages for the taking, all stapled to autumn leaves—a cheerfully helpful idea the floor's Resident Assistant clearly had not thought through. Best were the cutesy individual dry-erase boards on which young women would leave each other messages of love in big, loopy handwriting and notes about where they'd gone. How nice to briefly live in such a world, I thought, where friends might actually come looking for you and worry if you were not in your room.

FOR ALL my complaints and criticisms, I couldn't bear to miss trick-or-treating even once. The boys were more deliriously excited for Halloween than even for birthdays, so how could I miss out? I feared being associated with Benny, but this was a children's holiday, I kept reminding myself: If I was not responsible for the kids' choices when they lied about homework or cursed on the bus, was I responsible for an adult's? I couldn't think about it too closely.

And I knew too well the way things worked. Benny told Jessica what to do, and Jessica didn't have to let me be there—or anywhere in their lives. We all knew I would walk circle upon circle of eggshells to keep things going. How else could I still be there when things fell apart?

ON HALLOWEEN when Michael was thirteen, I won him a rainbow lava lamp at the mall by guessing how many candy corn pieces were in a jar. It was a Friday and our first Halloween completely alone—Jessica was living elsewhere in the state, and Ryan, who'd been promised he'd get to split Michael's candy haul, was shivering on the sidelines of an away high school football game. We live in the country, and the town is filled with candy-less student apartments, but this year we'd found an actual downtown family neighborhood to go to after the mall. Michael reminded me that it was the first year he'd ever gone to trick-or-treat at actual houses, and doing this amazed him. He was older than any other kid he saw, but it was just the two of us together, making up for lost time. Snow was on the ground and in the night air; the hills were steep and slippery, but the porches and paths were lined with orange lights, like runways. One family had built a giant Scooby-Doo model in their yard, and signs on every corner invited everyone to a homemade and not-too-spooky haunted house. The orange glow reflected off the snow, which in itself seemed like an uncouth blending of holidays, rushing us on to Christmas, which the Walmart shelves already were doing.

For once, though, I felt I had Michael to myself again, after all these years of shared Halloweens; for once I could hug him in the dark, my hand slipping over the shiny stretch fabric of the costume. His hand still clutched the same orange plastic pumpkin he'd always used, one of the few objects that have lasted and crossed both worlds of our lives, the before and the after of custody, from guarded fear to tenuous safety. That pumpkin still sits above the fridge from October to Christmas each year, as the candy gets raided and eaten in order of desirability, until only the stale, peppery hard candies and useless mini-erasers are left.

MONSTER BASH

Down in the foothills, two counties away, a beloved but way-outdated Christmas-in-July-themed amusement park opened back up after its season and allowed fraternities and sororities from a small local college to rent it out and make the park over into a Halloween experience. Each year a different charity was chosen to receive the profits, and each year the student groups outdid each other to transform the safe and gentle North Pole world into ever more grotesque and terrifying displays of horror—with enough kiddie activities thrown in that people would still bring their children.

Come 7:30 on the last Saturday night of October, the park's red and green was bathed in orange light and all the Santa's Workshop and pseudo-Swiss Elf Village nostalgia was gone. There was no attempt to reconcile these clashing holidays—how could there be?—it was frenetic millennial Halloween overlaid on a fading Burl Ives version of Christmas of the 1950s. When had Halloween become an adult holiday? Was it all a plot by Walmart to double the market for costume sales? I'd heard that after Christmas, it was the second-most-profitable holiday period for chain stores.

For all the summer season's jingling cheer, reasonable admissions price, and prospect of Christmas card–ready family photos in Santa's mammoth sled, Monster Bash seemed like a much bigger draw, judging by the number of people we waited with outside the gates. Once inside the park, the crowd would mill through the town square of the spotlit Christmas village, its windows drifted with permanent plaster snow, then jostle into indistinct lines and shove aboard the blacklit roller coaster and haunted hayride, pulled by horses that were apparently inured to the black-clad ninjas who would jump out along the forest path wielding (I hoped) dulled swords. I hated roller coasters, even this relatively low-rise one, and I couldn't handle having things jump out and surprise me.

I'd visited this park once with Michael's family in its summer incarnation, but they had been coming to Monster Bash here for years before I knew them. They sometimes won tickets off the radio, but one way or another, the money for tickets was always found. They rarely ventured out of the mountains otherwise, except for occasional hunting trips, but going to the Monster Bash was as much a tradition as their Christmas venison roast and gift swap. I never said no to going with them, hoping both to take the boys home with me for that long drive up the mountains at midnight and to shield Michael from the family's compulsory haunted house visit.

ALCOHOL WAS not allowed through the candy cane–striped gates, but things often felt just one shove or spilled drink shy of a brawl. There were always plenty of wasted-looking, leather-clad adults swept by strobe and orange spotlights. Sorority members circled the crowd dressed as slinky, cat-eyed Christmas elves, while others danced on top of wooden boxes to keep themselves out of reach.

There were some token elements for kids, mainly in the form of trick-or-treat stations outside each gift store and the chance to ride the merry-go-round with a college-aged Mrs. Claus. Students and younger adults were the target audience, however, and every element of the evening was cranked up. Those college students who were not running events promenaded between the bikers in steampunk top hats and dusters, brandishing clawed walking sticks, or vamp-tramp corsets; there were always a few Dr. Who's and Star Wars creatures as well. The brittle, jittery energy of adults looking for their money's worth made me feel like I was loitering in the doorway of the Magic Theater from *Steppenwolf*—definitely not for everybody, and certainly not for me.

For Michael, and perhaps for Ryan, who proudly walked without holding the railing through The Black Hole's spinning spiral tunnel of stars, I imagined these nights to be a three-dimensional manifestation of the fear, confusion, and uncertainty in which I believed they lived every day. The epitome of this chaos was the fraternities' signature haunted house, a year in the making, with themes inspired by the worst imaginable campy torture-horror movies. Set inside the black-draped Santa's House, it was clearly labeled for adults, and its line wound far beyond the candy-cane stanchions where parents and kids would normally wait to share their out-of-season Christmas list with Santa. I wouldn't have dared go into that haunted house myself, dreading as I do the certainty that something would sneak up behind or jump out in front of me. But the macho thing in Michael's family was to make their kids—including toddlers—go through the haunted house with them. It was a forced rite of passage: hilarious to the men and infuriating to me.

The first time we went to Monster Bash, when Michael was three or four, I wanted to keep him outside the haunted house, not even suspecting how bad it really was. There was a canopy-covered space to wait and watch as clumps of people were ejected from the attraction—they always ran out screaming, through an exit shaped like Santa's fireplace chimney, as if propelled by a jet of air. Jessica was grimacing tentatively, as though she too wanted to leave her baby outside with me. But Benny dismissed us both, with "Naw, naw, that's okay" and insisted on carrying Michael on his shoulders, while Ryan, who liked a scare even at that age, stuck by his mother's side to defend her. Raucous and teasing, they lined up to go in, while I, ever the chicken, waited outside.

The haunted house was meant for high school studs and their cute, shrieking dates—even at the entrance, they discouraged bringing in kids, warning that the fiends wouldn't give them a break. Michael came out on Benny's shoulders, shrieking and tearful as Benny laughed. Something had grabbed at Michael, then the corpse on an operating table had convulsed, monster-eyed, and lunged after them. As soon as Michael's feet touched the ground, I hugged him to me. He was still whimpering and just wanted to leave. The next year, the kids knew better: Ryan still wanted to go inside the haunted house, but Michael and Madison, a female cousin Michael's age, begged to wait outside with me. But just as we thought Michael was safe, Benny gleefully swept him out of my grip and away, as if I was making Michael soft, depriving a preschooler of his hardcore macho birthright. To this day Michael still remembers the Headless Horseman lunging down after him.

Even the one year we took Cody along as an older teen, he had the sense not to go into it, knowing these terrors already haunted his dreams. He was freaked out enough by the giant elf statues and a thigh-high chattering skeleton marionette he'd seen one of the steampunks walking down the park path; nothing Benny or Jessica's brother said would shame Cody into going through the haunted house, but once again Michael had no choice.

Just to look like I wasn't a complete coward on these nights, and was there to do something more than try ineffectually to anchor the children in this craziness, I'd clutch my way through the revolving Black Hole tunnel and the black light maze, where only I could have gotten lost. Same with witnessing the Freddy vs. Jason wrestling match on the fairytale lagoon bridge, which was always the kids' favorite stop, full of amplified grunting and groaning and awkward staged-combat maneuvers. But mostly I did a lot of waiting. Not just outside the haunted house and haunted forest, but also beside the clacking roller coaster and tilt-a-whirl, which I also couldn't handle in broad daylight.

THE WORST Monster Bash I remember—and the one I can't forget—came a few years after Isabelle had moved to live with Grandma Irene. She had recently turned twelve, and she must have agreed to spend a rare weekend with Jessica and Benny, with this Monster Bash trip as the bait. Isabelle was still angry with Benny, as silkily as he spoke to her in front of us, yet visiting her mother's house while Benny was there was the only way her mother would see her, or perhaps could.

The threat of early snow was in the air and everyone was wearing winter jackets; Isabelle wore hers over a pale pink tutu. Somehow the glitter of real snow flurries in the night looked like one more fake effect here. The crowd was already pumped up; two carnival freaks had leered out at us along the way in. The town square was mobbed by adults, a number of whom carried sleeping infants. The summer kids' kingdom of Frosty, Rudolf, frozen hot chocolate, and grandmotherly ride operators had vanished with the snap of autumn. Even though it was much closer to actual Christmas than to July, it felt like the summer welcome had been overstayed and the magic had drained away, exposing the harsh, gray underpinnings. The park was a place for grownups now, and so crowded that when one person leaned, I felt everything moving.

Techno music pulsed like a migraine, on and on, everywhere. With the palm of my hand, I absorbed the warmth of Michael's neck and cheek, while watching Benny from the corner of my eye. He'd been drinking more than his usual subsistence level, I suspected—his voice roared and frayed, even bigger and brassier than usual.

It was less crowded at the second grouping of rides, where the boys rode cars on spokes and tilting, spinning snowballs. Behind us were dart booths, where three dollars bought three shots at a balloon. As in any real carnival, you could never win the giant stuffed Coke polar bears that hung from the ceiling, but invariably the kids would win garish placard pictures in crummy frames and prop them above the woodstove in their living room. These pictures were of the usual suspects—SpongeBob, Pokemon, and monster trucks—but the boys would always pick the snarling cartoon pitbull wrapped in the inevitable rebel flag—or just the plain rebel flag picture itself. With Benny here, laughing at their success, there was little I could say to object and they knew it.

We moved along to the third block of rides, past the reindeer petting park, which was mercifully shut for the animals' good. This area still looked like a kids' zone so it clashed all the more with Benny's unmistakable smell of alcohol. Alcohol and whatever else. It was dark, but by the glow of stringed orange minibulbs, Grinch-green icicle lights, and the glare of a white security streetlamp, I saw Benny hugging Isabelle from behind and laughing, rocking until they both almost fell over. Isabelle smiled weakly as he called her Tinkerbell, roaring this nickname as if he'd never driven her down the road and threatened to return her to foster care. Isabelle, who was wearing a puffy pink jacket and tiara, still had the body of a twig, but the way Benny was hugging her made me move a step closer and cringe. As Jessica watched the boys pilot helicopters, Benny leaned down over Isabelle like the Big, Bad Wolf about to smother her in one big, bad, harmless joke.

Isabelle didn't freeze up, but she didn't play along either, just laughed uncomfortably and rolled her eyes, like this was one more embarrassment to wait out, like she was used to this. Every time Isabelle would ease away, Benny would grab her again. Over the mechanical racket of the rides soared the drunken siren of his voice, sounding so good-natured that even someone braver than I, with much less to lose, might not have known how to go up and intercede.

But a tuning fork of unease had been struck: a sickening note vibrated through the air as the lights of the ride streaked up and around, tilting away into the night. Forcing myself not to look away from Isabelle and Benny, I stared as if my gaze had the power to shame him, or at least to freeze the action. But I had no superpower laser vision, so I simply stood, complicit, watching.

It made me dizzy and sick—most at myself and my stasis. My stomach chilled: surely, I wasn't seeing what I was seeing—I always over-imagined everything, didn't I? Jessica busily checked that the boys were still strapped into their helicopters, then waved and whooped as they circled around again. *Please, turn around and see this,* I silently begged her. *You're the mother. Do something. Take this burden off of me.*

That Jessica kept watching the boys seemed a sign that she knew—and believed herself helpless to stop this. *Tag, you're it,* I could almost hear her say. Yet what could I do? March up and say, "Excuse me, Benny, perhaps you don't realize you are hugging Isabelle too much?" Or "Hey, Isabelle—come over here, there's something I want you to show you." But in this near-deserted section of the park, what was there to see?

Today, a decade later, with my 20/20 moral hindsight, what would I do differently? Even if I wasn't sure what I was seeing; and even though my knee-jerk reactions were a constant joke to Michael's family? From our current secure position of having custody, it's so easy to think in absolutes now; so easy to fly back through time to the rescue.

But then I saw Lillian, a county librarian who was the mother of a child in Michael's kindergarten. Although we were a ways from home, many people made the drive for this event, so I felt queasy with guilt but not surprised. Jessica wasn't watching Benny and Isabelle, but Lillian sure was. And, worse yet, watching me watch.

Despite the darkness, I saw every judgment in Lillian's concerned, repelled expression: Benny was drunk, he was ill, he was clearly not this child's father, and no one wanted to see a grown man hug a pretty, tiny twelve-year-old girl like this.

Lillian stared, knowing she knew me: *Why are you sitting there? How could you let him?* The disgust I saw was directed not just at Benny but at me. Then she swept her child away, as everyone else seemed to have done. How were we so alone there, in this almost sold-out park? Why was Jessica's back still turned as the boys spun and flew out into the darkness?

I was used to double takes at our mix of age, class, culture, whatever, when I spent time with what we all liked to call our family. I'd return my own challenging, even cocky gaze—yes, what *was* I doing with these people? What's it to you? Yes, we are all one family. *But not tonight, not like this.*

For years to follow, I wanted to make excuses every time I ran into Lillian, to succumb and say, "You know how it is, these people," to tell her I'd done something brave and outspoken after she'd left . . . but I never did. She'd seen what she'd seen of me, mutely standing and watching—and there was no excuse.

What I did do: shortly after Lillian and her son cleared out with that damning look, I eased up to Jessica and tried to whisper over the whirring ride machinery. Yes, to Jessica, who was so easily offended, so dangerous when crossed. I did this not with Joan of Arc bravery but with nauseated, freezing weakness, as would be the case for so many tests I would face in the future. I searched for words both diplomatic and crystal clear, subtle yet unmistakable, straining to pack it all into one urgent sentence: "Benny's too close to Isabelle—I think she's getting scared. It's scaring *me*."

Jessica got it, I could see. Maybe she was relieved I'd spoken up, or maybe she'd hoped I'd have had the manners, or the fear, to ignore what was so obviously right in front of me.

She didn't fight me, just nodded, and for a moment, I breathed. "I'll say something to him," she told me.

"Just please let Isabelle come with me." I must have begged, because Jessica agreed. Both of us were aware, I believed, that it wasn't only the crushing hugs of the moment from which we had to save Isabelle but from what could happen later that evening. And even though Jessica had planned to keep her daughter for the weekend, two hours later she packed her into my car with Michael, Ryan (whom I was already planning to drop at their Grandma Irene's), and me. I had girded myself for a parking-lot confrontation, but there was little fanfare—no explanation, no excuses. Just as if this had been the plan all along. Isabelle herself did not even speak.

I didn't say much to Irene when I dropped Isabelle and Ryan after midnight and watched as they both ran through her opened screen door and into the TV's gray glow. Then, too, I should have spoken up, although I knew Ryan might be quizzed back home about anything I said. Holding only an easily revocable guardianship of Isabelle, along with an absolute distrust of Benny, their grandmother surely would fill in the rest. I hoped so.

I expected severe payback, once Benny figured things out and blamed me. But the unaddressed stalemate that followed was almost scarier. The next day I told Irene that Benny had been in a mood or drinking—because what had I seen, really? And Jessica had quickly nodded agreement, promising to stay alert for signs of unnamed trouble in the future. I knew she did not want that to happen, however powerless she might believe herself to prevent it. Whatever *that* might be.

But this outcome was nothing to feel good about. Even if I didn't lose my visits with Michael, this was just one night, just one situation I'd happened to see. I was sick with dread—this one night might take a different course, but what of all the other visits that lay ahead? But this one night, I'd sensed something irreversible would have happened, and if I'd said nothing, my silence would have caused endless suffering. No one but Isabelle—and Lillian—might have known what I'd seen and stifled, but I too would have known and that burden would all have been on me.

THAT NIGHT I couldn't wait to leave the Monster Bash; couldn't wait to pack Michael, Ryan, and Isabelle into the temporary safety of my car's backseat; couldn't wait to drive back up into the mountains and never see another orange light or feel the twinge of foil and caramel stuck to my teeth. But we had two hours to go before I could take Isabelle and her brothers away with me. Two hours during which Jessica, having initially placated me, could quickly mumble "Benny's okay now" and whisk Isabelle back into the night, away from me. I stumbled through those two hours, expecting to hear exactly those words; two terrible hours of watching the Ferris wheel turn up into the night, the whirling snowballs, the orange glow over the plaster North Pole; two hours of enduring the sick dizziness of it all, flashing and screaming and spinning.

ALL SAINTS

Three years later came the Halloween that changed everything.

The boys' uncle Jonah, who was now divorced, and his girlfriend stayed in what once was Ryan's room, which was the size of a closet with a washing machine in it. I was friendly with Jonah's ex-wife, and the new girlfriend, Drema, made me uneasy. She had recently materialized with Jonah for Michael's birthday party at our house; they had hijacked that occasion by taking the boys down to our pond and sharing the news that she was pregnant, so they would be getting a new cousin. This was the part I did know.

What I didn't know until much later was that shortly before that year's Monster Bash trip—the first one I'd ever skipped—Ryan had found, hidden somewhere in the trailer, an old zippered pencil case that concealed a needle and shooting works.

Uncle Jonah

—Michael

I HAD a favorite uncle. His name was Jonah Jackson. Jonah loved to fish, hunt game and ginseng, build houses, and fix cars, and I too like to do most of this. Jonah seemed like the coolest guy ever to me, because he was strong, had a beard, sometimes wore sunglasses, drove four-wheelers, and sometimes drove a truck. We used to shoot off fireworks for his son's birthday, which seems like a cool way to celebrate a birthday. Jonah is hard to describe, because I have not seen him in a long time. I will share some memories of what he was like.

One day I rode in the car with my mother to pick up Jonah, her brother and my uncle, from my grandmother MeMa's house. This was after Jonah was divorced. As he got in the car, he pulled out a pack of cigarettes and asked my mom, "Hey, Jessica, you got a light?" Then my mother passed back her Led Zeppelin lighter. Jonah lit his cigarette. I remember driving down that road, which was Dry Creek Drive, so many times, with so many cigarettes lit, and so many ashes flicked. Jonah liked the Marlboro brand, but he smoked Pall Mall cigarettes, I think because they were cheaper. I looked over to see Jonah flick his cigarette ashes out his window. I listened to the random jokes he was telling over the Lynyrd Skynyrd blasting out of the speakers.

"Where are we going?" I asked Jonah.

"Wally World," he said.

We knew a guy with an eye patch called Wally and we called him One-Eyed Wally. At first I thought that Jonah meant Wally World was a planet full of Wallys, but when we got there, I realized Jonah had been talking about Walmart, so I laughed. As we were going through the parking lot, trying to find a spot, I turned to see Jonah cursing people who were driving slowly or stealing a parking place. He acted this way with everyone, and the way he cursed was kind of funny. He acted the same around everyone, although some people act differently around different people. Sometimes this was good for Jonah, but sometimes it caused him to get into trouble.

Jonah was in a band once. This band was full of alcoholics. Actually, I am not going to mention their names. Sometimes us kids and our adult family members and some friends would sit in lawn chairs, and the band would play for us from the shed, with the doors wide open, like a stage, but we knew that they had not practiced at all. Instead of practicing, they would always stay in the shed and drink. The music they played was always the same songs, like covers of songs by Lynyrd Skynyrd, Nickelback, and Kid Rock, and southern rock or any classic rock. The stereo was always on because they wanted to play with the music.

Jonah did drugs and drank beer, but on him it just seemed normal. After his and my mom's parents lost their house, Jonah came and lived with us in a trailer on Deer Trace Trail. His girlfriend, Drema, also lived with us. I was fine with that because Drema was nice sometimes and funny. It made things more crowded, and my brother and I had to sleep in the living room with my mother and her boyfriend, Benny, on a couple of the mattresses we used as a couch. Jonah got more addicted to drugs, and a few days before Halloween, Jonah died of a drug overdose.

We go to see Jonah's gravestone every year in the family cemetery. When we go to his gravestone, we put flowers on his grave. Jonah was cremated, and they gave my brother two little pouches of ashes to keep or scatter. Even though he is dead and there is nothing we can do, I still think about Jonah and still love him, just like everyone else who knew him loves him.

ALL SOULS

It was a Sunday morning, the day before our annual dorm trick-or-treat journey, which would fall on actual Halloween this year. Ryan was spending the weekend with Luke and his girlfriend in the next county, and Michael, who was living with us weekdays, was spending a rare Saturday night with Jessica and Benny. It was almost the last weekend he would stay there, as it turned out, to his continual disappointment and my great relief.

On that quiet Sunday morning my phone rang at 8:30. It was Jessica's second cousin Pinky. We were friendly, and I thought Pinky was just calling me for a ride; as she hesitated on the phone, I began concocting practical excuses why I couldn't run across the county and take her to a home health client's house. But it wasn't that at all.

"Jessica's not answering her phone," Pinky said. "I can't get her to pick up."

I wasn't surprised—it was Sunday morning, early, and maybe Jessica's phone wasn't even charged. At other times that might have alarmed me, but I didn't think she and Benny would be awake anyway.

"So, like, Jonah died," Pinky said.

Jessica's brother. The boys' favorite uncle. Their closest cousins' dad.

My brain sprang into instinctive, irrational superlogic, trying to explain away what it couldn't start to believe. This was a mistake. Didn't Jonah stay there, crowded in with Michael's family most of the time? Wouldn't Jessica know it? How did Pinky?

"Isn't he there?" I said stupidly.

"No, they took him to the hospital," Pinky said, then told me he'd been at the home of his girlfriend's great-aunt—hardly the safe haven it sounded like.

But I'd just seen Jonah in the line at Home Depot a few days earlier.

"Are you sure?" I said, again with that stupid reality reflex, as if anyone would phone with news like this if they weren't absolutely positive. I pictured the hospital staff loading his body into some refrigerated drawer. "So he's at the hospital? Do you think they've really checked?" Maybe it was just a mistake—a common oversight—that they hadn't noticed he was actually breathing.

But of course the news was true, and he had died of an overdose. Jonah had overdosed before, and we all knew he'd used serious drugs and done major drinking—even the children had seen the evidence. His roofing business, which had sustained itself and the extended family for a couple of years, seemed to have fallen apart after the separation with no one to figure out the billing and keep accounts straight for him. Jonah was the uncle the boys idolized, especially Ryan: no matter what Ryan had known and seen of Jonah, what canceled out the negative was Jonah's wild man love for hunting, bow hunting, camping, and fishing, a picture that grew only more legendary in the boys' minds, even as truth and rumors emerged. The day before, Jonah had received an insurance settlement for an accident, and now the cash had vanished. With Jessica adamant that it should be tracked down and given to his children, suspicion and bitterness further clouded the days of mourning.

The funeral was in the small country Baptist church where his family's milestones were marked, with Lynyrd Skynyrd songs played on a portable CD player, as they no doubt had been played for many funerals over the decade. No one sang "Go Rest High," but it was that kind of mood. Across the aisle I saw the person rumored to have sold Jonah what killed him, and I felt alternately sick and then guilty for believing it. And as at so many of the funerals I went to anymore, its main purpose seemed to be not the comfort of his children but the ancient preacher's altar call—this terrible loss just one more part of God's plan to get new and lapsed souls chalked up on the green slate scoreboard.

A LONG winter and summer later, we would be at the mountaintop family cemetery—just me and the boys and the cousins and their mother, along with a seminary intern from their church, walking up through a steep, soft, orange-rutted cow pasture. Jessica and Benny had gone south months before. And because of even more estrangement and blame, the grandparents—Jonah's (and Jessica's) parents—wouldn't be there at the same time as we all were, although they lived close by and would come soon after we'd left. Jonah's ashes had been buried with a marker, but now the headstone his ex-wife had bought for the kids' sake was finished and ready to set. Who knew they would have to mix the concrete powder and set it themselves? Who knew a headstone would be so hard to get straight?

BUT ALL this was to come. It was still morning, 8:35, the day before Halloween, the favorite holiday of Jonah and his whole family. How could the universe let it be forever ruined for them?

But then I realized the worst part. Pinky wasn't just calling to tell me. She was calling because it was on me to do something. To take the next step. To go tell Jessica, who now lived only twelve minutes away from me. No. To wake her up and tell her the worst thing anyone possibly could, about the person she loved and needed most in the world, other than her kids, I'd have bet. "But Jessica's dad should tell her," I argued. It wasn't my place at all. But no, apparently her dad was sitting right there, and he was the one who had asked Pinky to send me. Maybe he couldn't bear it, or maybe there was no gas money.

But still, why? I felt so sorry for myself. Why did I have to be the one to share this? I was the worst person to tell Jonah's sister what could only be the worst thing for her to hear. It felt so wrong, and yet in that moment Jessica felt like my sister. I hated this responsibility, and I fought it, but there was nothing to push against.

And then a worse thought—yes, Jonah had been staying over there because he'd been kicked out of all the other places he might have stayed. But hadn't Jessica also brought him in, and now his girlfriend, not just to help them out and to hang out but to run interference? To be the buffer between Jessica and Benny when his rage inevitably hit? And now Jonah was gone, the pregnant girlfriend would retreat during the furor over missing money, and both Michael and Ryan would have to stay with me for safe distance from the mourning and whatever emotional storm it would set off for Benny, who had long been one of Jonah's best friends. Leaving Jessica alone with Benny, as she hadn't been in so long. "My defender" was what she would call Jonah that morning, before we'd even stepped off the porch.

I HAD rounded up my husband, Will, to follow me over to Benny and Jessica's place—but he would only wait in the car for Michael to come out. The morning was sharply blue, and in a field below, a cow mooed out its usual complaints.

It was the most dreaded knock on a door—a Sunday morning door—I've ever had to make. I knocked and knocked and then finally just had to turn the unlocked doorknob and go in. They were all asleep in the living room, as I knew they would be, but for once it wasn't pumping with classic rock radio or staticky TV. Michael was sitting up, shirtless, from the heap of sleeping bags and blankets on the living room floor, rubbing his eyes, giddily happy to see me. I had to ask Jessica to come out on the porch, and I remember standing before her, my gaze on the scratched green fridge that ran off an extension cord. And then she misunderstood the news I relayed. She thought I'd come to take her to the hospital, that her brother was sick.

"Jonah overdosed," I repeated.

She didn't question how I knew that or why.

"I'll get my purse," she must have said. That's when I realized that my words still had not been enough, that she'd taken them to mean he'd just overdosed again, and that Jonah was alive—that we were going to the hospital so that she could help him through it.

WILL WOULD take Michael back to our house—and we'd expected Ryan to go with them as well, because we did not realize he was away with Luke, still blissfully ignorant of what would shatter his year. At least we could shield Michael from another awful scene. But I did have to drive to the hospital, where the family would do what was needed and make their decisions. And sit in a circle in a terrible room that I hope never to see again. It didn't look like a room where they put families, nor was it some sterile conference space. Maybe all those were occupied by other families that had suffered other deaths that brightly cold October morning. Rather, the room looked like some kind of employee workspace, with papers piled on tables and chairs pushed into a ring around the walls. Fourteen or so adults and kids were already sitting there when we arrived, and then a nurse quietly handed around styrofoam cups of black coffee.

A funeral home always feels unreal, false and cushioned, but this hospital workroom felt realer than real. Adults sat in a rare near-silence while the children circled from person to person and played hide-and-seek under the tables. Michael's cousin Madison, Jonah's daughter, asked for him, and no doubt Michael's absence was seen by adults as yet more evidence that I was sheltering him—as I was indeed trying my best to do. Michael's sister, Isabelle, who at that point showed up only for holidays and births, was there. And since I had driven Jessica and Benny and might have to drive them again, so was I. I'd envisioned just dropping them off with the relatives who had stood smoking outside the ER doors, but after the silent hugs I realized it would be worse to turn around and go. So as little as I thought I belonged, I was there, waiting on something, much as I ached to be home, hugging Michael and doing my pile of Sunday grading. Surely they'd be going other places with other family members, but I could hardly pipe up and ask if they could find a ride for later, like I had somewhere better and happier and more urgent to be.

I mumbled my offer—a barely disguised plea—to keep the boys indefinitely, knowing how hard things would be: Jessica said thank you, yes, and I felt immensely relieved. Except that Ryan later chose to spend what turned out to be a scarring last night at home after he returned from the home of his father's girlfriend. But after school the next day, he reappeared at our house for what would be many weeks, thankfully.

THIS WAS when the entire family fell apart. The cousins would be fatherless; come winter, Benny and Jessica would leave, moving to the deep South with the understanding that the boys would follow; Jessica's parents would implode with grief, pulling back even further from the world.

For months in his room in our house Ryan would make little shrines to Jonah; he hung up and kept the pouches of Jonah's ashes until he could give one to his mother. Jonah's sleeveless T-shirts, pieces of his hunting bow, and knives and wrist guards became unassailable relics, even as they sparked my pitiless rage. I tried to be sympathetic and sometimes drove Ryan out to visit the gravesite while I waited in my parked car down the hill, but it drove me crazy to witness hero worship of someone who had died at his own hand—not as a suicide but from a money-flooded overdose. As if it were up to me to judge whether he had died the right way to be mourned—and, I admit, I didn't always bite my tongue. But in Ryan's mind and Michael's, Jonah in death was now larger than life, and he was again the hunter, the builder, the joker, the favorite—the person he sometimes was and might yet have been.

But nothing stopped Halloween, even that year that Jonah died. A death inquiry had to happen and then cremation, so the funeral would not be for about another eight days. It was okay, and maybe even a comfort, to follow the routine.

None of the kids sat out Halloween the next night, which was another relief to me: they had their costumes and sorely needed the candy and diversion. The sad, surreal new normal had not yet begun to sink in. Thank goodness these kids could have their holiday still, I thought, without having that taken from them as well. Let parents "check" half the candy; let Freddy Kruger and Jigsaw chase children from the haunted house—but at least let the kids keep this magic evening for themselves. At five o'clock the day after Jonah had stopped breathing, Michael, Ryan, and I trick-or-treated through the dorms with Jonah's children and their mother, a year past the divorce driven by Jonah's addictions. There were giggles and waves to friends and the clattering of candy into buckets, as though everything had not yet changed for them all.

HALLOWMAS: ALL Hallows, All Saints, All Souls. It's that dusk of the year when a door is cracked open—spirit birds fly into houses and panic; deer leap from roadside shadows; and the last luna moths cling through the night to the screens of our lighted windows.

ARREST

Back at the university dorms, fate caught up the next Halloween, a year after Jonah's death. Jessica had recently accompanied a shaken Ryan back from her new home in the south, although she would return there again. She and Benny had both left our state when they had pending court dates, all car-related. Jessica had believed she would go to jail for that alone, on the basis of what one judge had threatened—but when it came down to it, she'd only been fined. No, the bigger problem was missing a much-delayed court date and being a fugitive. Once Jessica was back in our state, it was bound to catch up with her.

This night was the one time I was going to miss the dorm trick-or-treating, much as I didn't want to. I was hosting a long-ago friend who was speaking at the university, and I had planned this dinner and his presentation a good half-year before. It had to be on a Thursday, and I had to be there. Jessica's father would bring her to meet Michael in the dorm parking lot, and she would have this year's event all to herself, along with Ryan, who was staying with his mom at her parents' house. So I was to meet them, then go to the restaurant across the street to meet the speaker.

But it was getting late as we just stood in the parking lot, watching other cars pull in. I had to go, yet I knew that Jessica wouldn't miss this. She had no phone now, and the minutes were ticking by. I had that dual sensation familiar to many foster parents—frustration with the parent and wondering if she's going to be a no-show while trying to ease the child's rising tension and anxiety: *Is that her? Is that Poppa's truck? Why isn't she calling you? Why can't you call her on MeMa's phone?* The siren of anxiety rises inside—all to be forgiven and forgotten in the tumble of relief and excuses when the parent arrives, until the next time. But at Michael's age, with what had come before, I knew he was not just worrying that Mom had forgotten him—he was worrying through every possible worse option.

Much as I yearned to stay and reassure him, I had to leave and host the dinner and event I was supposed to be presenting. I left Michael with his "good" aunt, Grace, the ex-wife of the late Jonah. She definitely did not want to get caught up again with Jonah's family, and tried to keep her daughter, Madison, apart, but Grace agreed to let Michael trick-or-treat with Madison and their mutual friend Keisha until his mom arrived; both girls were greenish-white–faced in their Monster High schoolgirl outfits and perfect gray wigs. I was happy and grateful that Michael could go with them, and if need be Grace offered to drop him off at Grandma Irene's on her way home, where I'd planned to pick him up all along. I found out later that Jessica and Ryan did arrive to meet Michael before the first hour of dorm trick-or-treating was up, but I could never have waited that long for them myself.

So off Michael went with Madison, Keisha, and Aunt Grace, swinging his plastic pumpkin, in his age-appropriate zombie wear, with a rib cage, sternum, and heart showing through its grayish-green rags. His sadness at Jessica's absence seemed to evaporate in a flood of silly chatter with his cousin and friend, and off I went to be an adult again.

THREE HOURS later I took my friend back to his hotel after his speech, and as we were sitting in the sinking leather chairs of the lobby, making plans to see the famous fall foliage the next day, my phone started ringing but cutting in and out. It had to be time to go pick up Michael.

When I got to Grandma Irene's place, no one came to the door, and I ended up pushing it open. No sister, no grandmother, no Michael. I was baffled. Had he not come there? Had Mom taken him off somewhere with her family? I tried to call Irene's cell phone, but it rang right there on the table—she hadn't taken it. Michael's candy-filled pumpkin sat on a table, the black triangle eyes looking cheerfully at me.

I just stood around and waited. What had happened would remain confusing—either Ryan had called from the gas station, or Isabelle had called to say he was out walking along the road in the dark and Irene and Michael had gone to look for him.

I never could follow all the details, but somehow Jessica's father's truck, which often ran on the five dollars' worth of gas he would borrow from successive family members, had run dry at a defunct business down the road with the back of the pickup full of kids and teens. Ryan and his grandfather had walked down the road in the dark with a gas can in hand, but while they were gone, sheriff's deputies had stopped to check on the truck and had recognized Jessica, who was waiting there with the rest of the kids. The warrant for her arrest had been outstanding since the previous spring.

If only the boys had missed this whole experience—but when Irene and Michael had been searching for Ryan along the dark roadside, they had picked him up near the gas station, alone by that point, and then had seen the blue lights flashing. Michael had recognized the outline of Jessica's father's truck and spotted his mother standing beside it. Jessica's arrest had been inevitable, for after trying to keep her return to the area largely secret, she had let herself be seen on the main street downtown. Because she limped from a poorly set broken ankle and her tendoned hands were always twisting a cigarette to and from her lips, she was easily recognizable, even with her usually blonde hair dyed brown. "I'm going, I'm going," she told the deputies, who let her smoke a cigarette and hug the boys once her dad returned, then told everyone to drive away so the kids wouldn't have to see them put her in the patrol car.

I learned all this when Michael and Irene returned home, where I still waited, twenty minutes later. Michael was ghostlike and stunned, still in the zombie costume top, with its yellow bones and shriveled heart. He was ready just to throw his candy away. He didn't want anything more to do with anything sweet or kind or childish in his life. He was done.

Ryan had been staying with Jessica's parents, so I drove Michael home to our house alone, guilty for making him sit by himself in the back, which I did whenever it was dark and I thought there was a greater chance of being hit by drunks or simply of my own tired eyes' failing on our two-lane highway. I wished I could have reached back over the seat to clutch his fingers instead of keeping both hands gripped to the wheel as my eyes sought the faded yellow line.

That night Michael had no adults to "check" his candy and to take the crazy feast of sweetness he'd collected away from him. I couldn't do it. His fists clutched rolls of Smarties, while his pumpkin sat beside me in the front seat as I drove, totally jangled. For once I let the Milky Way squares and Sugar Babies be and instead prayed for some steady future, all the dark and quiet way home.

Make It Stop Now

—Michael

Rain was everywhere now.
The rain was a shallow pond.
It felt like pebbles bouncing off my head.
The black powder smoke clouds above
My head. Make it all stop now.
The rain hit ten or twelve times.
Then the rain stopped.

Coda

Coin in the Air

AT THIS point in the story of their lives, Michael is fourteen and Ryan a recent eighteen. We could not be prouder of both of them and of the hard work they continue to do to make their lives healthy and whole. Even as it has been our joy to have them with us, like any nonbiological parents, we know that joy comes at a loss to their biofamily and to the boys themselves. They continue to see and speak with their mother, and they have long understood that it was because of her love for them that she put their physical and emotional safety above all else and allowed them to come to us; they also regularly visit and speak with their father, who remains in prison but assures Michael he will be out in time to attend his high school graduation—a bright place on the horizon for both of them.

Both boys remain very close with Grandma Irene, who has nurtured and supported them from the start—they visit her at least weekly, talk with her frequently, and take pride in helping her with lawn mowing and repairs. She is always there to celebrate their successes, and always ready to give a ride or a word of advice or comfort when they need it. Although the boys wouldn't use these words, I think they prize the normalcy and spontaneity of this relationship, which meets so many needs that we never could have met from outside the family. I surely lean on Irene as much as they do. We are so lucky that she lives close by, although that is the norm here, so that's one thing at least that the boys can take for granted. Frequently, they see their now adult sister with Irene, as well as Irene's daughter and her family, and more geographically distant relatives.

Sadly, the boys' maternal grandmother passed away at a fairly young age due to the convergence of several chronic conditions, which were surely made worse by the heartbreak of losing her son; their maternal (and only living) grandfather has moved farther away and they now see him more rarely. While it is an addition and not a substitute, of course, Will's and my own families have happily absorbed Michael and Ryan as well. That very first summer that Michael was in foster care, my parents made a long trip to visit him at our house, in case that turned out to be all the time we got with him; soon after we found that our relationship could continue, our families also welcomed Ryan, Isabelle, Irene, Jessica, and cousins. With my family and Will's, the boys became grandchildren, nephews, and cousins all over again.

From their biofamily, from Will and me, and from our extended families, they have so much love—and while every fostering and adoption book cautions from the outset that love is not enough, at least it's a start. And we keep working from every angle on the rest of what the "enough" is, although the real key is that there can never be enough of whatever it is that "enough" may be.

In addition to all the medical, emotional, and other supports that we (and, thankfully, Medicaid) can give them, we've tried to just keep making their world bigger. We've taken the boys all over the country, not only to visit our scattered family members but also to see worlds in the West they could never have imagined, and to make concrete and visible the myriad worlds possible for their futures.

NOTHING IS easy, but they continue to amaze us all.

Ryan has fulfilled his often-voiced dream of being the first in his family to graduate high school, and he has the great good fortune to be going on to a college that has the mission and capacity to support students like him, who have had to hew the road to their own future. He plans to make a career out of reaching back to help other young people like himself, and he has already racked up considerable work and volunteer experience to this end. Through his high school years, he found special strength through his faith and a church family that empowered him with unconditional acceptance and support; his experience of traveling abroad on a church mission seemed to cement his sense of purpose in life. He is persistent and dedicated to whatever tasks and goals he takes on, and he is loyal to his family and Appalachian roots. Ryan has had the additional gift of being a teen who connects powerfully with adults—many at school, at church, and in the community have recognized his drive for personal success and have gone out of their way to help him with opportunities and recognition.

Michael's great gifts, I believe, are first, his lifesaving ability to express himself and give voice to his experience with honesty and insight, both aloud and in writing; and second, an almost uncanny mechanical ability to repair or reconfigure any piece of equipment he touches. Like Mary Poppins, things fly together in his hands—a gift all the more amazing to me as objects seem to fall apart in mine. He couldn't feel more accomplished than when his grandmother calls to ask for his help in fixing her vacuum, fencing her yard, or replacing the ceiling. He has so many energetic enthusiasms, from rocks and climbing to music, photography, and reading, to pigs (in the abstract) and his dog and cats to the TV series *The Fosters* and *The Simpsons*—and all this enthusiasm is among the benefits of the hyperfocus that is the undervalued reward for struggling with ADHD as he does. Michael has a strong sense of outrage at injustice and a love of practical service work. And the greatest gift, which is the ability to feel, verbalize, and show a deep love for his family and for us as his second set of parents. Many days he seems to be making up for lost time with us, exulting in love and sharing affection that many a teen might shy away from. As much as he is challenged by the lingering effects of trauma, in many ways he is living out a second childhood, which I believe can only be restorative—for both him and us.

Like Ryan, Michael has had the benefit of extraordinary teachers who have encouraged creativity, shown patience with his different ways of getting work and projects done, insisted on kindness to and respect for peers, and had a keen understanding of all the stresses so many students carry into and out of school with them. He (and we) have been especially lucky to have solution-focused teachers, both past and current, with a cutting-edge understanding of trauma's impact on learning and instinct; he was also blessed to have a middle-school language arts teacher who assigned her students to write numerous memoirs; she pushed Michael not only to craft and revise, but most of all to use these explorations to gain insight and healing. It was from this set of memoirs that Michael's prose pieces included here were drawn.

I OFTEN feel that we're living in a parallel universe—or more accurately, one superimposed on the typical universe. As many who have adopted or fostered will recognize, chronological age means little when there are ages and stages a child needs to revisit, and sometimes the unstoppable conveyor belt of education and expectations moves them forward on a schedule that doesn't yet fit. And, again, as many adoptive parents will understand, our getting custody was just the beginning of the story and not the end, for it's only once children are in a place of what you hope is unshakeable safety that they have the freedom to begin to let past trauma surface and slowly deal with the new forms it takes, which are often as indirect and inscrutable as any dream logic.

When I try to measure the boys' lives in concrete achievements or setbacks, the effort feels myopic and I lose the perspective of the proverbial big picture: it's often only through metaphor that I can take a step back and understand the larger patterns. It's metaphor that gives me peace, at times, and hope for the future. I'm finally realizing that trauma and resilience are flip sides of the same coin—but not a coin that has landed and been declared heads or tails; rather, a tossed coin that keeps turning in the air, eternally, suspended just out of reach. As parents, we all want to grab that coin out of the air and slap it heads up and hold it that way—but of course, as our society is slowly coming to realize, that can't be done, no matter how hard you wish it and how determinedly you grasp. You just have to watch it keep turning—through hope and fear, joy and pain, love and loss and love—and keep waiting, hands outstretched beneath your child's hands to catch it.